THE DESIGN BOOK

1000 NEW DESIGNS FOR THE HOME
AND WHERE TO FIND THEM

Jennifer Hudson

Candleholder, Valencia
Jaime Hayon
Crystal glass, sandblasted
by hand
H: 23.4cm (9in)
Diam: 10.6cm (4⅛in)
Gaia & Gino, Turkey
www.gaiagino.com

THE
DESIGN
BOOK

1000 NEW DESIGNS FOR THE HOME
AND WHERE TO FIND THEM

Jennifer Hudson

LAURENCE KING PUBLISHING

LAURENCE KING

Published in 2013 by
Laurence King Publishing Ltd
361–363 City Road, London,
EC1V 1LR, United Kingdom
T +44 (0)20 7841 6900
F + 44 (0)20 7841 6910
enquiries@laurenceking.com
www.laurenceking.com

Text © 2013 Laurence King Publishing Ltd

A catalogue record for this book is available from the
British Library.

ISBN: 978-1-78067-099-7

Design: Eleanor Ridsdale
Picture research: Fredrika Lökholm

Printed in China

Front cover: Johnny B. Butterfly lighting, Ingo Maurer
(see p. 240)
Back cover: Sparkling indoor/outdoor chair, Marcel Wanders
(see p. 68)

Acknowledgements
I would like to dedicate *The Design Book* to Laurence King,
who has shown me so much support over the years, and to
thank the following people for their invaluable help in the
making of this book: all the designers featured, especially
those who I interviewed and who took the time to give such
interesting replies to my questions; Eleanor Ridsdale for her
patience and skill in not only organizing over 1000 designs
into some kind of order but also in making the pages look
good as well; Jodi Simpson, my editor, for her keen eye and
expertise and John Jervis for his copy-editing, as well as our
production department here at LKP for getting everything
into a publishable state. But, once again, above all I would
like to thank Fredrika Lökholm, without whose advice, hard
work and patience this book would not have been possible.
Well, Fredrika, I think it's now time for a mojito, don't you?
JH

CONTENTS

INTRODUCTION

Interviewed on the eve of her thought-provoking 2008 exhibition 'Design and the Elastic Mind', Paola Antonelli, Senior Curator of Architecture and Design at the Museum of Modern Art, New York, spoke of the relevance of designers today: 'I believe designers are so important to society because they are like the worms that eat the earth and then digest and expel it as something fertile to make the terrain more fruitful. They are great synthesizers, very curious of all different viewpoints. The best designers enjoy design as an affirmation of life and a way to discover the world. And they render back to the world what they have learned.'[1]

The show gathered together over 200 objects, projects and concepts that explored the relationship between design and science on every scale from the microscopic to the cosmological, from nanodevices to vehicles, from appliances to interfaces, and from pragmatic solutions for everyday use to provocative ideas meant to influence our future choices. The aim was to focus on the designer's ability to grasp momentous changes in technology and social mores and convert them into products and systems that we as consumers can understand and use.

More than ever before, the significance we give to design in our everyday life is becoming apparent. Designers may not be able to change the world, but they will, as interpreters of innovation, increasingly become the catalyst for that change. Design is a broad-ranging discipline that today is recognized not only in the objects that you will find in the pages that follow but in its ability to build bridges between invention and real life.

The word 'design' has for too long been contaminated by the notion of decoration rather than what it could be: a vehicle for cultural, social and economic development. The strength of the designer is in his or her ability to take many different sources and ideas and amalgamate them into an object, scenario or service that has a clear intention and function. Over recent years, with the advent of design thinking and critical design—the former redefining what it means to be a good designer to include systems and strategies as well as enhanced skills in observation, analysis and communication; the latter using designed artefacts as an embodied critique or commentary on existing values, morals and practices in culture—the designer's intellectual focus is no longer solely on producing tangible things but on applying thought processes to ethical, social, environmental or humanitarian problems. The designer's purpose is to achieve the goals that are assigned to him or her, whether that be in the products that surround us, in technological innovations, in information processing or in a broader sense, sitting on panels to bring their 'elastic minds' to advise on such concerns as health, poverty, aging or long-term unemployment. The designer's role is to use the means available in a way that is relevant, logical, economical, elegant, expressive of us and the current zeitgeist, and most importantly, given the environmental crisis we are suffering, that champions sustainability.

The definition of design is changing. It is much more expansive and fluid than it used to be, and it comes with increased responsibility. For designers involved primarily with the process of producing objects, it is now no longer enough to make something that looks good and functions; they also have to create products that last, have the minimum impact on the environment, appeal to our sentiment and use technology and materials in an ingenious and imaginative way.

At the beginning of the 1970s, the designer Victor Papanek wrote in his rabble-rousing book *Design for the Real World*: 'There are professions more harmful than industrial design, but only a few.'[2] He went on to encourage designers to satisfy real needs rather than 'phony wants' without depleting the world's resources and ignoring their social and moral responsibilities. This directive is as influential now as it was then, if not more so. In an age where the ecological future of our planet is threatened, and in a period of bruising, ongoing global recession, the throwaway age has ended. Although inevitably the design media and the general conversation at Milan's Salone Internazionale del Mobile (the world's barometer of contemporary design) are full of the next new name, style, trend or headline, there is an ever-growing and underlining emphasis on the accountability of designers. They need to consider the whole life cycle of a product—whether it is designed, developed, manufactured shipped and disposed of responsibly—and to create products with longevity that will be handed down from generation to generation. The days of churning out 'stuff' that will find itself in landfill within a few years of appearing on the shelves are well and truly over. In humanitarian terms too there is a marked increase in craft-based objects produced in collaboration with third-world non-profit organizations that illustrate the duty Western designers are demonstrating in their contributions to developing countries. This caring, sustainable, considered and inclusive approach to design is evidenced again and again throughout this book and emphasized in the telling responses of the designers interviewed on being asked, for example, what they consider to be the main challenges currently facing a designer, what they understand as the definition of 'sustainable design' and whether design can contribute to social change.

The atmosphere of the 2012 Salone (the last before this publication went to print) was subdued, demure and conservative, reflecting the austerity of the times and the realization that consumer demand is for less rather than more. The end users of design products, instead of choosing many objects of a kind, are selecting just one that resonates emotionally and that they will want to keep for a long time. The most talked-about exhibitions were not the ones showcasing jaw-dropping furniture aimed at the luxury market but those that highlighted the need for design to be accessible to and understandable by the person in the street; these exhibitions addressed the growing interest in collaborative design, hacked design (the contemporary concept of appropriation, alteration and transformation), and open-source design (the free-sharing of technological information with its concomitant need for transparency and plurality), and emphasized the processes that lead up to the finished object.

The design agenda for the foreseeable future will be beset by many challenges and complex issues. But with the growing acknowledgement of designers' innate creative attitude, their ability to work in teams, their multidisciplinarian and experimental minds, along with the potential they have, in brain-storming with other disciplines and organizations, to tackle societal problems, this is a period of unparalleled opportunities.

While artists may choose whether to be responsible to and work for other people, designers, by definition, whether designing for our furnished environment or troubleshooting existing production or sustainability problems, must accept the 'primacy of the human scale'. As Paola Antonelli puts it, 'Designers always work from a center of gravity, which is the human being.'[3]

1. Pierre Alexandre de Looz, 'Curators Voice: Paola Antonelli on Design and the Elastic Mind', *Artinfo*, April 21, 2008, http://www.artinfo.com/news/story/27328/curators-voice-paola-antonelli-on-design-and-the-elastic-mind/.
2. Victor Papanek, *Design for the Real World: Human Ecology and Social Change* (New York: Pantheon Books, 1971).
3. De Looz, 'Curators Voice: Paola Antonelli on Design and the Elastic Mind'.

1.

TABLES
AND
CHAIRS

Chair, Spun (Coriolis)
Heatherwick Studio
Steel with black acid finish,
or bronzed brass
H: 65cm (25in)
W: 90cm (35in)
Haunch of Venison Gallery, UK
Marzorati Ronchetti, Italy
www.haunchofvenison.com
www.marzoratironchetti.it

Night table,
Small Ghost Buster

Philippe Starck
PMMA
H: 40cm (15¾in)
L: 50cm (19in)
D: 33cm (13in)
Kartell SpA, Italy
www.kartell.it

Coffee table, Quark

Emmanuel Babled
Plexiglass
H: 30cm (11¾in)
W: 102.5cm (40in)
L: 208cm (82in)
Emmanuel Babled Studio,
The Netherlands
www.babled.net

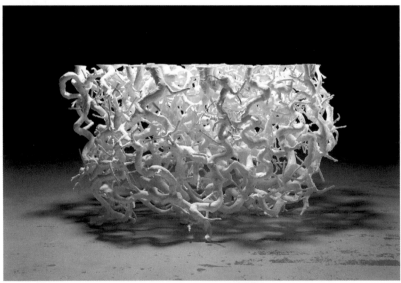

Table, Bonsai Structure

Anke Weiss
150 bonsai trees, epoxy resin
H: 50cm (19in)
Diam: 80cm (31in)
Studio Anke Weiss,
The Netherlands
www.ankeweiss.com

Writing desk,
Pirandello

Jasper Morrison
Transparent extra-light glass
or double-faced extra-light
acid-etched glass, tempered
and thermo-welded;
aluminium
H: 83cm (32in)
L: 80 or 110cm (31 or 43in)
D: 49cm (19¼in)
Glas Italia, Italy
www.glasitalia.com

Table, Oyster I
Marco Zanuso Jr
Polished stainless steel
H: 72cm (28in)
W: 60cm (23in)
D: 60cm (23in)
Driade, Italy
www.driade.com

**Indoor/outdoor stool/
side table, Hexagon**
Steven Holl
Lecce stone, okoume wood
H: 42cm (16 ½in)
W: 40 or 44cm
(15 ¾ or 17⅜in)
L: 43 or 51cm
(16⅞ or 20in)
Horm, Italy
www.horm.it

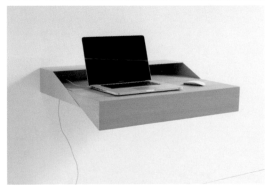

**Wall-hung table/cabinet,
Deskbox**
Raw Edges
Steel with epoxy lacquer,
solid wood
H: 13cm (5⅛in)
W: 80cm (31in)
D (closed): 44cm (17⅜in)
D (open): 60cm (23in)
Arco, The Netherlands
www.arco.nl

Table, Silver Crush Table
Fredrikson Stallard
Glass, steel, aluminium
H: 34cm (13⅜in)
W: 100cm (39in)
L: 130cm (51in)
Fredrikson Stallard, UK
www.fredriksonstallard.com

Blow resulted from a collaboration between Italian glass company Venini and British contemporary design brand Established & Sons (see page 184). Konstantin Grcic's design exploits Venini's artisan handblown glass to create a voluptuous organic shape that explores the limits of the technique. The main body of the table is conceived as a free-form bubble, onto which the table top of sheet glass is attached. The fascination of the piece lies in the scale of the blown glass, as well as the combination of translucent Venini colours.

Tables, Blow
Konstantin Grcic
Handblown Venini glass
H: 41.5 and 51.5cm
(16½ and 20in)
L: 50cm (19in)
D: 45cm (17¾in)
Established & Sons, UK
Venini SpA, Italy
www.establishedandsons.com

Coffee table with indoor/ outdoor removable top, Oppiacei Papaver
Diego Grandi with
Manolo Bossi
Glazed ceramic
H: 46cm (18⅛in)
Diam (base): 40cm (15¾in)
Diam (plate): 58cm (22in)
Skitsch, Italy
www.skitsch.it

Table, Zipte Table
Michael Young
Aluminium
H: 73cm (28in)
Diam: 85cm (33in)
Ostbahn, Hong Kong
www.ostbahn.com

Table with folding top, Double Size
Matali Crasset
Birch marine plywood,
scratch-resistant
lacquered wood
H: 72cm (28in)
L: 170cm (66in)
Danese Milano, Italy
www.danesemilano.com

Table, Fleur de Novembre
Fabio Novembre
PMMA, polycarbonate
H: 72cm (28in)
Diam: 120cm (47in)
Kartell SpA, Italy
www.kartell.it

Table, Source
Xavier Lust
Mirror-polished aluminium
H: 73cm (28in)
Diam. 70cm (27in)
Driade, Italy
www.driade.com

Table, Central
Ronan and Erwan Bouroullec
Die cast aluminium
H: 72cm (28in)
D. 60cm (23in)
Magis SpA, Italy
www.magisdesign.com

Dressing table, Chandlo
Doshi Levien
Solid ash, steel, mirror, MDF,
plywood
H: 143.5cm (56½in)
W: 165cm (65in)
D: 65cm (25½in)
BD Barcelona Design, Spain
www.bdbarcelona.com

Table, Drain
Marcel Wanders
Aluminium
H: 75cm (29in)
Diam: 170cm (66in)
Cappellini, Italy
www.cappellini.it

Table, Bac
Jasper Morrison
Ash wood
H: 72cm (28in)
Diam: 125cm (49in)
Cappellini, Italy
www.cappellini.it

Table, Blow Up
Xavier Lust
Cristalplant, steel
H: 73cm (28in)
W: 80cm (31in)
L: 210cm (82in)
Skitsch, Italy
www.skitsch.it

Low table, Ponte
James Irvine
White Carrara marble
H: 35cm (13¾in)
W: 50cm (19in)
L: 150cm (59in)
Marsotto Edizioni, Italy
www.marsotto-edizioni.com

Table, Arctic Rock
JSPR
Solid mahogany wood
finished with Piano Lacquer
H: 75cm (29in)
W: 100cm (39in)
L: 250cm (98in)
JSPR Production,
The Netherlands
www.jspr.eu

Coffee tables, Black Sheep
Emmanuel Babled
Black Marquinia marble
H: 40cm (15¾in)
W (large version):
94cm (37in)
L (large version):
177cm (70in)
Nilufar, Italy
www.nilufar.com

Table, XY
Karel de Boer
Wood
H: 74cm (29in)
W: 210, 240 or 270cm
(82, 94 or 106in)
D: 90cm (35in)
Montis, The Netherlands
www.montis.nl

**Indoor/outdoor table,
Table B**
Konstantin Grcic
Extruded aluminium, stone
H: 73.5cm (29in)
W: 120cm (47in)
L: 180, 240, 300 or 360cm
(70, 94, 118 or 141in)
BD Barcelona Design, Spain
www.bdbarcelona.com

Console, Topkapi
Konstantin Grcic
White Carrara marble
H: 72cm (28in)
W: 50cm (19in)
L: 200 or 240cm (78 or 94in)
Marsotto srl, Italy
www.marsotto-edizioni.com

Table, Tense
Piergiorgio and Michele
Cazzaniga
Composite tabletop
(aluminium, polystyrene) with
steel legs, clad in acrylic resin
H: 73 cm (28in)
W: 120cm (47in)
L: 400cm (157in)
MDF Italia, Italy
www.mdfitalia.it

Tables, Rock
Tom Dixon
Forest Brown Indian Marble
H: 30cm (11¾in)
Diam: 70cm (27in)
Tom Dixon, UK
www.tomdixon.net

Table, Cobogò
Fernando and Humberto
Campana
Terracotta, resin,
varnished steel
H: 74cm (29in)
Diam: 137cm (54in)
PlusDesign srl, Italy
www.plusdesigngallery.com

**Table and chairs, 100
Table and 100 Chair**
Michael Young
Leather, wood
H (table): 70cm (27in)
W (table): 70cm (27in)
L (table): 128cm (50in)
H (chair): 78cm (30in)
W (chair): 63cm (24in)
D (chair): 58cm (22in)
Trussardi, Italy
www.trussardi.com

Table, Tobi-Ishi
BarberOsgerby
Baydur®, wood,
cement grout
H: 73.5cm (29in)
Diam: 160cm (63in)
B&B Italia, Italy
www.bebitalia.it

Table, Twaya
Ferruccio Laviani
Solid oak wood
H: 76cm (29in)
L: 270 or 320cm
(106 or 126in)
D: 120cm (47in)
Emmemobili, Italy
www.emmemobili.it

Table, Kami
Claesson Koivisto Rune
Solid bamboo
H: 71cm (28in)
W: 100cm (39in)
L: 240cm (94in)
Discipline srl, Italy
www.discipline.eu

Chair and table, Österlen
Inga Sempé
Ash wood
H (chair): 83cm (32in)
W (chair): 43.3cm (16⅞in)
D (chair): 49.3cm (19¼in)
H (table): 73cm (28in)
W (table): 70cm (27in)
D (table): 70cm (27in)
Garsnäs, Sweden
www.garsnas.se

Chair and table, Ami Ami
Tokujin Yoshioka
Polycarbonate
H (chair): 85cm (33in)
W (chair): 41cm (16⅛in)
D (chair): 50cm (19in)
H (table): 72cm (28in)
W (table): 70cm (27in)
D (table): 70cm (27in)
Kartell SpA, Italy
www.kartell.it

**Chair and table,
Lancaster Chair and Table**
Michael Young
Cast aluminium, ash wood
H (chair): 77cm (30in)
W (chair): 51cm (20in)
D (chair): 47cm (18½in)
H (table): 72cm (28in)
W (table): 76–122cm
(29–48in)
D (table): 124–183cm
(49–72in)
Emeco, USA
www.emeco.net

Tables, V-table
Xavier Lust
Lacquered steel and
aluminium
H (table): 73cm (28in)
H (side table): 63cm (24in)
Tacchini, Italy
www.tacchini.it

High table, Crossing
Patricia Urquiola
Laminated tempered
transparent extra-light glass
with three-dimensional
polychromatic decoration
H: 74cm (29in)
L: 200 or 250cm (78 or 98in)
D: 90cm (35in)
Glas Italia, Italy
www.glasitalia.com

**Folding table,
Grand Central**
Sigrid Strömgren,
Sanna Lindström
Plywood, MDF, textile
H: 46cm (18⅛in)
Diam: 79cm (31in)
Sigrid Strömgren and Sanna
Lindström, Sweden
www.sigridstromgren.se
www.sannalindstrom.com

Table, Black Forest
Outofstock
Solid wood, stainless steel
H: 72cm (28in)
W: 72cm (28in)
D: 60cm (23in)
Ligne Roset, France
www.ligneroset.com

Low table, Drawn Table
Naoto Fukasawa
Transparent glass
H: 36cm (14⅛in)
W: 85cm (33in)
L: 140cm (55in)
Glas Italia, Italy
www.glasitalia.com

Home workstation, Strata
Karim Rashid
Glass
H: 80cm (31in)
W: 60cm (23in)
L: 120cm (47in)
Tonelli Design, Italy
www.tonellidesign.it

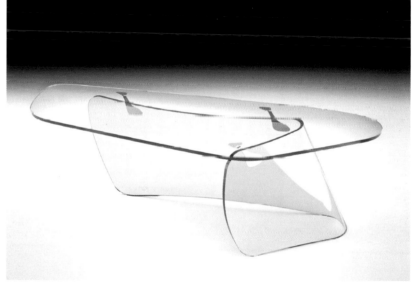

Desk, Graph
Xavier Lust
Glass, stainless steel
H: 74cm (29in)
L: 220cm (86in)
D: 80cm (31in)
Fiam Italia, Italy
www.fiamitalia.it

Coffee table, Newton
Dan Sunaga, Staffan Holm
Wood, glass
H: 40cm (15¾in)
Diam: 92cm (36in)
Karl Andersson & Söner,
Sweden
www.karl-andersson.se

Desk, Reti Fragili
Matteo Pastori
Maple wood, cotton strings,
cardboard, scratch-resistant
lacquered multiplex
H: 72cm (28in)
W: 90cm (35in)
Danese Milano, Italy
www.danesemilano.com

Desk, Pontus
Russell Pinch
Walnut, oak, painted finish
H: 75.5 + 25.5cm
(29 + 10¼in)
W: 180cm (70in)
D: 75cm (29in)
Pinch, UK
www.pinchdesign.com

Table, Stabiles
Alfredo Häberli
Veneered plywood,
solid wood
H: 75cm (29in)
W: 100cm (39in)
L: 235cm (92in)
Alias SpA, Italy
www.aliasdesign.it

Writing desk, Ponti
Claesson Koivisto Rune
Oak
H: 71cm (28in)
W: 50cm (19in)
L: 140cm (55in)
Arflex, Italy
www.arflex.com

Desk, Treviso
Matthew Hilton
Oak
H: 86cm (33in)
W: 122cm (48in)
D: 59cm (23in)
Ercol, UK
www.ercol.com

**Dining Table,
Lily Dining Table**
Leif.designpark
Solid American black walnut,
Corian®
H: 75cm (29in)
W: 190cm (74in)
D: 85cm (33in)
De La Espada, Portugal
www.delaespada.com

Table, Aki Table
Alfredo Häberli
Oak, linoleum
H: 72cm (28in)
W: 120cm (47in)
L: 240cm (94in)
Fredericia Furniture A/S,
Denmark
www.fredericia.com

**Lightweight portable
table, Nomad**
Jorre van Ast
Wood
H: 75cm (29in)
W: 95cm (37in)
L: 190, 210 or 240cm
(74, 82 or 94in)
Arco, The Netherlands
www.arco.nl

Table, Peggy
Pearson Loyd
Ash
H: 72.5cm (28in)
W: 100cm (39in)
L: 200cm (78in)
SCP, UK
www.scp.co.uk

Outdoor table, Railway
Luca Nichetto
Natural teak, steel, stainless
steel, powder coating
H: 74cm (29in)
Diam: 140cm (55in)
De Padova srl, Italy
www.depadova.it

Extendable table, Oyster
Mario Bellini
Lacquered aluminium,
tempered serigraphed glass
H: 73cm (28in)
L (closed): 190cm (74in)
L (open): 250cm (98in)
D: 90cm (35in)
Kartell SpA, Italy
www.kartell.it

**Coffee table,
Rememberme**
Tobias Juretzek
Jeans, cotton, resin, metal
H: 75cm (29in)
W: 75cm (29in)
D: 75cm (29in)
Casamania, Italy
www.casamania.it

Table, Baguettes
Ronan and Erwan Bouroullec
Die-cast aluminium
H: 72cm (28in)
L: 205cm (80in)
Magis SpA, Italy
www.magisdesign.com

Table, 360°
Konstantin Grcic
Aluminium, steel,
painted MDF
H: 73–95cm (28–37in)
W: 90cm (35in)
L: 140cm (55in)
Magis SpA, Italy
www.magisdesign.com

Extending table, Vanity
Stefano Giovannoni
Aluminium, tempered glass
H: 74cm (29in)
W: 90cm (35in)
L: 160–220cm (63–86in)
Magis SpA, Italy
www.magisdesign.com

Table, Bamboo Steel Table
Nendo
Handwoven stainless steel
H: 70cm (27in)
Diam: 60cm (23in)
Yii, Taiwan
HAN Gallery, Taiwan
www.yiidesign.com
www.han-gallery.com

Table, Palio
Ludovica and Roberto Palomba
Particle board with a stained
ash wengé veneer, leather
H: 74cm (29in)
W: 91cm (35in)
L: 210cm (82in)
Poltrona Frau SpA, Italy
www.poltronafrau.com

Table, Faint
Patricia Urquiola
Transparent extra-light glass
with tempered top
H: 74cm (29in)
W: 90cm (35in)
L: 200 or 230cm (78 or 90in)
Glas Italia, Italy
www.glasitalia.com

Dining table, Babel
Marcel Wanders
Varnished beech veneer,
varnished solid wood
H: 73cm (28in)
W: 90cm (35in)
L: 180cm (70in)
xO, France
www.xo-design.com

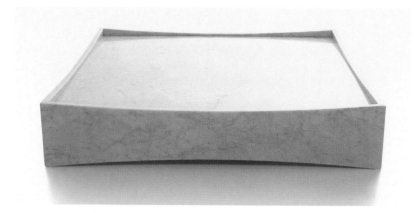

Low table, Gallery
Claesson Koivisto Rune
White Carrara marble
H: 20cm (7⅞in)
W: 100cm (39in)
L: 100cm (39in)
Marsotto Edizioni, Italy
www.marsotto-edizioni.com

**Outdoor table and
seating, Moma**
Javier Mariscal
Polyethylene
H (table): 45cm (17¾in)
W (table): 100cm (39in)
L (table): 115cm (45in)
Vondom, Spain
www.vondom.com

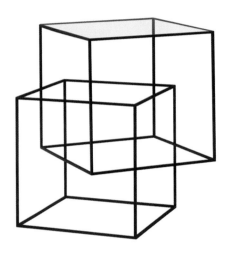

**Side table,
Thin Black Table**
Nendo
Glass, steel
H: 51cm (20in)
W: 47cm (18½in)
D: 46cm (18⅛in)
Cappellini, Italy
www.cappellini.it

Coffee table, Rota
Denis Santachiara
Aluminium
H: 31.2cm (12¼in)
L: 120cm (47in)
D: 80cm (31in)
Diam (wheel):
30cm (11¾in)
Pallucco srl, Italy
www.pallucco.com

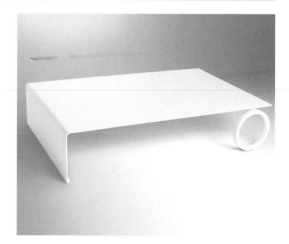

**Modular table system,
Colonnade**
David Chipperfield
White Carrara marble
H: 72cm (28in)
W: 98cm (38in)
L (symmetrical):
150cm (59in)
L (asymmetrical):
116.5cm (46in)
Marsotto srl, Italy
www.marsotto-edizioni.com

Coffee table, Anodized Table

Max Lamb
Anodized aluminium with
steel fixtures and rubber feet
H: 32cm (12⅝in)
W: 64cm (25in)
L: 64cm (25in)
Deadgood, UK
www.deadgoodltd.co.uk

Table, Big Table

Alain Gilles
Painted steel, wood
H: 74cm (29in)
W: 100cm (39in)
L: 200–320cm (78–126in)
Bonaldo, Italy
www.bonaldo.it

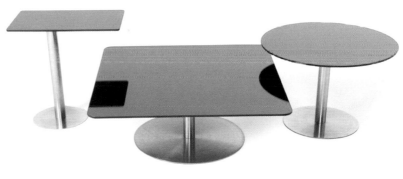

Table, Arc Table

Foster & Partners
Glass, concrete composite
(Ductal)
H: 73cm (28in)
Diam: 140cm (55in)
Molteni&C, Italy
www.molteni.it

Tables, Flash

Tom Dixon
Mirrored bronze, brass plated steel
H (Flash Rectangle): 50cm (19in)
L (Flash Rectangle): 50cm (19in)
D (Flash Rectangle): 30cm (11¾in)
H (Flash Square): 30cm (11¾in)
L (Flash Square): 80cm (31in)
D (Flash Square): 80cm (31in)
H (Flash Circle): 40cm (15¾in)
Diam (Flash Circle): 60cm (23in)
Tom Dixon, UK
www.tomdixon.net

Transformable table, Shuffle

Mia Hamborg
Lacquered MDF, solid beech, solid oak
H: 69cm (27in)
Diam: 45cm (17¾in)
& Tradition, Denmark
www.andtradition.com

Side tables, Time Piece

Jaime Hayon
Bronze
H: 43 or 58cm
(16⅞ or 22in)
Diam: 30 or 20cm
(11¾ or 7⅞in)
Sé, UK
www.se-london.com

Side tables, Gillespie

Samuel Chan
Oak or walnut, glass
H (small): 45cm
Diam (small): 35cm
H (medium): 55cm
Diam (medium): 45cm
H (large): 65cm
Diam (large): 55cm
Channels, UK
www.channelsdesign.com

Side table, Birignao

Ferruccio Laviani
Solid fir wood
H: 52cm (20in)
Diam: 55cm (21in)
Emmemobili, Italy
www.emmemobili.it

Table, Spool

Missoni Home Studio
Wood with high-gloss finish, viscose thread with resin finish
H: 39cm (15⅜in)
Diam: 80cm (31in)
Missoni Home by T&J Vestor SpA, Italy
www.missonihome.com

Pedestal dining table, Gabion
Benjamin Hubert
Granite ballast, steel, ash
H: 74cm (29in)
Diam: 130cm (51in)
De La Espada, Portugal
www.delaespada.com

Coffee table, Peggy Leggy
Richard Hutten
Massive wood, oak stained in
white or black
H: 40cm (15¾in)
Diam: 80cm (31in)
David Design, Sweden
www.daviddesignfurniture.se

Low tables, Marbelous 34 and 50
Naoto Fukasawa
White Carrara marble
H: 34 and 50cm
(13⅜ and 19in)
Diam: 45cm (17¾in)
Marsotto Edizioni, Italy
www.marsotto-edizioni.com

Table, Layer
Luca Nichetto
Glass, wood
H: 75cm (29in)
Diam: 150cm (59in)
Gallotti & Radice, Italy
www.gallottiradice.it

Coffee table, Float
Luca Nichetto
Aluminium, stainless steel
with mirror finish
H: 31cm (12¼in)
D: 118cm (46in)
La Chance, France
www.lachance.fr

Side table, CT09 Enoki
Philipp Mainzer
Marble, powder-coated steel
H: 40cm (15¾in)
Diam: 40cm (15¾in)
H: 30cm (11¾in)
Diam: 55cm (21in)
e15 Design and Distributions
GmbH, Germany
www.e15.com

Table, Alone in a crowd
Rolf Sachs
Oak, mild steel, toughened
glass, metal clock hands
and movement, 511
miniature figures
H: 72cm (28in)
W: 300cm (118in)
D: 120cm (47in)
Rolf Sachs Studio, UK
www.rolfsachs.com

Table, Patchwork Table
Arik Levy
Steel
H: 35.5cm (14⅛in)
Diam: 110cm (43in)
Established & Sons, UK
www.establishedandsons.com

Table, Udukuri Table
Jo Nagasaka
Douglas fir coated in resin
H: 73cm (28in)
L: 238cm (94in)
D: 100cm (39in)
Established & Sons, UK
www.establishedandsons.com

**Table and chairs,
Floating Table**
Ingo Maurer
Tabletop: Ash-faced plywood
Chairs: Solid ash, stain, steel
runners, inset castors
H (table top): 73.5cm (29in)
Diam (table top):
130cm (51in)
Established & Sons, UK
www.establishedandsons.com

Table, Briccole Venezia
Matteo Thun
Reused briccola oak wood
H: 76cm (29in)
W: 70/90cm (27/35in)
L: 290/340cm (114/133in)
Riva 1920, Italy
www.riva1920.it

Riva 1920 was founded almost one hundred years ago at Cantu, in the heart of the Italian furniture manufacturing district of Brianza, and is now being run by the third generation of the Riva family. Starting out as a small craft workshop producing bespoke wooden pieces, today it is internationally recognized, not only for its timeless, high-end and beautifully crafted products but also for its unswerving commitment to green design. The company uses solid wood from sustainable forests and natural finishes to create furniture that suffuses the home with the scent of timber, wax and oils. Riva's philosophy of 'natural living' goes hand in hand with its understanding of the cultural importance of wooden furniture, as well as the emotional quality of the material.

Building on the success of the Kauri collection, which saw 30,000-year-old wood that had been excavated from the ancient swamps of New Zealand turned into tables and chairs that showed traces of the fossilized timber's former life,

the Tra le Briccole di Venezia series similarly reinterprets an extraordinary material. So far thirty-four designers have been asked to conceive objects made from the reclaimed chestnut oak trunks that once formed mooring posts in the Venetian lagoon. Each post is at least 10 metres (32 feet) tall and has an average life span of five to ten years. Over time, as the tides rise and fall, the wood is invaded by micro-organisms and provides a home to the sea's flora and fauna. Once eroded, the posts are replaced but, by reusing this deformed but strangely beautiful timber, Riva has breathed new life into a resource that would otherwise have been discarded. The products that resulted from this initiative are a blend of design, art, craft and ecology that comment on the passing of time. Matteo Thun's table is made from sections cut from the full length of the posts. The legs are fixed at an angle, recalling the iconography of the Venice waterfront. A further example from the project can be seen in table mats designed by Philippe Starck (see page 175).

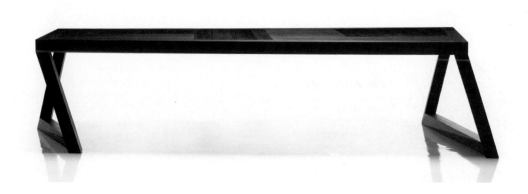

Table, Rotor
Piero Lissoni
Wood
H: 74cm (29in)
W: 123cm (48in)
L: 303cm (119in)
Cassina, Italy
www.cassina.com

Piet Hein Eek

You made your name with your graduation project, the scrap-wood cupboard (right). Could you describe the concept?

The project was inspired by timber that I found in a lumberyard. In Holland we have a rich tradition of recycling wood from demolished buildings, but it had never before been used for domestic design purposes. As a student I found it a beautiful and cheap resource and one I could process in the school workshop. In fact, this is still the way I work. Materials, technique, craftsmanship and availability are the main inspirations for my designs.

How would you say your approach to design has evolved over the years?

In essence nothing has changed. I always work with deep respect for materials and develop the best ways to use them naturally without wasting energy. Any evolution is in terms of perfected craftsmanship and the ability to arrive at better solutions, and in recognizing good ideas.

How do you manage to combine your philosophy with a growing business?

As I work in a pragmatic way, using down-to-earth production processes and as little energy and material as possible, the company has grown naturally. It's necessary to be mindful of labour costs and material resources when producing in Europe. I recognized the importance of the latter long before it was a topic of discussion in the design world.

Top right: Classic Cupboard in Scrapwood (1990)

Chunky Beam Chair No. 1 (2011)

You maintain that concern for resources and the environment is not a primary motive in your reuse pieces. Do you consider yourself a sustainable designer?

I regard myself as a sustainable person. I don't like the meaningless consumption of energy and materials. But I find the discussion of sustainability flawed, as almost everybody talks about the subject from the perspective of maintaining the way we live and consume. The only solution is to accept that we have to cut back by at least 10–15 per cent. We should be prepared to pay the same amount of money and receive less, which means the economy will survive. We have to accept the truth that things have to change and not be scared.

You have previously said that the combination of the techniques and materials you use results in a logical form. Can you expand on this statement?

The scrap-wood cupboard is based on the idea that longer pieces of scrap wood are difficult to use because they're often damaged or twisted. The solution of making frames in which it's possible to fit even the smallest fragments allowed me to use almost every piece.

The tube furniture (page 97) was inspired by a previous project, the big beam furniture (left). I had a huge amount of beams and at first I didn't know what to do with them, until I suddenly thought I could simply pile them up like a child playing with blocks. It then dawned on me that I could do a similar thing with the pipes that we had left over from the restoration work on our premises.

The aluminium curved, modular cabinet (page 106) is highly developed and seems to be a departure from your usual work. Would you agree?

We are known for our work in scrap wood, but our first aluminium collection was already in production in 1995. The cabinet is as much a part of my way of working as all my other designs. It is a celebration of the quality of the materials

we used, it's pragmatic in the way it's constructed and it's beautiful. The project started as a commission for a boutique and the shape was influenced by the need for a curved profile. The solution was to make an aluminium glass cupboard to match the balance of materials, colours and transparency in the shop. The combination of curved (aluminium) and straight (glass) forms lends the design its modern art deco feeling.

You have said that you want to create a recognizable brand with your work. Was the move to your current premises (right), which combine a workshop with a restaurant, a gallery and a shop, a part of that decision?

When we started in 1993 it was already evident that the designer was becoming more important than the producer (take Philippe Starck, for example). We decided to use my name against everything we did and to produce and distribute ourselves. We like to be in control of the whole process from first idea to communication with the consumer. It was difficult at first, but once you develop a way of working it becomes easier. A product is successful if everything is done well. Not just the aesthetics but also the pricing, the quality, the presentation, the transport. If you have to think about all these things, it's not surprising that you should want to control them. People often ask me what I consider to be my best design. I would now reply it's our own studio. In my final degree thesis I wrote if you want to make good things, or to function well, you should create a stimulating environment. This we have done in Eindhoven. In our previous premises we were a fishbowl but now we are an aquarium.

As a Design Academy Eindhoven alumnus of 1990, you are often described as a conceptual designer. Does this concern you?

It does bother me because I don't feel attached to that school of thought. I believe it's important to consider design in general. Designers should think and act as individuals whilst still being connected to their environment and culture. Dutch conceptual design was successfully promoted and I did benefit from that, but I have a problem with the way it was done. I don't agree with the term 'conceptual design' (with reference to Dutch design). It's more of a mentality. Many of the designers working in this way are not producing good design that will last but are making a statement. What the Dutch did in the 1990s was to show simplicity in a time of wealth and extravagance. After the confusion following the fall of the Twin Towers this same simplicity was embraced again, but for a different reason.

What do you consider to be the main challenges facing a designer today?

That he should not think of himself as a specialist but as a generalist. In the coming decade, designers should take more responsibility for the whole process. At this time there's a huge demand for people who are able to think differently, which is the challenge for all creative people.

Piet Hein Eek's studio, Eindhoven

Table, Troy Town Table
Hendzel & Hunt
Discarded roof trusses with
stained pieces of reclaimed
pallet wood inlays
H: 72cm (28in)
W: 96cm (37in)
L: 299cm (118in)
Hendzel & Hunt, UK
www.hendzelandhunt.com

The current trend for handicraft, sustainable design and
upcycling is highlighted in the work of young British designers
Jan Hendzel and Oscar Hunt, whose Made in Peckham range
is constructed entirely from reclaimed and waste materials
sourced from the streets and yards of the SE15 district of
London. These raw materials are transformed into elegant
pieces of bespoke or one-off furniture, with close attention
to detail. All the joints are dovetailed using traditional
cabinetmakers' techniques, and without the use of metal
fixings of any kind. The Troy Town Table and its benches are
built entirely from discarded roof trusses, with stained pieces
of recovered pallet wood inlayed into the table top. The joinery
is inspired by age-old Japanese woodworking methods.

**Posture kneeling stool
and desk, Knelt™**
Tim Spencer
American walnut veneered
moulded ply, coloured card
writing pad
H (desk): 42cm (16½in)
W (desk): 60cm (23in)
D (desk): 54cm (21in)
H (stool): 15cm (5⅞in)
W (stool): 43.5cm (17⅜in)
D (stool): 23cm (9in)
ubiquity design studio, UK
www.ubiquitydesignstudio.co.uk

Table, Frog Table
Hella Jongerius
Walnut wood, blue
transparent enamel
H: 120cm (47in)
W: 210cm (82in)
D: 105cm (41in)
Galerie kreo, France
www.galeriekreo.com

Stool, Senta
Fernando Brízio
Agglomerated cork, wood
H: 44.3cm (17⅜in)
Diam: 25.5cm (10¼in)
Amorim Cork Composites, S.A,
Portugal
www.corkcomposites.amorim.com

Nesting stool, AP
Shin Azumi
Curved plywood
H: 50cm (19in)
W: 47cm (18½in)
D: 37cm (14⅝in)
Lapalma srl, Italy
www.lapalma.it

**Children's furniture,
Wonder Box**
Monica Förster
Lacquered MDF, green
blackboard
H: 50cm (19in)
H (seat): 30cm (11¾in)
W: 70cm (27in)
D: 35cm (13¾in)
Richard Lampert, Germany
www.richard-lampert.de

**Side table/stool/step,
Maia**
Matthew Hilton
American black walnut or
American white oak
H: 35cm (13¾in)
W: 36cm (14⅛in)
D: 30cm (11¾in)
De La Espada, Portugal
www.delaespada.com

Chair, Gun Metal Chair
Xavier Lust
Anodized aluminium
H. 78cm (30in)
W: 47cm (18½in)
L: 51cm (20in)
Xavier Lust design studio,
Belgium
Carpenters Workshop Gallery,
UK
www.xavierlust.com
www.cwgdesign.com

Chair, Nara
Shin Azumi
Solid timber
H: 83.5cm (33in)
W: 49.5cm (19in)
D: 53cm (20in)
Fredericia Furniture A/S,
Denmark
www.fredericia.com

Chair, Lox
PearsonLloyd
Steel, leather
H: 79cm (31in)
H (seat): 46cm (18⅛in)
W: 70cm (27in)
D: 70cm (27in)
Walter Knoll, Germany
www.walterknoll.de

**Armchair, Bridge
Ora-Gami**
Ora-Ito
Polyurethane
H: 77cm (30in)
W: 66cm (26in)
D: 69cm (27in)
Steiner, France
www.steiner-paris.com

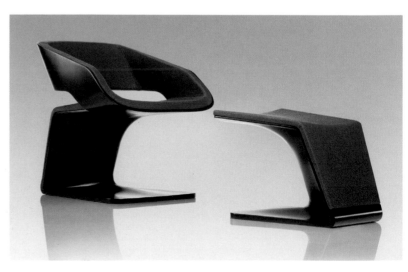

Chair, Cyborg Elegant
Marcel Wanders
ABS, wicker
H: 84cm (33in)
W: 56cm (22in)
L: 53cm (20in)
Magis SpA, Italy
www.magisdesign.com

Dining and lounge chairs, Kite
Shin Azumi
Solid beech wood,
polyurethane, fabric
H (dining chair): 80cm (31½in)
W (dining chair): 54cm (21in)
L (dining chair): 55cm (21in)
H (lounge chair): 70cm (27in)
W (lounge chair): 67cm (26in)
L (lounge chair): 66cm (26in)
Fornasarig srl, Italy
www.fornasarig.it

Chair, Monster
Marcel Wanders
Fire retardant synthetic
leather
H: 88cm (34in)
W: 62.5cm (24in)
D: 58cm (22in)
Moooi, The Netherlands
www.moooi.com

Chair, Vad Wood
Luca Nichetto
Natural solid oak,
polypropylene, fabric/leather
H: 78cm (30in)
W: 59cm (23in)
D: 60cm (24in)
Casamania, Italy
www.casamania.it

Chair, Felicerosa
Karim Rashid
Rotomoulded polyethylene,
fabric
H: 70cm (27in)
W: 73cm (28in)
L: 85cm (33in)
Felicerossi, Italy
www.felicerossi.it

Armchair, Sunshare
Emmanuel Babled
Carrara marble
H: 82.3cm (32in)
W: 120.6cm (47in)
D: 76cm (29in)
Studio Babled,
The Netherlands
www.babled.net

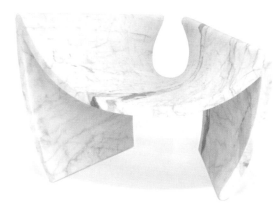

Chair, Eddy
PearsonLloyd
Upholstery
H: 75cm (29in)
W: 61cm (24in)
D: 63cm (24in)
Tacchini, Italy
www.tacchini.it

Armchair, 4801
Joe Colombo
Transparent technopolymer
thermoplastic
H: 59cm (23in)
W: 62cm (24in)
D: 64cm (25in)
Kartell SpA, Italy
www.kartell.it

Armchair, Apps
Richard Hutten
Wood, foam, fabric
upholstery
H: 77cm (30in)
W: 90cm (35in)
D: 76cm (29in)
Artifort, The Netherlands
www.artifort.com

Chair, Jumper
Bertjan Pot
Powder-coated steel, beech
ply, foam, felted wool
H: 74.5cm (29in)
L: 73.5cm (29in)
D: 70cm (27in)
Established & Sons, UK
www.establishedandsons.com

Chair, Avalon Chair
Michael Young
Steel tubing, moulded high-
resilience foam
H: 71cm (28in)
W: 78cm (30in)
D: 70cm (27in)
Swedese, Sweden
www.swedes.se

**Swivel armchair and
ottoman, Grande Papilio**
Naoto Fukasawa
Upholstery
H (armchair): 102cm (40in)
W (armchair): 83cm (32in)
D (armchair): 87cm (34in)
H (ottoman): 42.5cm (16⅞in)
W (ottoman): 70cm (27in)
D (ottoman): 50cm (19in)
B&B Italia SpA, Italy
www.bebitalia.com

Armchair, Tulip
Marcel Wanders
Upholstered polyurethane
H: 160cm (63in)
Diam: 86.3cm (33in)
Cappellini, Italy
www.cappellini.it

Portable and stackable outdoor seating, Fedro
Lorenza Bozzoli
Dedon fibre
H: 74cm (29in)
W: 75cm (29½in)
L: 101cm (40in)
Dedon, Germany
www.dedon.de

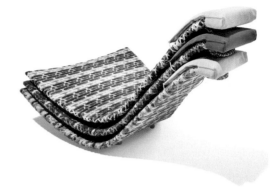

Armchair, Binta
Philippe Bestenheider
Steel, polyurethane foam, polypropylene
H: 95cm (37in)
W: 62cm (24in)
D: 62cm (24in)
Moroso SpA, Italy
www.moroso.it

Armchair, Crash
Konstantin Grcic
Powder-coated tubular steel, foam, upholstery
H: 80cm (31in)
L: 100cm (39in)
D: 72cm (28in)
Established & Sons, UK
www.establishedandsons.com

Rotating chair, Blaster Chair
James Irvine
Steel frame, foam, sustainable upholstery
H: 80.5cm (31in)
W: 92.7cm (36in)
D: 80.5cm (31in)
NgispeN, The Netherlands
www.ngispen.nl

Armchair, Shadowy
Tord Boontje
Plastic threads
H: 160cm (63in)
W: 105cm (41in)
D: 90cm (35in)
Moroso SpA, Italy
www.moroso.it

Armchair, Book Chair
Richard Hutten
Books, epoxy resin
H: 80cm (31in)
W: 110cm (43in)
D: 75cm (29in)
Richard Hutten Studio,
The Netherlands
www.richardhutten.com

Armchair, Antler
Nendo
Wool felt, solid olive
ash wood
H: 72cm (28in)
W: 64cm (25in)
D: 65cm (26in)
Cappellini, Italy
www.cappellini.it

Outdoor seating, Dala
Stephen Burks
Powder-coated extruded
aluminium mesh, strands
of ecological fibre
H: 80cm (31in)
Diam: 96cm (37in)
Dedon, Germany
www.dedon.de

Chair, Bac
Jasper Morrison
Solid ash wood and plywood
H: 73cm (28in)
W: 52.5cm (21in)
D: 51cm (20in)
Cappellini, Italy
www.cappellini.it

Chair, Vigna
Martino Gamper
Metal, bi-injection-
moulded plastic
H: 84cm (33in)
W: 43cm (16⅞in)
D: 49cm (19¼in)
Magis SpA, Italy
www.magisdesign.com

**Armchair, The
Secret Clubhouse**
Martin Vallin
Pinewood, felt-
covered cushions
H: 153cm (60in)
W: 98cm (38in)
D: 92cm (36in)
Cappellini, Italy
www.cappellini.it

**Chair, No. 14 Anniversary
Edition**
Michael Thonet
Antiqued walnut, 100%
hand-woven Viennese straw
H: 89cm (35in)
W: 41cm (16⅛in)
D: 49cm (19¼in)
Gebrüder Thonet Vienna
(trademark of Poltrona Frau
SpA), Italy
www.thonet-vienna.com

Chair, 5 O'Clock Chair
Nika Zupanc
Solid beech, Skai leather
H: 80cm (31in)
W: 49cm (19¼in)
D: 42cm (16½in)
Moooi, The Netherlands
www.moooi.com

Chair, Wolfgang
Luca Nichetto
Wood
H: 70cm (27in)
W: 49cm (19¼in)
D: 42cm (16½in)
Fornasarig srl, Italy
www.fornasarig.it

**Rocking chair, Domestic
Tales Scissor Chair**
Kiki van Eijk
Iron, polyurethane, wood
and lycra
H: 78cm (30in)
W: 100cm (39in)
D: 61cm (24in)
Skitsch, Italy
www.skitsch.it

Chair, Chair-4a
Michael Young
Aluminium
H (seat): 44cm (17⅜in)
W: 37cm (14⅝in)
D: 37cm (14⅝in)
Ostbahn, Hong Kong
www.ostbahn.com

**Outdoor armchair,
Crinoline**
Patricia Urquiola
Polyethylene weave, natural
fibre or bronze string
H: 155.5cm (61in)
W: 101cm (40in)
D: 75cm (29in)
B&B Italia SpA, Italy
www.bebitalia.com

Stefan Diez

Your work has been described as functional, elegantly simple and accurately crafted, and as such could be tagged as belonging to the Germanic school of design. In an increasingly global environment, do you think one can talk of national style characteristics?

That sounds to me like a definition of good design. International companies collaborate with designers from all over the world and, as such, it's difficult to track a national style in a manufacturer's, often globally homogenous, portfolio. I use technology and materials that are accessible around me, which results in my work having a certain locality. This is the thread that runs through all my designs.

Do you think your training as a cabinetmaker has affected the way you work?

Learning things from scratch is not unusual in Germany. The Academy of Arts in Stuttgart demanded a solid training in metal- and woodwork before I could study there. The importance of an education in craft techniques helps a designer understand materials and be able to communicate with producers. We use our hands to form a design through all the stages of development and to learn about the emerging product by making models and prototypes. I can absolutely not imagine working without this kind of knowledge or thinking.

What did you learn from the periods you spent in the studios of Richard Sapper and, later, Konstantin Grcic?

Top right: Shuttle containers for Rosenthal-Thomas (2006)

Prototype 404 F Chair for THONET (2007)

As a student I worked first with Richard Sapper, and then afterwards for two years in Konstantin's studio. Each has influenced the way I think about design. Richard's perspective was towards technical complexity. His work is informed by careful observation and an enormous knowledge of manufacturing and materials. Konstantin is totally honest and conscious about everything he does. His work adds a personal and intellectual aspect to an industrial product. I am grateful to have had such teachers.

You primarily collaborate with manufacturers that have their routes in high-tech industrial production, such as THONET, but with the Houdini family you worked with e15 (page 54), which is orientated more towards handcraft. Did your approach alter?

THONET is a good example of how a proprietary manufacturing technique can shape the picture we have of a company. They have twice invented distinct production processes with a design language that has become the DNA of any of their bent-wood or bent-metal products. Working for THONET was, ergo, not so much about designing a chair but rather designing for a process [to manufacture chairs]. This was a crucial discovery for me and has influenced the way I think and work for other clients. With each new project I try to define a relevant field of experimentation, which the studio then explores during design development. Collaborating with a relatively young manufacturer such as e15 therefore produces completely different answers than those generated whilst working for an industrial manufacturer like Wilkhahn (opposite page, right) or the elderly Lady Thonet.

You employ innovative techniques and push the limitations of the materials you use. To what extent does this influence your designs?

With each project we develop an experimental playground with the aim of finding something the client can own afterwards. Considering both materials and production processes helps, especially if we find new applications for both, or an innovative way to combine the two. We are constantly searching for answers with a contemporary, relevant and surprising quality. Once our initial ideas become clearer, we start to fathom the boundaries. For me, the challenge of design is vertical not horizontal.

Can you describe two pivotal projects of your studio?

I can't view my work in this way. Ideally every project opens up a new universe.

You have said that you are reluctant to work with Chinese manufacturers. Why?

European companies with poor ideas but good distribution channels have used China as a way out. They have taken the opportunity to manufacture their products for half the price and so earn double the profit. Others have gone to China in order to diversify their portfolio. The problem is that only a few Chinese manufacturers, offering standard processes to both their old and new clients, are now responsible for many of the objects that surround us. As a designer it's difficult to be innovative in such an environment, which is widely characterized by generic rather than proprietary knowledge. Still, there are some great Chinese manufacturers and I have been lucky to work with some of them during my collaboration with Rosenthal (opposite page, top right) and Authentics (above).

You talk a lot about the effect living in India has had on you and how you would like to collaborate with Indian manufacturers. Can you explain your interest?

Since I was an apprentice, one of my very best friends has been an Indian from Pune. We were taught in the same school and woodworking workshop. I first visited his family in 1994 and from that time onwards have been a big fan of his country. The Cultural Revolution in China extinguished any links that country had with its cultural heritage, whereas India has direct access to thousands of years of culture, which is still alive and forms a strong spiritual foundation in society.

I started working with an Indian manufacturer of household goods and modular kitchens in 2011, and we launched our first product range in May 2012. I know that I will have a lot to learn to fit the expectations of such a different market, but I have an enthusiastic and proud collaborator who is willing to undertake the risk of an experimental approach. Looks like I always find reasons to play it the hard way rather than follow a comfortable guarantee of success.

What do you think a good project for the future would be in terms of sustainability?

One that has a high degree of refinement and sophistication paired with durability and efficiency. The many designers and manufacturers that are aiming to make a living whilst respecting the planet should also follow Dieter Rams's dictum 'less, but better'.

What is the most important role a designer can play?

Our role is often the representation of an idea that has been invented and carried out by many. This being the case, it is necessary for us to keep the spirit of an optimist and be clear about our values and utopias.

Left: Kuvert casual bags for Authentics (2006)

Right: Chassis Chair for Wilkhahn (2008)

Armchair, Scratch

Patrick Norguet
Solid ash-wood slats, multi-
density polyurethane foam
H: 67.5cm (26in)
W: 69cm (27in)
D: 55cm (21in)
Cappellini, Italy
www.cappellini.it

Easychair, Oscar Bon

Philippe Starck
Carbon fibre
H: 78cm (30in)
W: 56cm (22in)
D: 65cm (25in)
Driade, Italy
www.driade.com

Chair, Flower Cup Chair

Leif.designpark
Plywood with oak or walnut
veneer, solid American black
walnut or American white
oak, upholstery
H: 77cm (30in)
W: 53cm (21in)
D: 52cm (20in)
De La Espada, Portugal
www.delaespada.com

Outdoor lounge chair and table, Swa

Setsu and Shinobu Ito
Oak
H (chair): 71cm (28in)
L (chair): 63cm (24in)
D (chair): 79cm (31in)
H (table): 38cm (15in)
L (table): 63cm (24in)
D (table): 50cm (19in)
Fornasarig, Italy
www.fornasarig.it

**Chair, Woodware
Lounge Chair**
Max Lamb
Maple, walnut, ash, beech,
cherry, tulip, oak
H: 69cm (27in)
W: 74cm (29in)
D: 63cm (24in)
Max Lamb, UK
www.galleryfumi.com

Armchair, Pebble
Osko & Deichmann
Foam, fabric, steel
H: 75cm (29in)
W: 85cm (33in)
D: 103cm (41in)
Blå Station Sweden
www.blastation.com

Armchair, Maritime
Benjamin Hubert
Solid oak ply
H: 75.5cm (29in)
W: 53cm (20in)
D: 53cm (20in)
Casamania, Italy
www.casamania.it

**Outdoor chair,
Impossible Wood**
Doshi Levien
Injection-moulded
thermoplastic composite
(80% wood fibre,
20% polypropylene)
H: 75cm (29in)
W: 65cm (25in)
D: 53cm (20in)
Moroso SpA, Italy
www.moroso.it

Chair, Comback Chair
Patricia Urquiola
Batch-dyed technopolymer
thermoplastic
H: 90cm (35in)
L: 56cm (22in)
D: 61cm (24in)
Kartell SpA, Italy
www.kartell.it

Swivel chair, Nub
Patricia Urquiola
Solid beech, chromed steel
finished in lacquer
H (small version): 85.5cm (33in)
W (small version): 64cm (25in)
D (small version): 58cm (22in)
H (large version): 89cm (35in)
W (large version): 78.5cm (31in)
D (large version): 61cm (24in)
Andreu World, Spain
www.andreuworld.com

Chair, Branca
Industrial Facility
Solid wood
H: 82cm (32in)
W: 57cm (22in)
D: 54cm (21in)
Mattiazzi, Italy
www.mattiazzi.eu

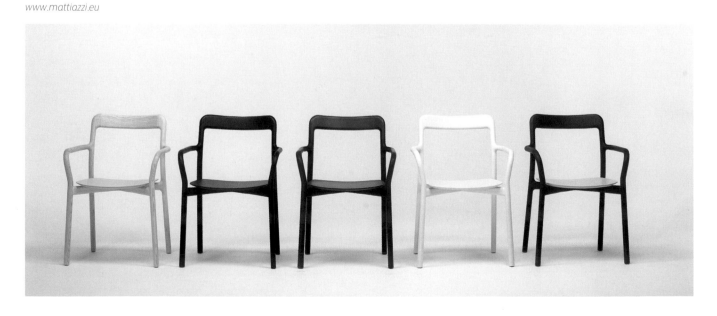

Foldable lounge chair, Clip Chair
Osko & Deichmann
Beech wood
H: 74cm (29in)
W: 80cm (31in)
D: 67cm (26in)
Moooi, The Netherlands
www.moooi.com

Dining chair, Straw Chair
Osko & Deichmann
Steel tube
H: 84.5cm (33in)
W: 47.5cm (18⅞in)
D: 59.5cm (23in)
Blå Station, Sweden
www.blastation.com

Armchair, Fildefer
Alessandra Baldereschi
Polyester-coated iron rod
H: 112cm (44in)
L: 78cm (30in)
D: 70cm (27in)
Skitsch, Italy
www.skitsch.it

Chair, Masters
Philippe Starck with
Eugeni Quitllet
Modified batch-dyed
polypropylene
H: 84cm (33in)
W: 57cm (22in)
D: 47cm (18½in)
Kartell SpA, Italy
www.kartell.it

Bench, 10 Unit System
Shigeru Ban
UPM ProFi wood plastic
composite
H: 84cm (33in)
W: 80cm (31in)
D: 44cm (17⅜in)
Artek, Finland
www.artek.fi

Stool, Alodia
Todd Bracher
Metal tube, steel sheet, plastic
H: 70 or 80cm (27 or 31in)
W: 46cm (18⅛in)
L: 54cm (21in)
Cappellini, Italy
www.cappellini.it

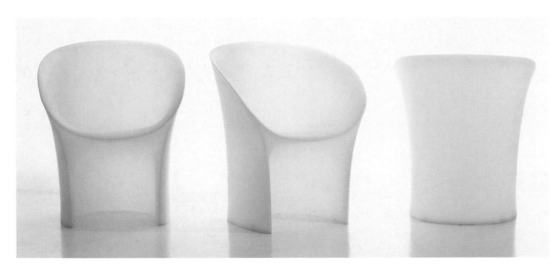

Armchair, Moon
Tokujin Yoshioka
Rotationally moulded 100%-
recyclable polyethylene
H: 73cm (28in)
W: 61cm (24in)
D: 62cm (24in)
Moroso SpA, Italy
www.moroso.it

Privacy chair, Pod
Benjamin Hubert
Sound-dampening PET
felt technology
H: 130cm (51in)
W: 103cm (41in)
D: 83cm (32in)
De Vorm, The Netherlands
www.devorm.nl

Chair, Instant Seat
Matali Crasset
Plywood beech
H: 73.5cm (29in)
W: 45.5cm (18⅛in)
D: 61.5cm (24in)
Moustache, France
www.moustache.fr

**Armchair, The Invisibles
Light Collection**
Tokujin Yoshioka
Transparent technopolymer
thermoplastic
H (seat): 42cm (16½in)
H: 70cm (27in)
W: 60cm (23in)
D: 57cm (22in)
Kartell SpA, Italy
www.kartell.it

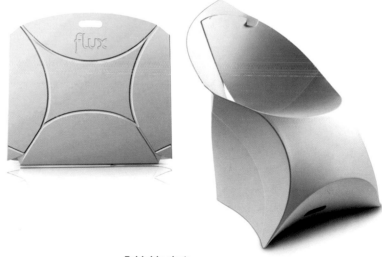

**Foldable chair,
flux® chair**
Tom Schouten and
Douwe Jacobs
Polypropylene
H: 84cm (33in)
W: 66cm (26in)
D: 67cm (25⅔in)
Flux Furniture,
The Netherlands
www.fluxfurniture.com

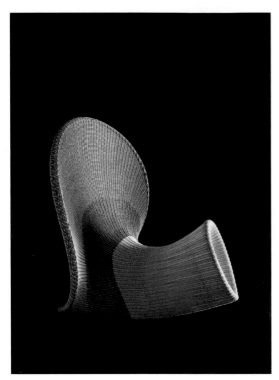

**Outdoor chairs
and table, Sunrise**
Ludovica and Roberto Palomba
Lacquered aluminium
H (chair): 83cm (32in)
W (chair): 46cm (18⅛in)
D (chair): 52cm (20in)
Driade SpA, Italy
www.driade.com

Outdoor rocking chair, 56 h
Fabio Novembre
Aluminium structure covered
with woven plastic
H: 123cm (48in)
W: 112cm (44in)
D: 107cm (42in)
Driade SpA, Italy
www.driade.com

Armchair, Altair
Daniel Libeskind
Stainless steel
H: 86cm (33in)
W: 80cm (31in)
L: 120cm (47in)
Sawaya & Moroni, Italy
www.sawayamoroni.com

Chair, Phalène
Marc Sadler
Iron rod
H: 82cm (32in)
W: 52cm (20in)
D: 55cm (21in)
Robots SpA, Italy
www.robots.it

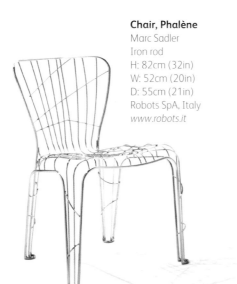

Chair, Z-Chair
Zaha Hadid
Stainless steel
H: 91cm (35in)
W: 60cm (23in)
L: 95cm (37in)
Sawaya & Moroni, Italy
www.sawayamoroni.com

**Chair, The Ghost
of a Chair**
Valentina Gonzalez Wohlers
Polyester
H: 95cm (37in)
W: 80–100cm (31–39in)
L: 80–100cm (31–39in)
D: 80–100cm (31–39in)
Valentina Gonzalez Wohlers, UK
www.valentinagw.com

Chair, The Cloud Chair
Richard Hutten
Polished aluminium, rhodium
H: 85.5cm (33in)
W: 120cm (47in)
D: 90cm (35in)
Richard Hutten Studio bv,
The Netherlands
www.richardhutten.com

Chair, The Reverb Chair
Brodie Neill
Mirror-polished and hand
formed nickel-plated
aluminium
H: 74cm (29in)
W: 100cm (39in)
D: 84cm (33in)
The Apartment Gallery, UK
www.theapartmentuk.com

Armchair, Memory
Tokujin Yoshioka
Cotton-fibre fabric with an
aluminium core
H: 83cm (32in)
H (seat): 48cm (18⅞in)
W: 88cm (34in)
D: 75cm (29in)
Moroso SpA, Italy
www.moroso.it

Chair, Tip Ton
BarberOsgerby
Plastic
H: 78.6cm (31in)
W: 50.9cm (20in)
D: 55.5cm (22in)
Vitra AG, Switzerland
www.vitra.com

Chair, Canteen
Utility Chair
Andre Klauser and
Ed Carpenter
Beech plywood, steel tube
H: 80.5cm (31in)
W: 49.5cm (19in)
D: 45.5cm (18⅛in)
Very Good & Proper, UK
www.verygoodandproper.co.uk

Stackable armchair,
Monza
Konstantin Grcic
Ash wood, polypropylene
H: 76cm (29in)
W: 54cm (21in)
D: 49cm (19in)
Plank Collezioni srl, Italy
www.plank.it

Stackable chair, Wogg 50
Jörg Boner
Plywood
H: 81cm (31in)
W: 52cm (20in)
D: 50cm (19in)
Wogg AG, Switzerland
www.wogg.ch

**Nesting folding indoor/
outdoor chair, Piana**
David Chipperfield
100% recyclable
polypropylene reinforced
with fibreglass
H: 78cm (30in)
W: 46cm (18⅛in)
D: 52cm (20in)
Alessi SpA, Italy
Lamm SpA, Italy
www.alessi.com
www.lamm.it

Stackable chair, Peg
Tom Dixon
Solid birch
H: 78cm (30in)
W: 53cm (20in)
L: 54cm (21in)
Tom Dixon, UK
www.tomdixon.net

Stackable chair, Florinda
Monica Förster
Solid beech, transparent
acrylic varnish, polycarbonate
H: 83cm (32in)
W: 48cm (18⅞in)
D: 51cm (20in)
De Padova srl, Italy
www.depadova.it

**Chair with armrest,
CH04 HOUDINI**
Stefan Diez
Oak or walnut-veneered
plywood, lacquered,
upholstery
H (seat): 46cm (18⅛in)
W: 57cm (22in)
D: 40cm (15¾in)
E15, Germany
www.e15.com

**Stackable chair,
Ahrend 380**
Ineke Hans
Recyclable plastic
H: 81.5cm (32in)
W: 51cm (20in)
D: 51.5cm (20in)
Ahrend, The Netherlands
www.ahrend.com

Chair, EC04 LEO
Stefan Diez
Walnut-veneered plywood,
lacquered
H (seat): 40cm (15¾in)
W: 57cm (22in)
D: 46cm (18⅛in)
E15, Germany
www.e15.com

Chair, Pebble
Benjamin Hubert
Rotational moulded
polyethylene, oak
H: 84cm (33in)
W: 46cm (18⅛in)
D: 40cm (15¾in)
Devorm, The Netherlands
www.devorm.nl

Chair, Jill
Alfredo Häberli
Plywood
H: 85cm (33in)
W: 49.1cm (19¼in)
D: 51.7cm (20in)
Vitra AG, Switzerland
www.vitra.com

**Indoor/outdoor armchair,
Waver**
Konstantin Grcic
Tubular steel, fabric
H: 99cm (39in)
W: 78.5cm (31in)
D: 87cm (34in)
Vitra AG, Switzerland
www.vitra.com

Chair, Green
Javier Mariscal
Recycled polypropylene,
wood
H: 79cm (31in)
W: 50cm (19in)
D: 50cm (19in)
Mobles 114, Spain
www.mobles114.com

Barstool, Bentboo
Chen-hsu Liu
Laminated bamboo
H: 75cm (29in)
W: 38.5cm (15⅜in)
Yii, Taiwan
HAN Gallery, Taiwan
www.yiidesign.com
www.han-gallery.com

Stools, Tom and Jerry
Konstantin Grcic
Solid beech wood, plastic
H: Adjustable
Diam (seat): 34cm (13⅜in)
Magis SpA, Italy
www.magisdesign.com

Stool, 5°
Tomás Alonso
Oak, rope
H: 49cm (19¼in)
W: 45cm (17¾in)
D: 25cm (9⅞in)
Nils Holger Moormann
GmbH, Germany
www.moormann.de

Stool, Stool
Aldo Bakker
Wood
H: 35cm (13¾in)
W: 34cm (13⅜in)
D: 33cm (13in)
Particles, The Netherlands
www.particlesgallery.com

**Stackable stool, NOM
(Nature of Material)**
Bakery Studio
Laser-cut aluminium sheet
H: 44.5cm (17¾in)
W: 37.5cm (15in)
D: 37.5cm (15in)
Cappellini, Italy
www.cappellini.it

Stool, Zen Cap
Ludovica and Roberto Palomba
Canadian solid-wood
red cedar
H: 45cm (17¾in)
Diam: 40cm (15¾in)
Exteta, Italy
www.exteta.it

Chair, 3DWN1UP
Aldo Bakker
Wood
H: 88cm (34in)
Diam: 42cm (16½in)
Particles Gallery,
The Netherlands.
www.particlesgallery.com

Stool, Eden
Marcel Wanders
Ceramic, shiny finish
H: 46cm (18⅛in)
Diam: 33cm (13in)
xO, France
www.xo-design.com

Barstool, Bambool
Yu-jui Chou
Bamboo
H: 73cm (28in)
W: 45cm (17¾in)
Yii, Taiwan
HAN Gallery, Taiwan
www.yiidesign.com
www.han-gallery.com

Revolver is a four-legged bar stool that rotates thanks to integrated ball bearings in the lower ring. It was designed to encourage social interaction – the footrest moves with the seat so that the user can swivel through 360 degrees, allowing the whole body to turn at once.

Rotating barstool, Revolver

Leon Ransmeier
Steel tubing, punched steel sheet
H: 76.7cm (30in)
Diam: 45cm (17¾in)
Established & Sons, UK
www.establishedandsons.com

Stools, Noughts and Crosses

Michael Sodeau
Oak, metal
H: 82.5cm (32in)
Diam: 51cm (20in)
Modus, UK
www.modusfurniture.co.uk

Chair, Stubborn Chair

Studio Makkink & Bey
Polyester
H: 86cm (33in)
W: 51cm (20in)
D: 56cm (22in)
NgispeN, The Netherlands
www.ngispen.nl

Stool, Stool

Fernando and Humberto Campana
Steel and wood structure covered in ostrich leather
H: 50cm (19in)
Diam: 30cm (11¾in)
Klein Karoo, South Africa
www.kleinkaroo.com

Chair, Medici

Konstantin Grcic
Wood
H: 79.5cm (31in)
W: 68.5cm (27in)
D: 75cm (29in)
Mattiazzi srl, Italy
www.mattiazzi.eu

Design today is being challenged to develop lasting solutions that achieve a balance between 'people, planet and profit'. But, in industries built on and pushing the idea of consumption, this is not always straightforward, as large manufacturing companies have to consider commercial viability and factory demands. New attitudes and approaches need to be set in place to change the way a product is devised and for its lifecycle to be re-evaluated in all areas, including how it is eventually disposed of or recycled. Forward-thinking market leaders are rising to the challenge, including Coca-Cola, which is committed to exploring a sustainable approach for reusing their PET bottles. In 2009 the company set up the rPET merchandise line, which, in collaboration with designers and producers, seeks to motivate people to recycle by showing them how plastic bottles can be upcycled and transformed into high-end design products.

Despite the considerable expense involved in re-engineering a core product, Emeco was excited to be involved in turning something many people throw away into an item that is strong, durable and has a long shelf life. The Navy Chair is an iconic design, created in 1944 for the US Navy. The new 111 Navy Chair is made from at least 111 recycled bottles, in combination with other materials including pigment and glass fibre that make up less than 40 per cent of its composition. In the first year of production, the chair diverted 3.5 million bottles out of landfills. Gregg Buchbinder, chairman and CEO of Emeco, speaks enthusiastically about the project: 'Unlike other companies which use virgin materials and produce stylish designs in trendy colours with the message that you can consume and recycle, we keep consumer waste out of landfills and upcycle it into something that does not need to be recycled for a long time. Our Navy Chair design is over six decades old. You can buy our 111 Navy Chair this year or next year or in ten years to come, it will never go out of style.'

After local collection of used bottles, the PET is processed in Coca-Cola's recycling plant and turned into a proprietary mix before being sent to Emeco's manufacturing plant for moulding in a robotic four-part tool that replicates exactly the sections of the original aluminium chair. Once cooled and set, the new chair is presented to a factory worker who smoothes any imperfections before manually installing its H-brace and feet. This personal touch gives a unique quality to a product in which twenty-first-century recycling technology is married to a handmade aesthetic, producing an object that is both old and new – in more ways than one. The 111 Navy Chair has an expected thirty-year life span, after which it can be recycled to make new chairs.

Chair, 111 Navy Chair®
Emeco
65% recycled plastic bottles,
35% glass fibre
H: 86cm (34in)
W: 39cm (15½in)
D: 50cm (19½in)
Emeco, USA
www.emeco.net

Xavier Lust

You made your name with a new technique for the precision folding and bending of metal, which you call the '(de)formation of surfaces'. Could you explain this technique?

The idea came to me in 1999. Until then I was producing my own designs, primarily welding and folding steel. I worked with many specialist factories and gained a lot of experience in the limitations of the machines being used. (De)formation is a simple technique, and cost-effective as there is no investment in moulds. By distorting the metal through progressive shapes from the flat to the curved, the material is allowed to speak for itself and defines the end result. The process is also economical in the amount of metal it uses, as it's the precision folding that adds strength to the object. The following year I exhibited at SaloneSatellite during the Milan Furniture Fair. It was an important year for me as I was collaborating with MDF Italia, who went on to produce and distribute Le Banc (opposite page, bottom left), which is now a collector's item.

Can you briefly describe two of the pivotal projects of your studio and explain why they have influenced the way you work?

Apart from Le Banc and the PicNik table for Extremis, both of which are key examples of the (de)formation process, an important early piece is the Turner candleholder (below) for Driade. It's ironic that a company specialising in moulding called me. Turner is pivotal because it was a change in direction. Although it is still informed by the material, in this case aluminium, it was designed in 3D on the computer and sent to the client as a CAD model. It's become a classic and is still my bestseller in terms of the number of pieces produced. As far as more recent work is concerned, the Gamete (page 222) and Algue lights for MGX by Materialise have shown me what it is to work with a technique that is boundless. I normally use technological limitations as a guideline, but with stereolithography virtually any form is possible.

Top right: Baobab coat stand for MDF Italia (2005/2008)

Turner candleholder for Driade (2003/2004)

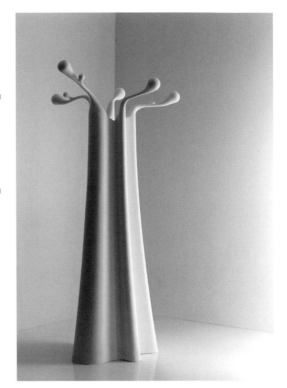

You say that all your designs have been inspired by nature. Can you explain what you mean?

Although some of my designs reference nature in an evident way, such as the Gamete light and the Baobab coat stand (above), I'm alluding to another, microscopic level of inspiration. Nothing in nature is without a function and similarly everything in my designs is there for a reason, like Darwin's theory; it's an evolutionary process.

You design both mass-produced products and limited-edition pieces. How important is it to keep a balance between the commercial and experimental?

Design for me is a dialogue between four parameters: function, aesthetics, culture and technology. They form a closed circuit with one linking to the other. When all four are well balanced, I'm satisfied. When you design a limited-edition piece it presents the opportunity of working in a way you couldn't for industrial production, but I think it's possible to be innovative as well as affordable and commercial. To create something that makes sense and is beautiful is the ultimate goal. It's nice to make luxury but it's nicer if you can make it for every terrace.

You maintain that innovation is not the antithesis of tradition. Can you expand on this?

It's impossible to go against tradition because we are all informed by influences from the past. This is the basis of creativity. You can only go further and add to it. When I was a student I was sick of hearing that everything had already been created and it was only possible to be innovative through

new technology. Technological advances are fantastic but they are not everything. You can be totally original and make new things without sidestepping tradition. I want the work I'm doing today to be the tradition of tomorrow.

You recently won the Urban Street Furniture Competition for the Brussels region. What attracted you to this commission?

About nine years ago I started to be interested in the idea of designing street furniture. Many of my designs don't get made because they would be too expensive to manufacture, but street furniture is always linked to the cost of production. More importantly the humanist element appealed to me. I wanted to make something as banal as waiting for a bus a pleasurable experience. Every detail counts. I was surprised that I won the competition because it's not my nature to apply political pressure. My work is either the best or it's not. I don't sell myself; my work sells me. There were a lot of practical, as well as health and safety, considerations to take on board and many different bodies to please. It has been a long and difficult process. I had to reply meticulously to the brief, but I like to work within constraints as they offer guidelines, and I'm pleased with the result (right).

Do you think Belgian design has a voice? Is it helpful to talk about national styles?

I'm Belgian and proud of it, but five or six years ago the concept of Belgian design was born and I think it doesn't apply. We are a small country and our power lies in being open to the world. I think the message should be international. I like the idea of an object speaking a universal language; it's the way I work. If you start to talk about an imaginary 'Belgian' style, you reduce the discourse.

Do you believe that designs assists in the creation of a better world?
Yes.

What are your thoughts on sustainable design?

Something has to change. Manufacturers have to produce the object and make it as commercially as possible, and the majority of suppliers just want to sell. They don't care about the rest. I was recently in discussion with one company about the possibility of using a more ecological, vegetable-based plastic alternative to polypropylene, but although they said they could obtain it, it was twelve times more expensive!

What do you consider to be the main challenges facing a designer today?

To consider the planet as much as possible and to create designs that are aesthetic as well as functional but, above all, that make sense. Products should be durable in terms of their wear and tear but also timeless, so they survive the vagaries of fashionable trends.

Left: Le Banc for MDF Italia (2000/2001)

Right: Street furniture for Region Brussels-STIB-MIVB (2012)

Chair, Zuiderzee Chair
Richard Hutten
Beech wood
H: 77cm (30in)
W: 43cm (16⅞in)
D: 42cm (16½in)
NgispeN, The Netherlands
www.ngispen.nl

Armchair, Flow
Jean-Marie Massaud
Oak, polyester, expanded
polyurethane
H: 78cm (30in)
L: 60cm (23in)
D: 56cm (22in)
MDF Italia, Italy
www.mdfitalia.it

Chair, PLC Series
PearsonLloyd
Plywood
H: 73.5cm (29in)
W: 60.2cm (23in)
D: 55.3cm (21in)
Modus, UK
www.modusfurniture.co.uk

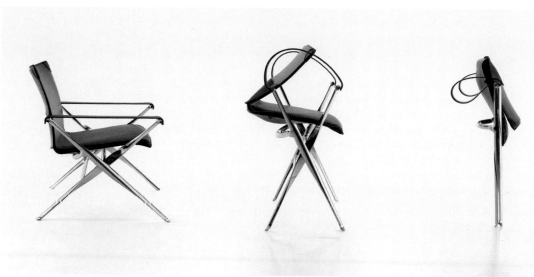

Folding armchair, Beverly
Antonio Citterio
Aluminium alloy,
leather/fabric
H: 78cm (30in)
W: 69.5cm (27in)
D: 74cm (29in)
B&B Italia SpA, Italy
www.bebitalia.com

Armchair, M-collection
Van Eijk & Van der Lubbe
Hand-laminated polyester,
glossy finish, upholstery
H: 95cm (37in)
W: 80cm (31in)
D: 79cm (31in)
Lensvelt b.v., The Netherlands
www.lensvelt.nl

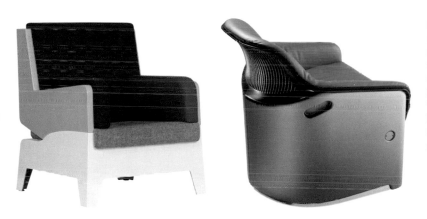

Lounge chair, Avus
Konstantin Grcic
Plastic, polyurethane
foam (flame retardant),
natural leather
H: 80cm (31in)
W: 73cm (28in)
D: 73cm (28in)
Plank Collezioni srl, Italy
www.plank.it

**Indoor/outdoor
armchair, Nemo**
Fabio Novembre
Polyethylene
H: 135cm (53in)
W: 90cm (35in)
D: 83cm (32in)
Driade, Italy
www.driade.com

**Indoor/outdoor
chair, Piña**
Jaime Hayon
Wood, wire, cushion
H: 81cm (31in)
W: 53cm (20in)
D: 53cm (20in)
Magis SpA, Italy
www.magisdesign.com

**Dining chair,
Bamboo Steel**
Nendo
Steel
H: 82cm (32in)
W: 50cm (19in)
D: 54cm (21in)
Yii, Taiwan
HAN Gallery, Taiwan
www.yiidesign.com
www.han-gallery.com

Lounge chair, Coracle
Benjamin Hubert
Leather, steel
H: 65cm (25in)
W: 90cm (35in)
D: 90cm (35in)
De La Espada, Portugal
www.delaespada.com

Armchair, Arpa
Jaime Hayon
Tubular powder-coated steel
frame, upholstery
H: 120cm (47in)
W: 75cm (29in)
D: 100 cm (39in)
Sé, UK
www.se-london.com

Seating, Superheroes
Glimpt
Bent and welded metal,
sea grass, thread
H (big stool): 31cm (12¼in)
Diam (big stool): 70cm (27in)
Cappellini, Italy
www.cappellini.it

Armchair, Juliet
Benjamin Hubert
Solid wood, polyurethane
foam, polyester wadding,
Pelle Frau® leather
H: 85cm (33in)
W: 101cm (40in)
D: 80cm (31in)
Poltrona Frau, Italy
www.poltronafrau.com

Chair, Wave
Fernando and Humberto
Campana
Bamboo stalk
H: 86cm (33in)
W: 50cm (19in)
D: 84cm (33in)
Yii, Taiwan
HAN Gallery, Taiwan
www.yiidesign.com
www.han-gallery.com

**Indoor/outdoor armchair,
Pavo Real Outdoor**
Patricia Urquiola
Tubular aluminium, braided
plastic, outdoor upholstery
H: 130cm (51in)
W: 110cm (43in)
D: 89cm (35in)
Driade, Italy
www.driade.com

Multifunctional chair,
Library Chair
J. Schotte/groupDesign
FSC birch plywood
H: 90cm (35in)
W: 36.6cm (14⅝in)
D: 48cm (18⅞in)
groupDesign, UK
www.groupdesign.co.uk

Armchair, Grinza
Fernando and Humberto
Campana
Steel, polyurethane, eco-fur
H: 75cm (29in)
W: 106cm (42in)
D: 88cm (34in)
Edra SpA, Italy
www.edra.com

Cantilever chair, A-chair
Werner Aisslinger with
Tina Buyaprasit
Steel tube, metal mesh
H: 79.7cm (31in)
W: 52.8cm (20in)
L'abbate, Italy
www.lacollection.it

Indoor/outdoor chair,
Gothic Chair
Studio Job
Rotational moulded
polyethylene
H: 90cm (35in)
W: 44.5cm (17¾in)
D: 46cm (18⅛in)
Moooi, The Netherlands
www.moooi.com

Stackable chair, JO
Alfredo Häberli
Sandblasted stainless
steel, plywood
H: 84cm (33in)
W: 50cm (19in)
D: 57cm (22in)
Lapalma srl, Italy
www.lapalma.it

Easy armchair, Bloom
Kenneth Cobonpue
Microfibre, resin, steel
H: 87cm (34in)
W: 105cm (41in)
D: 98cm (38in)
Kenneth Cobonpue,
Philippines
www.kennethcobonpue.com

Chair, Hide Chair
Matthew Hilton
Plywood, fabric
H: 68.5cm (27in)
W: 91cm (35in)
D: 100cm (39in)
De La Espada, Portugal
www.delaespada.com

**Seating, Second
Skin Chair**
Quinze & Milan
Leather, oak wood
H: 84.3cm (33in)
W: 86.6cm (34in)
D: 81.6cm (32in)
Quinze & Milan, Belgium
www.quinzeandmilan.tv

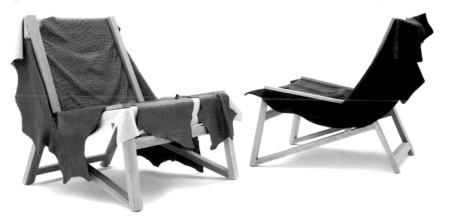

Outdoor chair, Pattern
Arik Levy
Recyclable steel
H: 85cm (33in)
W: 61cm (24in)
D: 56cm (22in)
Emu Group SpA, Italy
www.emu.it

By employing the process of blow moulding, Marcel Wanders's Sparkling chair uses a minimum of materials – in this case 100 per cent PET, making it fully recyclable. The technique is common in the production of water bottles, but unusual in the manufacture of furniture. After the legs and seat have been formed, the hollow space inside them is filled with high-pressure air to strengthen the components. The chair is therefore very light, weighing in at only 1 kilogram (just over 2 pounds), reducing its carbon footprint. As the legs are screwed into the seat, the chair can be disassembled for transportation, which adds further to its green credentials.

**Indoor/outdoor chair,
Sparkling**
Marcel Wanders
Blow-moulded PET
H: 77cm (30in)
W: 42cm (16½in)
D: 49cm (19¼in)
Magis SpA, Italy
www.magisdesign.com

**Chair, Murano
Vanity Chair**
Stefano Giovannoni
Polycarbonate
H: 81cm (31in)
W: 40.5cm (16⅛in)
D: 49cm (19¼in)
Magis SpA, Italy
www.magisdesign.com

Chair, More or Less Chair
Maarten Baas
Steel, wood
Unique pieces
NgispeN, The Netherlands
www.ngispen.nl

Chair, Osso
Ronan and Erwan Bouroullec
Solid ash, solid oak
H: 77cm (30in)
W: 44cm (17⅜in)
D: 49cm (19¼in)
Mattiazzi, Italy
www.mattiazzi.eu

Chair, Robo
Luca Nichetto
Wood, steel
H: 77cm (30in)
W: 57cm (22in)
D: 53cm (20in)
Offecct, Sweden
www.offecct.se

Chair, Chassis
Stefan Diez
Sheet steel, fabric
H: 78cm (30in)
W: 54cm (21in)
D: 57cm (22in)
Wilkhahn, Germany
www.wilkhahn.com

Chair, 130
Naoto Fukasawa
Solid wood
H: 84cm (33in)
W: 49cm (19¼n)
D: 56cm (22in)
Thonet GmbH, Germany
www.thonet.eu

**Children's chair,
Codomo Chair**
Ichiro Iwasaki
Rattan, iron, cotton cushion
H: 54cm (21in)
W: 40.5cm (16⅛in)
D: 42cm (16½in)
Sfera srl, Italy
www.ricordi-sfera.com

Armchair, The Lounger
Jaime Hayon
Painted tubular steel,
varnished walnut plywood,
fabric/leather upholstery
H: 99cm (39in)
W: 76cm (29in)
D: 91cm (35in)
BD Barcelona Design, Spain
www.bdbarcelona.com

Armchair, Twenty.two
Jaime Hayon
Solid wood, upholstery
H: 89cm (35in)
L: 94cm (37in)
D: 72cm (28in)
Ceccotti Collezioni, Italy
www.ceccotticollezioni.it

**Chair, Prooff #001
EarChair**
Jurgen Bey,
Studio Makkink & Bey
Wood, MDF, foam,
fabric, leather
H: 149cm (59in)
W: 129cm (51in)
D: 100cm (39in)
Prooff, The Netherlands
www.prooff.com

Armchair, Husk
Patricia Urquiola
Moulded plastic,
leather/fabric
H: 110cm (43in)
W: 64cm (25in)
D: 60.5cm (24in)
B&B Italia SpA, Italy
www.bebitalia.com

Armchair,
Skate Deck Chair
Amanda and Lance Glover
Repurposed and recycled
skateboard decks, CNC-milled
clear maple plywood and
Fin Color Ply, stainless-steel
hardware
H: 79cm (31in)
W: 86cm (34in)
D: 89cm (35in)
Treehouse & Carlson Arts,
LLC, USA
www.treehousedsgn.com

The father/daughter design team of Lance and Amanda
Glover devised the Skate Deck Chair as a means of recycling
used skateboard decks. The basic idea was to refine the
spontaneity of ad-hoc 2 x 4 and plywood ski, skateboard and
snowboard furniture, drawing on the proportions of the classic
Adirondack chair, the functional clarity of model airplanes
and the ebullient free-forms of mid century moulded plywood
furniture. The design developed into two slightly different
forms: a kit, which allowed the customer's used skate decks to
be utilized with a frame made of CNC-milled Fin Color Ply, and
a complete version that shipped with clear maple skate decks
using a framework of CNC-milled clear maple plywood.

Stool, TWB
Raw Edges
Natural ash wood
H: 44 or 56cm
(17⅜ or 22in)
W: 74cm (29in)
D: 28cm (11in)
Cappellini, Italy
www.cappellini.it

Chair, Amateur Masters S
Jerszy Seymour
Polycaprolactone wax
H: 80cm (31in)
W: 45cm (17¾in)
D: 54cm (21in)
NgispeN, The Netherlands
www.ngispen.nl

Chair, 43
Konstantin Grcic
Hand-crafted bamboo
H: 77cm (30in)
W: 55cm (22in)
L: 54.5cm (21in)
Skitsch, Italy
www.skitsch.it

Chair, Spun (Coriolis)
Heatherwick Studio
Steel with black acid finish,
or bronzed brass
H: 65cm (25in)
W: 90cm (35in)
Haunch of Venison Gallery, UK
Marzorati Ronchetti, Italy
www.haunchofvenison.com
www.marzoratironchetti.it

Since founding his process-led company in 1994, Thomas Heatherwick has become known worldwide for ambitious and innovative use of both engineering and materials. His studio, where concept development, detailing and fabrication take place, is littered with models and prototypes, many of which are self-financed research and development exercises, such as the Spun chair. Heatherwick had long been interested in the traditional technique of metal spinning (used to make tubular parts by fixing sheet metal to a rotating mandrel, then stretching it until it takes the form of the tool). This process is normally associated with industrial components or small-scale objects, and also with the production of timpani drums. Heatherwick wondered whether it would be possible to use the method to create a chair that was completely rotationally symmetrical, with the same profile for all contact points with the body. The obvious shape was a cone, and tests were carried out to determine the ergonomic form that would allow an optimum balance between comfort and symmetry.

When the design was considered structurally and aesthetically viable, a working prototype was made in aluminium by a family-run metal-spinning workshop, with the seat, back and arms, as well as a stand to hold it up, all completed using just six tools. The project was then developed for limited-edition production in collaboration with the central London art gallery Haunch of Venison, which found a large-scale metal-forming company to produce the collector's piece. The final version, in either steel or brass (a warm metal not commonly used in furniture design), is not immediately apparent as a chair – when upright it looks more like a sculptural object. However, when tilted on its side, it forms a comfortable and functional seat in which the user can rock from side to side, or even turn in a circle. A plastic, mass-manufactured version is also available from Magis, the Italian furniture producer with whom Heatherwick has worked for many years. It is created using rotational moulding, an entirely different process but one that retains the notion of 'spinning'.

Outdoor rotating chair, Spun
Thomas Heatherwick
Rotational-moulded
polyethylene
H: 78cm (30in)
Diam: 91cm (35in)
Magis SpA, Italy
www.magisdesign.com

Swivel easychair, Oppo
Stefan Borselius
Steel, wood, moulded
polyurethane foam, fabric
H: 73cm (28in)
W: 70cm (27in)
D: 90cm (35in)
Blå Station AB, Sweden
www.blastation.com

Stool, Apple
Yu-jui Chou
Fibreglass, lacquer
H: 45cm (17¾in)
Diam: 53cm (20in)
Yii, Taiwan
HAN Gallery, Taiwan
www.yiidesign.com
www.han-gallery.com

Armchair, Spook
Iskos-Berlin
Heat formed fibre felt in
100% polyester
H: 61cm (24in)
W: 102cm (40in)
D: 93.5cm (37in)
Blå Station AB, Sweden
www.blastation.com

Seating, Blobina
Karim Rashid
Polyurethane, heat-moulded
polystyrene, elastic fabric
H: 43cm (16⅞in)
W: 63cm (24in)
L: 90cm (35in)
Meritalia SpA, Italy
www.meritalia.it

Pearson Lloyd

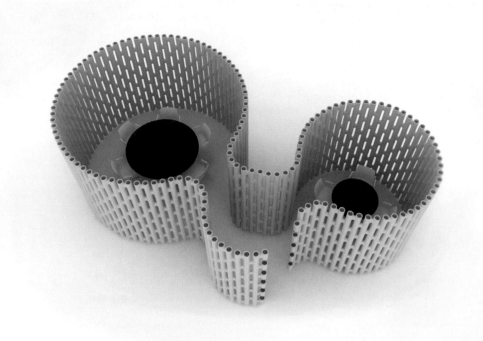

Where did you meet? What are the drawbacks and advantages of working as a design duo?

We met at the Royal College of Art in London. I graduated from furniture, Tom from product design. Interestingly, whilst undergraduates, we had both been on each other's respective courses and that synergy of background formed the basis of our early communication.

Top right: Link modular partitioning system for MOVISI (2007)

Upper Class seat for Virgin Atlantic (2006)

The drawbacks and strengths of a partnership lie in the disagreements. It's very important as a designer to be challenged and to always question one's thinking. As the studio grows we find we increasingly handle projects separately, but there is constant dialogue and review on the projects.

You are increasingly involved in designing for the public realm. How do you think design can contribute to social change?

Design at its best is always about social change. Either it elicits cultural or social change or it helps facilitate it. Design in the public realm is interesting in that the user often interfaces with 'the design' only at critical times. For example, in healthcare the interface is often when the patient is most vulnerable, and as a result the environment and context are uncompromising. Design has become a popular tag attached to many things, but very often it is not design at all but a kind of window dressing – ultimately, dull and uninspiring. We do believe that good design should improve our wellbeing.

Your work is very pluralist. How do you account for this wide-ranging approach?

The studio was always set up to do varied work and is essentially a place where we continue to learn and be stretched. We strongly believe the approach we undertake is transferable, and it is precisely the fact that we are pluralists that keeps things fresh. In practice this was difficult at times, as clients could be wary of us not having experience in a certain area. However, we now have many successful products under our belt and the wide-ranging portfolio is without doubt an advantage when we discuss the concept of cross-fertilization of ideas.

In 2011 the Aram Gallery's 'Then-Now' exhibition gathered together products from the graduation shows of fifteen designers, displaying the student projects alongside recent examples of work the designers were proud of. What point were you making with the pieces you selected?

The 'Then-Now' exhibition was very interesting as an idea. It not only captured a moment in time, in terms of design and certain individuals, but it was also fascinating as virtually all the designers chosen, even at an early age, presented a very clear thread of their DNA. I think we simply put in projects that for a number of reasons interest us now. The Link free-standing partition and room divider (opposite page, top right), the Cobi office chair (right) and the PLC chair were our choices. They perhaps represented investigations into materiality, ergonomic 'idea' and cultural archetype respectively. If we were asked to do the same now, the choices might be different. The studio and our thoughts are always evolving.

Can you describe two of the pivotal projects of your studio and why they have influenced the direction of your practice?

Many of the projects we have completed could be described as pivotal, but probably the two with the biggest impact in terms of market influence as well as design interrogation and process have been the Upper Class seat for Virgin Atlantic (opposite page, bottom) and the PARCS office furniture system for Bene (right). The Upper Class seat was a game changer in the industry in terms of art direction but also performance. PARCS is very different but has also been an industry changer. It positions itself interestingly because unlike most furniture, which is specified after an office interior is designed, architects are actually planning a space from the outset with PARCS in mind.

How would you describe the process you follow in designing and developing a product?

Design process in a studio such as ours is a difficult thing to explain or quantify. We are two partners who discuss our ideas continually with a team of full-time dedicated designers who work very closely with us to achieve our ambitions. It varies from historical influence and intuitive response to detailed analysis, with no idea what design will ultimately take form on the 'blank sheet of paper'. At the other end of the spectrum, we are far more involved in research and brief writing now. The

more complex the problem, the clearer you must be that you are indeed asking the right question in the first place.

The definition of sustainable design is difficult and contradictory. What is your understanding of the term?

It's far too difficult to define 'sustainable design' in a sentence or two. Moreover, the sands are always shifting in terms of knowledge. Sustainability should always be the aim. Reducing waste, energy consumption and material use are all components. In our view, chasing fashion with products is high risk as it promotes obsolescence. However, if an object becomes fashionable it can indeed prolong its life expectancy. It seems to us that our value system is most in need of recalibrating. Luckily our products seem to last a long time in the market. Make less, less often and better.

What do you consider to be the catalysts for design's development today?

Sustainability is without doubt a primary factor in product development now. We have saturated markets. Growth as an endgame in itself may not be a sustainable model. Innovation is vital. Seven billion is a lot of people to feed. Just because we can make it does not mean we should.

What is the main challenge facing a designer today?

I think the main challenge facing design now is the desire for speed and cheapness rather than true progress and value.

In the 1960s Ettore Sottsass was quoted as saying, 'For me design is a way of discussing society, politics, eroticism, food and even design. At the end, it is a way of building up a possible figurative utopia or metaphor about life.' How much do you agree with this?

Design has always reflected culture and responded to socioeconomic changes. At its best it can motivate, inspire, question and lead. It's what we do. It's what we are. It's structurally imprinted in and shapes our DNA.

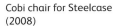

Cobi chair for Steelcase (2008)

Bottom: PARCS range of office furniture for Bene (2009)

2.
SOFAS
AND
BEDS

Bed, Temple
Claesson Koivisto Rune
Wood, fabric
H: 191cm (74in)
W: 210cm (82in)
L: 210cm (82in)
Cinova, Italy
www.cinova.it

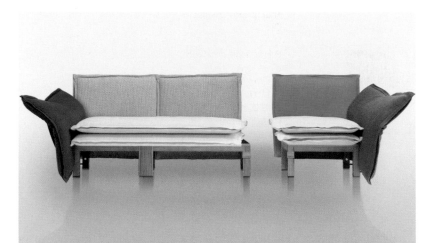

Modular seating, Xarxa
Martí Guixé
Wood, linen, jute, cotton,
viscose and polyester fabrics
H: 100cm (39in)
H (seat): 45cm (17¾in)
D: 80cm (31in)
Danese srl, Italy
www.danesemilano.com

Modular sofa system, Toot
Piero Lissoni
Aluminium, fabric upholstery
H: 42cm (16½in)
D: 85 or 100cm (33 or 39in)
Cassina, Italy
www.cassina.com

Sofa, Quilt
Ronan and Erwan Bouroullec
Metal structure, fibreglass
shell, foam and textile
H: 75cm (29in)
H (seat): 30cm (11¾in)
L: 210cm (82in)
D: 120cm (47in)
Established & Sons, UK
www.establishedandsons.com

**Indoor/outdoor sofa,
Out/In**
Philippe Starck
Polyethylene, anodized
aluminium
H: 82cm (32in)
H (seat): 44cm (17⅜in)
W: 202cm (80in)
D: 76cm (29in)
Driade, Italy
www.driade.com

Sofa, Hug 2-seater Sofa
Leif.designpark
Solid American black
walnut or American white
oak, fabric upholstery
H: 76cm (29in)
W: 166cm (65in)
D: 77cm (30in)
De La Espada, Portugal
www.delaespada.com

Sofa, Knokke
Carlo Colombo
Monoblock of multilayer
solid wood
H: 73cm (28in)
H (seat): 40cm (15¾in)
L: 215cm (84in)
D: 88cm (34in)
Emmemobili, Italy
www.emmemobili.it

Seating, Love Seat
Gareth Neal
Green Ash
H: 96cm (37in)
L: 103cm (41in)
D: 48cm (18⅞in)
Gareth Neal Ltd, UK
www.garethneal.co.uk

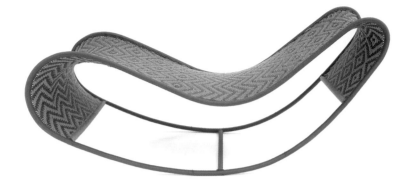

Seating, Bayekou
Birsel & Seck
Plastic threads
H: 63cm (24in)
W: 58cm (22in)
L: 135cm (53in)
Moroso SpA, Italy
www.moroso.it

Sofa, Doodle
Front
Leather
H: 104cm (41in)
H (seat): 46cm (181⁄8in)
W: 180cm (70in)
D: 80cm (31in)
Moroso, Italy
www.moroso.it

Sofa, Favn
Jaime Hayon
Upholstery, satin-
polished aluminium
H: 88cm (34in)
W: 221cm (87in)
D: 93cm (36in)
Fritz Hansen A/S, Denmark
www.fritzhansen.com

Seating, Scuba
Brodie Neill
Lacquered fibreglass
H: 77cm (30in)
H (seat): 45cm (173⁄4in)
L: 220cm (86in)
D: 88cm (34in)
Domodinamica, Italy
www.domodinamica.com

Bench, Reii
Patricia Urquiola
Plastic threads
H: 51cm (20in)
W: 42cm (16½in)
L: 120cm (47in)
Moroso SpA, Italy
www.moroso.it

Sofa, Sack
Marc Sadler
Polyurethane, cotton,
wood, rope, anti-slip
material, polyester
H: 80cm (31in)
W: 125cm (49in)
L: 260cm (102in)
Skitsch, Italy
www.skitsch.it

Sofa, Aviator sofa
Nigel Coates
Wood, polyurethane foam,
velvet, silk
H: 98cm (38in)
L: 210cm (82in)
D: 125cm (49in)
Poltronova, Italy
Cristina Grajales Gallery,
New York, USA
www.poltronova.com
www.cristinagrajalesinc.com

**Outdoor seating,
Tropez Collection**
Stefan Diez
Thermo-lacquered
aluminium, plastic fabric
Various dimensions
Gandia Blasco, Spain
www.gandiablasco.com

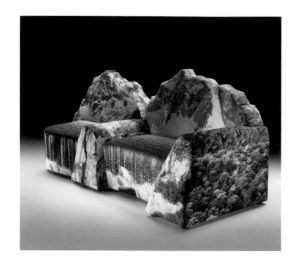

Sofa, Montanara
Gaetano Pesce
Polyurethane, fabric,
steel, wood
H: 110cm (43in)
W: 282cm (111in)
D: 94cm (37in)
Meritalia SpA, Italy
www.meritalia.it

**Outdoor chaise longue,
Tokyo (Cassina I Maestri
Collection)**
Charlotte Perriand
Wood
H: 65cm (25in)
L: 150cm (59in)
D: 55cm (21in)
Cassina, Italy
www.cassina.com

**Seating, Concrete
Chesterfield Sofa**
Jon Gray
Glass-reinforced concrete
H: 70cm (27in)
W: 80cm (31in)
L: 190cm (74in)
Gray Concrete, UK
www.grayconcrete.co.uk

Bench, Agranda Bench
Daniel Rose, David Angus,
Nicola Rose
Ash, aluminium,
stainless steel
H: 48cm (18⅞in)
W: 30cm (11¾in)
L: 120cm (47in), extending
to 180cm (70in)
RASKL, UK
www.raskl.co.uk

Sofa, Beetley Sofa
Jaime Hayon
Powder-coated steel,
upholstery
H: 95cm (37in)
W: 220 or 250cm
(86 or 98in)
D: 85cm (33in)
Sé, UK
www.se-london.com

Sofa, Paper Cloud
Tokujin Yoshioka
Injected flame-retardant
foam, steel, polypropylene
H: 60cm (23in)
H (seat): 35cm (13¾in)
L: 274cm (108in)
D: 95cm (37in)
Moroso SpA, Italy
www.moroso.it

**Seating, Two-Seater
Low Settle**
Studioilse
European chestnut, copper
H: 95cm (37in)
W: 121cm (48in)
D: 51.3cm (20in)
De La Espada, Portugal
www.delaespada.com

Seating
Peter Marigold and
Hinoki Kogei
Wood
H: 42cm (16½in)
W: 205cm (80in)
D: 39cm (15⅜in)
Japan Creative, Japan
www.japancreative.jp
www.petermarigold.com

**Modular sofa system,
Smallroom**
Ineke Hans
Cold foam wrapped with
flameproof fibre, frame
in wood, fixed upholstery
in fabric or leather, legs
in chrome
Various dimensions
Offecct AB, Sweden
www.offecct.se

Sofa, Ten
Michael Sodeau
Solid beech, birch
plywood, steel, anodized
aluminium, fabric
H: 76cm (29in)
H (seat): 39cm (15⅜in)
W: 102cm (40in)
L: 250cm (98in)
Modus, UK
www.modusfurniture.co.uk

Sofa, Munich Sofa
Sauerbruch Hutton
Solid wood, steel tubing
with rubber webbing,
polyurethane with polyester
fibre, leather
H: 74cm (29in)
H (seat): 40cm (15¾in)
L: 164cm (65in)
D: 81cm (31in)
ClassiCon GmbH, Germany
www.classicon.com

Chaise longue, Remix
Brodie Neill
Assorted plastics and woods
H: 43cm (16⅞in)
W: 75cm (29in)
L: 200cm (78in)
The Apartment Gallery, UK
www.theapartment.uk.com

**Sofa, Notturno a New York
(Nighttime in New York)**
Gaetano Pesce
Plywood, beech wood,
polyurethane foam, polyester
wadding, fabric
H: 124cm (49in)
H (seat): 44cm (17⅜in)
W: 103cm (41in)
L: 333cm (131in)
Cassina, Italy
www.cassina.com

**Modular sofa system,
Bricks**
Robert Bronwasser
Foam, wood, fabric
H (seat): 39, 43 or 47cm
(15⅜, 16⅞ or 18½in)
D: 75 or 89cm (29 or 35in)
Palau, The Netherlands
www.palau.nl

All covers are in a special fabric processed to resemble a tapestry;
a sophisticated weaving technique is used to produce 14,000
warp and weft stitches, generating extremely high-definition
images. Larger yarns are interwoven to achieve the three-
dimensional designs.

Sofa, Onkel
Simon Legald
Fabric, lacquered wood
H (side): 40cm (15¾in)
L: 235cm (92in)
D: 80cm (31in)
Normann Copenhagen,
Denmark
www.normann-copenhagen.com

**Sofa/chaise longue/
day bed, Single Sofa**
Maarten Baptist
Wood, foam, textile
H: 76cm (29in)
W: 255cm (100in)
D: 80cm (31in)
Joine/Maarten Baptist,
The Netherlands
www.joine.nl

Sofa, Soft Wood Sofa
Front
Stress-resistant polyurethane foam with differentiated densities, polyester fibre, wood frame
H: 85cm (33in)
H (seat): 44cm (17⅜in)
W: 194cm (76in)
D: 86 (33in)
Moroso SpA, Italy
www.moroso.it

Sofa, Bubble
Yu-jui Chou
Bamboo, metal rings, rubber
H: 52cm (20in)
H (seat): 35cm (13¾in)
W: 166cm (65in)
D: 70cm (27in)
Yii, Taiwan
HAN Gallery, Taiwan
www.yiidesign.com
www.han-gallery.com

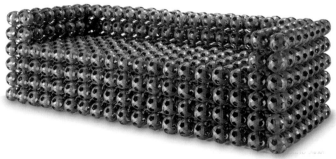

Modular seating, Bondo D
Harri Korhonen
Steel, upholstery
H: 76cm (29in)
H (seat): 45cm (17¾in)
W: 140cm (55in)
D: 73cm (28in)
Inno, Finland
www.inno.fi

Outdoor sofa, Rimini
Fredrikson Stallard
Painted aluminium structure covered with woven plastic
H: 69cm (27in)
H (seat): 40cm (15¾in)
W: 195cm (76in)
D: 68cm (26in)
Driade SpA, Italy
www.driade.com

Outdoor sofa, Borgos
Terry Dwan
Solid teak, quick-dry foamed cushions with outdoor removable cover
H: 110cm (43in)
H (seat): 45cm (17¾in)
W: 225cm (88in)
D: 95cm (37in)
Driade Spa, Italy
www.driade.com

Chaise longue, Glacier
Brodie Neill
Glass
H: 65cm (25in)
W: 58cm (22in)
L: 175cm (68in)
Patrick Brillet Fine Art, UK
www.brodieneill.com
www.patrickbrillet.com

Each example of Brodie Neill's work highlights this young Tasmanian designer's love of sculptural form and his innovative use of materials. Whether creating production pieces, such as the Clover light for Kundalini (page 234) and the Curve bench for Riva 1920 (page 97), or limited editions, such as the Remix chaise (page 84) and Reverb chair (page 51), his fluid lines and strong organic shapes have been refined through the use of advanced digital technology to create objects that are artistic yet technically involved. His designs are inspired by nature and science; the Glacier chaise longue is named for its resemblance to a solid piece of ice. Neill collaborated with the best Czech glass artists to hand-cast the 135 litres of clear glass, which was poured into a mould over 2 metres (7 feet) long. To guard against shattering as it hardened, the glass had to be cooled slowly over an 80-day period, allowing it to anneal and strengthen to certified standards. Once the glass had solidified, the plaster tool was chipped away and the master craftsmen began the laborious and highly skilled process of cutting back and honing the surface to a crystal-clear polish. Suspended bubbles and internal veiling – forever fossilized within the once-molten creation – are the only evidence that the chaise longue was made by hand. The result is pure and elegant, with an ethereal quality that belies its 300 kilogram (661 pound) weight.

Love seat, Gladis
Ayala Serfaty
Fabric cover, polyurethane foam
H: 72cm (28in)
W: 112cm (44in)
L: 155cm (61in)
Aqua Creations, Israel
www.aquagallery.com

Sofa, TST Sofa
Michael Young
Steel frame, foam,
sustainable upholstery
H: 69.4cm (27in)
W: 151.8cm (60in)
D: 62cm (24in)
NgispeN, The Netherlands
www.ngispen.nl

Sofa, Foliage
Patricia Urquiola
Batch-dyed technopolymer
thermoplastic, polyurethane
foam padding with quilted
elastic fabric covering
H: 90cm (35in)
L: 185cm (72in)
D: 90cm (35in)
Kartell SpA, Italy
www.kartell.it

Sofa, Conversation Sofa
Satyendra Pakhalé
Horse hair, cotton, wool, flax,
pine structure, steel springs
H: 80cm (31in)
W: 120cm (47in)
D: 75cm (29in)
Hästens, Sweden
www.hastens.com

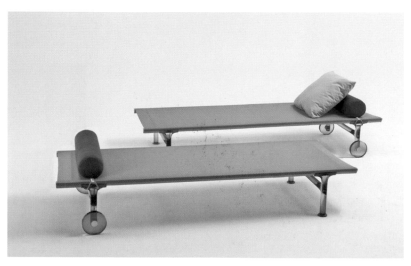

Outdoor lounger, O/K
Rodolfo Dordoni
Plastitex sling mattress,
aluminium, thermoplastic
H: 35cm (13¾in)
W: 200cm (78in)
D: 67cm (26in)
Kartell, Italy
www.kartell.it

Sofa, M-collection
Van Eijk & Van der Lubbe
Hand-laminated polyester,
glossy finish, upholstery
H: 95cm (37in)
W: 170cm (66in)
D: 79cm (31in)
Lensvelt b.v., The Netherlands
www.lensvelt.nl

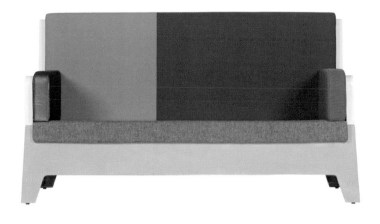

**Bench, Plaidbench
Collection**
Raw Edges
Wood
H (Plaidbench D):
44cm (17⅜in)
W (Plaidbench D):
75cm (29in)
L (Plaidbench D):
80cm (31in)
Dilmos, Italy
www.dilmos.it

Outdoor sofa, Canisse
Philippe Nigro
Polyethylene
H: 79cm (31in)
H (seat): 40cm (15¾in)
W: 173cm (68in)
D: 89cm (35in)
Serralunga srl, Italy
www.serralunga.com

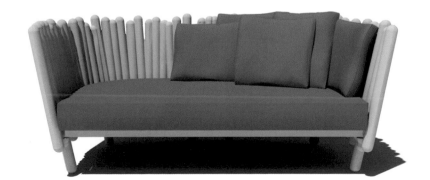

Sofa, Leo Leonis
Dominique Perrault,
Gaelle Lauriot Prevost
Laquered wood, fabric
H: 70cm (27in)
H (seat): 38cm (15in)
W: 90cm (35in)
L: 145cm (57in)
Sawaya & Moroni, Italy
www.sawayamoroni.com

**Indoor/outdoor chaise
longue and chair, BiKnit**
Patricia Urquiola
Wood, steel, knitted
polypropylene liner filled with
polyethylene and covered
with polyester and PVC
H (chaise longue):
92cm (36in)
L (chaise longue):
155cm (61in)
H (chair): 85cm (33in)
L (chair): 102cm (40in)
W: 64cm (25in)
Moroso SpA, Italy
www.moroso.it

Sofa, Button Down
Edward van Vliet
Wood, polyurethane foam,
polyester fibre, fabric
H: 85cm (33in)
H (seat): 42cm (16½in)
W: 190cm (74in)
D: 92cm (36in)
Moroso SpA, Italy
www.moroso.it

Sofa, Paddock
Michele De Lucchi,
Davide Angeli
Wood, polyurethane, leather
H: 70cm (27in)
H (seat): 40cm (15¾in)
W: 198cm (78in)
D: 80cm (31in)
Domodinamica srl, Italy
www.domodinamica.com

Sectional sofa, Bounce
Karim Rashid
Curved clear plastic, wood
covered with lasercut foam,
elastic fabric upholstery
H: 73cm (28in)
H (seat): 40cm (15¾in)
W (one section): 90cm (35in)
D: 94cm (37in)
Domodinamica srl, Italy
www.domodinamica.com

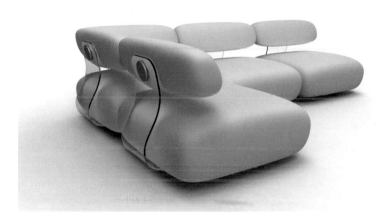

Sofa, Ploum
Ronan and Erwan Bouroullec
Fabric, foam,
steel structure
H: 76cm (29in)
H (seat): 36cm (14⅛in)
W: 245cm (96in)
D: 126.5cm (50in)
Ligne Roset, France
www.ligneroset.com

Sofa with adjustable backrest, Sfatto
Francesco Binfaré
Ultra-soft padding covered
in heavy fabrics
H: 66/88cm (26/34in)
W: 215/240cm (84/94in)
D: 103/115cm (41/45in)
Edra SpA, Italy
www.edra.com

Sofa, Cocoon Plan
Rock Wang
Bamboo
H: 80cm (31in)
W: 90cm (35in)
D: 100cm (39in)
Yii, Taiwan
HAN Gallery, Taiwan
www.yiidesign.com
www.han-gallery.com

**Outdoor hanging and
standing loungers,
Nestrest**
Daniel Pouzet, Fred Frety
Dedon Fiber, aluminium
H: 268cm (106in)
Diam: 200cm (78in)
Dedon GmbH, Germany
www.dedon.de

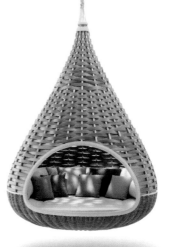

Sofa, Cipria
Fernando and Humberto
Campana
Metal tube frame,
Gellyfoam® and Dacron
wadding, ecological faux
fur covering
H: 84cm (33in)
H (seat): 40cm (15¾in)
W: 222cm (87in)
D: 128cm (50in)
Edra, Italy
www.edra.com

Sofa, Rive Droite
Christophe Pillet
Solid American walnut, fabric
H: 80cm (31in)
W: 290cm (114in)
D: 88cm (34in)
Ceccotti Collezioni, Italy
www.ceccotticollezioni.it

Sofa, Metro
Luca Nichetto
Aluminium, recycled elastic
viscose upholstery, wool
H: 40cm (15¾in)
L: 136cm (54in)
D: 85cm (33in)
Emmegi SpA, Italy
www.emmegiseating.com

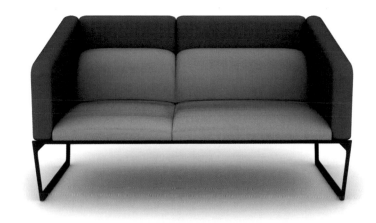

Bench, Table Bench Chair
Industrial Facility
Beech, natural waxed oak
H: 82cm (32in)
H (seat): 46cm (18⅛in)
L: 176cm (69in)
D: 54cm (21in)
Established & Sons, UK
www.establishedandsons.com

Sofa, Fergana
Patricia Urquiola
Solid ash, polyurethane
foam, fabric
H: 75cm (29in)
H (seat): 38cm (15in)
W: 200cm (78in)
D: 100cm (39in)
Moroso SpA, Italy
www.moroso.it

Sofa, Royeroid
Robert Stadler
Upholstered fabric
H: 74cm (29in)
L: 255cm (100in)
W: 148cm (58in)
Carpenters Workshop Gallery,
UK and France
www.cwgdesign.com

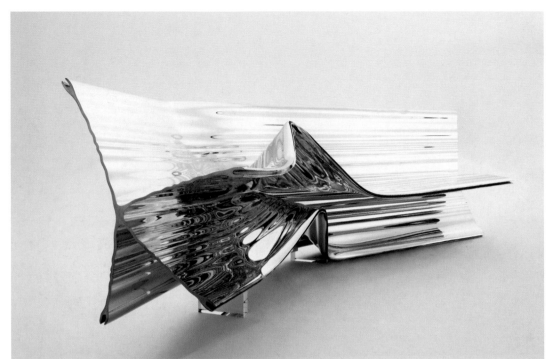

Bench, Extrusions
Heatherwick Studio
Aluminium
H: 75cm (29in)
L: 185cm (72in)
D: 110cm (43in)
Limited edition production
Haunch of Venison Gallery, UK
www.haunchofvenison.com

The Extrusions project was the first time British designer Thomas Heatherwick worked with the private, London-based art gallery Haunch of Venison, which helped fund and expand his ongoing personal research into a technique that he had already explored within the limitations of his studio (the second collaboration was the Spun chair; page 72). The original concept dates from Heatherwick's postgraduate days as a student at the Royal College of Art, London, when he was interested in the idea of simplifying the elements of a seat, which normally require numerous parts and involve complex manufacturing and assembly processes, into only one component made from one material: a single piece of aluminium without any fixtures or fittings. His idea was to use the technique of extrusion (an industrial manufacturing process whereby a material is pushed under high pressure through a die of the desired profile shape) to create L-shaped benches consisting of legs, seat and back.

The first experiments proved that his theory was viable, but it took a further eighteen years to locate a factory that had an extruding machine large enough to produce the unprecedented cross-sectional dimensions (the facility that Heatherwick eventually found in Asia usually makes aluminium products for the aerospace industry). From the beginning, Heatherwick saw the potential in the contorted, rough first and last lengths of an extrusion, which result from the abrupt stop-start process and are usually discarded. The seven experimental pieces that form the Extrusions project could have been sliced to create a pristine section, but instead these gnarled ends have been retained for their brutal, sculptural qualities. Although all the benches have been extruded from a single, specially designed die, each is unique, having been manipulated by hand when leaving the machine and then polished to a chrome-like finish. As the world's first extruded single-component furniture, the series pioneers aluminium technology, elevating a banal architectural component normally concealed in curtain walls to collectors' objects of extraordinary beauty.

Bench, Hopper Bench
Dirk Wynants
Galvanized steel
H: 74cm (29in)
H (seat): 44cm (17⅜in)
W: 68cm (26in)
L: 240 and 300cm
(94 and 118in)
Extremis, Belgium
www.extremis.be

Bench, Tube Bench no. 2
Piet Hein Eek
Old pipes
H: 90cm (35in)
L: 350cm (138in)
D: 98cm (38in)
Piet Hein Eek,
The Netherlands
www.pietheineek.nl

Bench, Offcut
Tom Dixon
Discarded wood
H: 44cm (17⅜in)
W: 37.5cm (15in)
L: 100cm (39in)
Tom Dixon, UK
www.tomdixon.net

Bench and stool, Ipe
Luca Nichetto
Panga Panga wood
H: 42.5cm (16⅞in)
L (stool): 45cm (17¾in)
L (bench): 100cm (39in)
D: 33cm (13in)
Mabeo, Botswana
www.mabeofurniture.com

**Indoor/outdoor bench
seat, Curve**
Brodie Neill
Wood
H: 42cm (16½in)
W: 180cm (70in)
D: 37cm (14⅝in)
Riva 1920, Italy
www.riva1920.it

Bed, Petalo
Luigi Caccia Dominioni
Polished cherry structure with
black lacquered edges
H: 105cm (41in)
W: 200–244cm (78–96in)
D: 210cm (82in)
Azucena, Italy
www.azucena.it

**Bed with flexible
headboard, Lelit**
Paola Navone
Poplar plywood,
polyurethane, polyester,
Pelle Frau® leather, velvet,
varnished aluminium
H: 140cm (55in)
L: 255cm (100in)
W: 231cm (91in)
Poltrona Frau, Italy
www.poltronafrau.it

Bed, Life
Claesson Koivisto Rune
Ash wood, 100% cotton,
plywood
H (frame): 29cm (11⅜in)
H (headboard): 88cm (34in)
W: 129, 149, 169 or 189cm
(51, 59, 67 or 74in)
L: 211cm (83in)
Cinova, Italy
www.cinova.it

Bed, Companions Bed
Studioilse
Chestnut with copper feet
Available in UK/USA/EU sizes
Queen and King
De La Espada, Portugal
www.delaespada.com

Bed, Suite Bed
Autoban
American black walnut or
American white oak with
veneered plywood headboard
lipped in solid oak or walnut,
upholstery
Available in UK/USA/EU sizes
Queen and King
De La Espada, Portugal
www.delaespada.com

Bed, Suu Bed
Leif.designpark
American black walnut
or American white oak,
upholstery
Available in UK/USA/EU sizes
Queen and King
De La Espada, Portugal
www.delaespada.com

Bed, Col-letto
Nuša Jelenec
Soft foam, stretch fabric
W: 100, 120, 152, 160
or 180cm
(39, 47, 60, 63, or 70in)
L: 200cm (78in)
Lago SpA, Italy
www.lago.it

Wardrobe, Kalahari Range
Claesson Koivisto Rune
Wood
H: 190cm (74in)
W: 118cm (46in)
D: 60cm (23in)
Mabeo, Botswana
www.mabeofurniture.com

**High rack,
Man Made series**
Peter Marigold
Sand-blasted douglas fir,
brass fixings
H: 180cm (70in)
W: 45cm (17¾in)
D: 30cm (11¾in)
Peter Marigold, UK
www.petermarigold.com

**Cabinet, Aluminium
Curved Cabinet**
Piet Hein Eek
Aluminium, glass
H: 100cm (40in)
W: 100cm (40in)
L: 150cm (59in)
Piet Hein Eek,
The Netherlands
www.pietheineek.nl

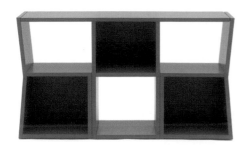

**Bookcase/console table
with two chairs, Trick**
Sakura Adachi
Beech plywood
H: 71cm (28in)
W: 45cm (17¾in)
L: 130cm (51in)
Campeggi srl, Italy
www.campeggisrl.it

Bookshelf and table, Portico
Claesson Koivisto Rune
Oak
H (bookshelf): 81cm (31in)
W (bookshelf): 172cm (68in)
D (bookshelf): 44cm (17⅜in)
H (table): 73cm (28in)
W (table): 90cm (35in)
L (table): 200cm (78in)
Living Divani srl, Italy
www.livingdivani.it

Bookshelf, Virgo
Xavier Lust
Mirror-polished stainless steel
H: 200cm (78in)
W: 125cm (49in)
D: 31cm (12¼in)
Driade, Italy
www.driade.com

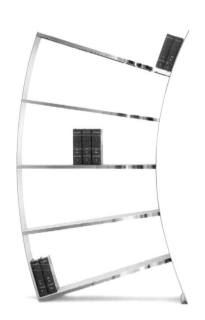

Containers, 360°
Konstantin Grcic
Glossy ABS, aluminium
H: 72 and 127cm
(28 and 50in)
W: 35cm (13¾in)
D: 46cm (18⅛in)
Magis SpA, Italy
www.magisdesign.com

**Modular storage
system, Inori**
Setsu and Shinobu Ito
Glass
H: 180cm (70in)
W: 240cm (94in)
D: 36.5cm (14⅝in)
Fiam Italia SpA, Italy
www.fiamitalia.it

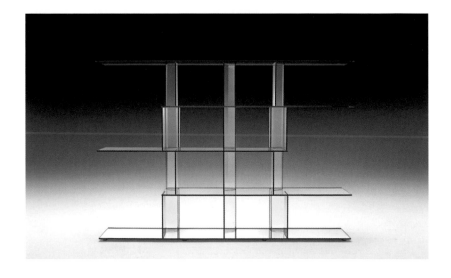

Modular shelving system with online modular construction program, Vita

Massimo Mariani with AedasR&D
MD wood fibreboards
L (each square element): 60cm (23in)
D: 22cm (8⅝in)
MDF Italia SpA, Italy
www.mdfitalia.it

Wall-mounted storage units, S-Cube

Ferruccio Laviani
Veneers, matt lacquering, metal, wood
W: 50 or 80cm (19 or 31in)
L: 50 or 80cm (19 or 31in)
Emmemobili, Italy
www.emmemobili.it

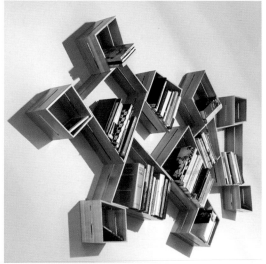

Modular system, Inmotion

Neuland Industriedesign
Varnished MDF
Various dimensions
MDF Italia SpA, Italy
www.mdfitalia.it

Wall-mounted asymmetrical shelving system, SUM

Peter Marigold
Solid cherry
H (small shelf): 18.5cm (7¼in)
W (small shelf): 19.5cm (7⅝in)
D (small shelf): 13cm (5⅛in)
H (medium shelf): 25.8cm (10¼in)
W (medium shelf): 28.9cm (11⅜in)
D (medium shelf): 13cm (5⅛in)
H (large shelf): 42.7cm (16⅞in)
W (large shelf): 37.5cm (15in)
D (large shelf): 13cm (5⅛in)
SCP, UK
www.scp.co.uk

Modular shelving system, Transistor

Barberini & Gunnell
Glass, anodized aluminium
L (minimal element): 30cm (11¾in)
D: 27cm (10⅝in)
Tonelli Design srl, Italy
www.tonellidesign.it

Armoire, Lowry
Russell Pinch
Douglas fir
H: 180cm (70in)
W: 132cm (52in)
D: 56.5cm (22in)
Pinch Design Ltd, UK
www.pinchdesign.com

Storage, Amsterdam Armoire
Scholten & Baijings
Fibreboard, printed laminate, steel, hand-blown glass
H: 172.5cm (68in)
L: 121.5cm (48in)
D: 60cm (23in)
Established & Sons, UK
www.establishedandsons.com

Modular storage, Collar
Nendo
Lacquered MDF or laminated chipboard, aluminium, sheet metal
H (one module): 40cm (15 ¾in)
D: 35cm (13 ¾in)
Quodes, The Netherlands
www.quodes.com

Workstation, Pivot Desk
Raw Edges
Solid oak
H: 74cm (29in)
W: 170cm (66in)
D: 50cm (19in)
Arco, The Netherlands
www.arco.nl

Coffee table and storage, Leigh Coffee
& Then Design
Solid blocked European oak, laminate
H: 46cm (18⅛in)
L: 137.2cm (54in)
D: 48.2cm (18⅞in)
& Then Design, UK
www.andthendesign.co.uk

Johanna Grawunder

You started your career working for Ettore Sottsass in 1985 when the Memphis Group was challenging the status quo of twentieth-century design. How do you think this early introduction to design influenced your work?

Sottsass has been the single most significant influence on my work. The cultural values, aesthetic and functional freedoms, and social and political consciousness of that experience inform everything I do at a very deep level. Starting from basic questions such as 'What is design?' to more philosophical problems like 'What is beauty?' Sottsass constantly questioned every premise, every decision, every conviction in a very liberated and un-neurotic way. On each occasion this lead to totally different and unexpected solutions. It is a difficult format to maintain through the years, but it is still my goal, in every situation.

You use a lot of colour and light in your product designs and also dematerialize form by working with transparency. What attracts you to these qualities?

These are the 'magical' qualities of our contemporary landscape. They have no weight or thickness. They are not directly derived from any kind of earthly mining or extraction. Yet they specifically either define or blur our visual and sensorial fields.

I think of colour and light as materials, so I treat them with the same (or sometimes more) respect and deference than I treat steel, acrylic or wood in a project. When I design a light-ceiling (opposite page), or furniture, or an interior, the colours and light are there from the beginning. In the case of transparency, I consider it a state of being of the material (such as crystal, acrylic or metal mesh) as opposed to an absence of materiality.

Innovations in materials and technological processes have advanced design over recent years. Which of these excite you the most and has been a driving force in your work?

I am interested in new technologies and materials and translating them into objects, interiors or architecture that do not necessarily exude 'technology' or 'new material'. I am interested in technology to the point that it can enable me to do new things or else old things in a better way, as opposed to using it for the sake of novelty.

For example, in recent years LED technology has allowed me to design things that would not have been possible before (below). Cast acrylic has given me the opportunity to conduct light through slabs of transparent colour (opposite page), an effect no other material can achieve. Chromalusion car paint, by DuPont, gives 3D colour-changing effects that seem to make a stable object sway (above), so that's a good material as well.

You are an architect as well as a designer. Do you find being active in both disciplines influences how you work?

The abstract quality of my work tends to be somewhat universal, scaleless and nondenominational. That said, architectural pretension definitely informs everything I do. In my opinion it is the mother of all design.

You advocate designing built space 'at eye level'. Could you explain this?

I call it 'The Barbie Way'. Little girls play with Barbie dolls and they learn how to move through spaces at eye level, making up the pathways as they go along. In architecture, this sort of point-to-point navigational method can lead to richly complex spatial relationships. Think Marrakech, or Barragan. It is a nonsculptural, though still abstract, way of approaching a problem. In design, this idea might translate more into a 'life is messy' approach. I never set out to design sculpture. I try to design spaces, or functions or light. The sculptural part sometimes happens due to the abstract architectural language. But the process is down there with Barbie.

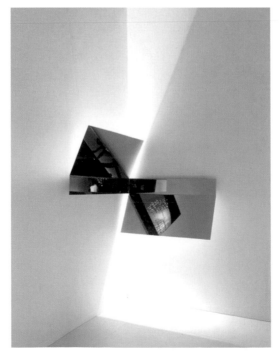

Top right: Percorso Illuminato, Weston offices, Paris (2006)

LED Corner Light for Carpenters Workshop Gallery (2011)

Why do you think there are so few internationally recognized female product designers?

'R-E-S-P-E-C-T...' or boys' club, take your pick.

You have offices in both America and Italy. How would you sum up the experience of working in both countries?

Generally speaking, in Europe, because of the cultural habits and the institutional structures in place, including the art fairs and design galleries, there are patrons and good design collectors. But design in the USA has traditionally been seen as a service for industry, not an artistic or sociocultural end in itself. Apple, revolutionary and incredible as it is, has helped perpetuate the American idea of what design should be. But thanks to Art Basel, Design Miami and other events that showcase limited-edition design, and also recently thanks to many American museums, which are accumulating fantastic contemporary design collections, the USA is coming around.

Personally, I set up my practice that way for lifestyle reasons more than as a career move (jury is still out on that one). But it is the perfect mix for me of design (Milano) and technology (San Francisco). I produce most of my pieces in Italy, with very professional and advanced artisans, who are still willing to try new things all the time. This is rare anywhere else in the world. Occasionally, I've worked with high-tech engineers here in SF to solve some difficult physics-type problems that have arisen with my pieces. The gallery that represents me now is Carpenters Workshop Gallery in Paris and London, and my 'patrons' and collectors are scattered all over the place.

Do you feel the way we consume design is altering?

I do not think we consume design so much as stuff.

In your opinion which current design trends will prove the most enduring?

Durability: designing things to last through more than one wash and more than one generation. We should be designing heirlooms, pieces that last forever and get handed down from generation to generation. And lightness-of-being: designing towards using the least amount of material possible for any given design requirement. Selecting the proper material to get the desired property, which means using all possible materials, even the 'evil' ones, but in the correct way. The goal should be to extract the least amount of raw materials from the earth.

Light-ceiling, Robert restaurant, Museum of Art and Design, New York (2010)

**Totem with magnetic
shelves, Myshelf**
Ronda Design and
A+N Design
Steel
H (shelf): 30cm (11¾in)
W (shelf): 30cm (11¾in)
D (totem): 2.8cm (1⅛in)
Ronda Design, Italy
www.rondadesign.it

Storage unit, The Object
Andreas Roth and
Mats Theselius
Corian®, brass, marble,
oak, glass
H: 90cm (35in)
W: 100cm (39in)
L: 140cm (55in)
Minus tio, Sweden
www.minustio.se

**Cabinet/shelving system,
Staircase_P1**
Danny Kuo
Spruce plywood
H: 260cm (102in)
W: 75cm (29in)
D: 55cm (21in)
Danny Kuo, The Netherlands
www.dannykuo.com

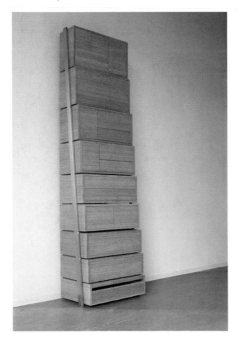

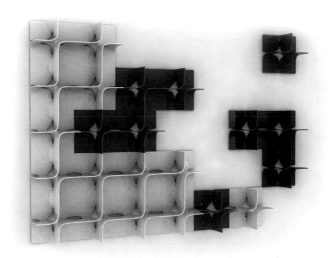

Bookcase, Melt
Thomas Sandell
White Carrara marble
H: 90cm (35in)
W: 37cm (14⅝in)
L: 70cm (27in)
Marsotto Edizioni, Italy
www.marsotto-edizioni.com

Series of hanging display cases, Heigh-Ho
Piero Lissoni
Transparent glass
H: 40, 60 and 130cm
(15¾, 23 and 51in)
Glas Italia, Italy
www.glasitalia.com

Modular shelving system, Tide
Zaha Hadid
Standard injection-moulded glossy ABS
H (each unit): 45cm (17¾in)
W (each unit): 45cm (17¾in)
D: 25cm (9⅞in)
Magis SpA, Italy
www.magisdesign.com

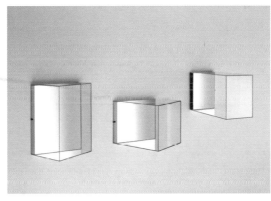

Coat stand, Peg
Tom Dixon
Solid birch
H: 180cm (70in)
Diam (max): 73.5cm (29in)
Tom Dixon, UK
www.tomdixon.net

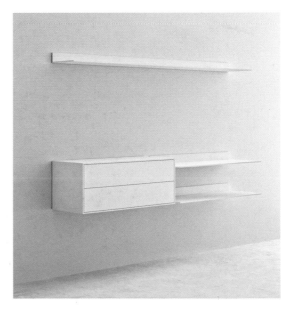

Modular system, Easy Wave
Bruno Fattorini & Partners
White acrylic solid surface
Various dimensions
MDF Italia SpA, Italy
www.mdfitalia.it

Modular wall-mounted cabinet system, Boxes
Studio Pastoe
Wood with basic lacquer of veneer
H: Various
W: Various
D: 36cm (14⅛in)
Pastoe, The Netherlands
www.pastoe.com

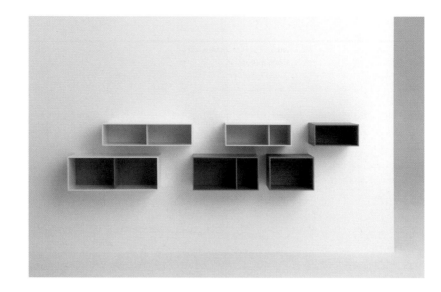

Chest of drawers, Scrigno
Fernando and Humberto Campana
Particleboard covered with brilliant laser-cut shards of acrylic (Colorflex)
H: 90cm (35in)
W: 113cm (44in)
D: 56cm (22in)
Edra, Italy
www.edra.com

Chest of drawers, Suitcase Drawers
Jamesplumb
Antique and vintage suitcases, aged steel, plywood
H: 131.5cm (52in)
W: 71.5cm (28in)
D: 44.5cm (17¾in)
Jamesplumb, UK
www.jamesplumb.co.uk

Coat stand with pocket emptier and tray, To'taime
Philippe Starck and Eugeni Quitllet
Aluminium
H: 175cm (68in)
W: 48cm (18⅞in)
D: 48cm (18⅞in)
Alias, Italy
www.aliasdesign.it

Modular bookcase, Speed
Paolo Grasselli
Steel, oak
H: 205cm (80in)
W: 29cm (11⅜in)
L: 275cm (108in)
Felicerossi srl, Italy
www.felicerossi.it

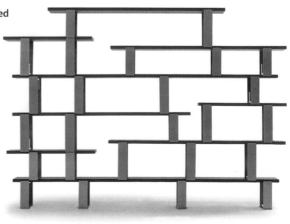

**Nest of boxes,
Cupboard of Secrets**
Jean-Michel Frank
Natural rye straw marquetry,
waxed
H: 52cm (20in)
L: 47cm (18½in)
Hermès (La Maison), France
www.hermes.com

Modular bookshelf, Unit
Itamar Burstein
Chestnut wood
H (each unit): 19cm (7½in)
W (each unit): 50cm (19in)
D: 28cm (11in)
Environment Furniture, USA
www.environmentfurniture.com

**Series of storage
furniture, Boxy**
Johanna Grawunder
Coloured mirror
H (vertical version):
29cm (11⅜in)
W (vertical version):
49cm (19¼in)
L (vertical version):
150cm (59in)
Glas Italia, Italy
www.glasitalia.com

Bookcase, Sundial
Nendo
Veneered lacquered
chipboard, PMMA
H: 165cm (65in)
L: 100cm (39in)
D: 35cm (13¾in)
Kartell SpA, Italy
www.kartell.it

Modular bookcase, Loggia
Jakob Timpe
Lacquered MDF
H (modular elements):
10, 30 and 40cm
(3⅞, 11¾ and 15¾in)
W (modular elements):
25, 50 and 75cm
(9⅞, 19 and 29in)
D (modular elements):
20 and 33cm (7⅞ and 13in)
Alias, Italy
www.aliasdesign.it

**Cupboard, Bookshelf
Cupboard**
Front
MDF
H: 210.5cm (82in)
W: 30.5cm (12¼in)
L: 86cm (33in)
Skitsch, Italy
www.skitsch.it

Storage, Satellite
BarberOsgerby
Lacquered MDF
H: 79cm (31in)
L: 135cm (53in)
D: 55cm (21in)
Quodes, The Netherlands
www.quodes.com

**Modular bookcase,
Home Kit Large**
Harry Allen
MDF
H: 185cm (72in)
W: 29cm (11⅜in)
L: 178cm (70in)
Skitsch, Italy
www.skitsch.it

**Wardrobe cabinet,
Homework Cabinet**
Nika Zupanc
Green ultrapas, breech wood,
polypropylene, paper, brass
H: 250cm (98in)
W: 75.5cm (29in)
D: 60.6cm (24in)
Nika Zupanc, Slovenia
www.nikazupanc.com

Shelving unit, Redivider
Peter Marigold
Wood, acrylic/gypsum
composite
H: 160cm (63in)
W: 50cm (19in)
D: 30cm (11¾in)
Peter Marigold, UK
www.petermarigold.com

Cupboard, Eco Storage
Giulio Patrizi
Varnished MDF and OSB
H: 120cm (47in)
W: 120cm (47in)
D: 45cm (17¾in)
Giulio Patrizi, Italy
www.giuliopatrizi.com

**Floor vase/umbrella
stand, Puddle Big**
Front
Stainless steel
H: 52cm (20in)
W: 38cm (15in)
L: 48cm (18⅞in)
Skitsch, Italy
www.skitsch.it

Storage system, Inverso
Jens Praet
Marble, particle board
H: 44.1cm (17⅜in)
L: 144cm (57in)
D: 34.8cm (13¾in)
PlusDesign srl, Italy
www.plusdesigngallery.com

**Shelf with sliding
screens, Folio**
Ronan and Erwan Bouroullec
Real wood oak veneer,
steel, felt
H (screen): 170cm (66in)
W (screen): 105cm (41in)
L (top shelf): 180cm (70in)
D (top shelf): 35cm (13¾in)
Established & Sons, UK
www.establishedandsons.com

Bookshelf, Weave
Chicako Ibaraki
Rubber-painted stainless steel
H: 160cm (63in)
W: 38cm (15in)
D: 38cm (15in)
Casamania, Italy
www.casamania.it

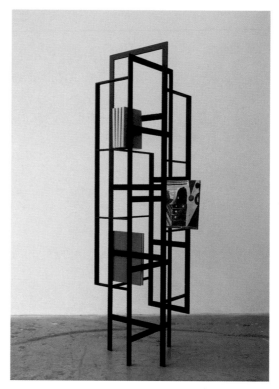

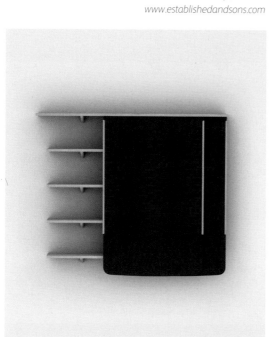

Shelving System
Naoto Fukasawa
Lacquered birch, painted
MDF, zinc, aluminium
H (tall version): 147cm (58in)
H (short version): 78cm (30in)
W (one unit): 86cm (33in)
D: 39.5cm (15¾in)
Artek, Finland
www.artek.fi

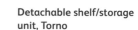

**Detachable shelf/storage
unit, Torno**
Inga Sempé
Agglomerated cork, metal
H (max, bowl): 10.3cm (3⅞in)
Diam (bowl): 14.1cm (5½in)
H (max, tray): 11.1cm (4⅜in)
Diam (tray): 18cm (7⅛in)
Amorim Cork Composites, S.A,
Portugal
www.corkcomposites.amorim.com

System of cases and cabinets, I Policromi
Alessandro Mendini
Wood, plastic laminate
H (tall bookcase):
221cm (87in)
W (tall bookcase):
35cm (13¾in)
D (tall bookcase):
42cm (16½in)
H (tall table): 79cm (31in)
W (tall table): 35cm (13¾in)
D (tall table): 42cm (16½in)

H (low bookcase):
79cm (31in)
W (low bookcase):
160cm (63in)
D (low bookcase):
35cm (13¾in)
H (low table): 58cm (22in)
W (low table): 35cm (13¾in)
D (low table): 42cm (16½in)
Domodinamica srl, Italy
www.domodinamica.com

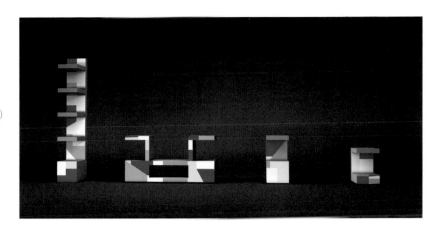

Coat stand, Hanahana
Setsu and Shinobu Ito
Ash wood veneer,
lacquered steel
H: 180cm (70in)
W: 48cm (18⅞in)
D: 48cm (18⅞in)
Swedese Möbler AB, Sweden
www.swedese.se

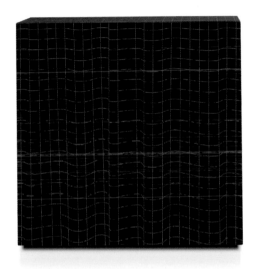

Cupboard, Black and White
Front
Particle board,
bleached maple
H: 183cm (72in)
W: 110cm (43in)
D: 48cm (18⅞in)
Porro, Italy
www.porro.com

Bookcase with shelves, table and sliding container, Grandi Legni GL 21
Andrea Branzi
Old reshaped wood, iron,
painting reproduction
H: 235cm (92in)
W: 400cm (157in)
D: 35cm (13¾in)
Design Gallery Milano and
Nilufar, Italy
www.nilufar.com

Magazine rack, Front Page
Front
Polycarbonate
H: 34cm (13⅜in)
W: 50cm (19in)
D: 35cm (13¾in)
Kartell SpA, Italy
www.kartell.it

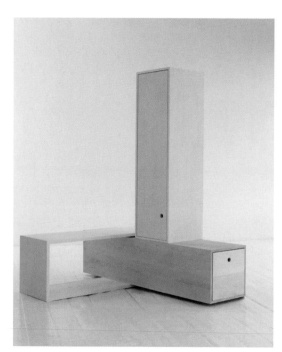

Multifunctional and modular cabinet, Container
Alain Gilles
Natural elm wood, lacquered MDF
H: 89cm (35in)
W: 229cm (90in)
D: 60cm (23in)
Casamania, Italy
www.casamania.it

Storage units, 11 Boxes
studio vit
Soaped maple/painted maple, matt and gloss white
H (long box with two drawers): 40cm (15¾in)
W (long box with two drawers): 40cm (15¾in)
D (long box with two drawers): 160cm (63in)
H (open box): 46cm (18⅛in)
W (open box): 135cm (53in)
D (open box): 40cm (15¾in)

H (tall box with hinged door): 140cm (55in)
W (tall box with hinged door): 40cm (15¾in)
D (tall box with hinged door): 40cm (15¾in)
studio vit, UK
www.studiovit.se

Occasional table/night table, White Shell
Salvatore Indriolo
Cristalplant, composite material based on resins
H: 39cm (15⅜in)
W: 64cm (25in)
D: 57cm (22in)
Zanotta SpA, Italy
www.zanotta.it

**Storage, Paesaggi
Italiani – Mirror**
Massimo Morozzi/
Fernando and Humberto
Campana
Mirrored methacrylate
H: 290.8cm (114in)
W: 339.6cm (133in)
D: 43.8cm (17⅜in)
Edra, Italy
www.edra.com

**Storage, Paesaggi
Italiani – Straw**
Massimo Morozzi/
Fernando and Humberto
Campana
Long strands of raffia
H: 194.8cm (76in)
W: 182cm (72in)
D: 112cm (44in)
Edra, Italy
www.edra.com

**Storage, Paesaggi
Italiani – Wood**
Massimo Morozzi/
Francesco Binfaré
Solid mahogany wood
H: 194.8cm (76in)
W: 144.3cm (57in)
D: 43.8cm (17⅜in)
Edra, Italy
www.edra.com

**Cupboard,
Bois de Rose**
Massimo Morozzi
Wood veneer, piano pedals
H: 120cm (47in)
W: 120cm (47in)
D: 48cm (18⅞in)
Edra SpA, Italy
www.edra.com

Barber Osgerby

What are the drawbacks and advantages of being a design duo, and how do you work together?

We met on the first day of our postgraduate architecture course at the Royal College of Art in London and hit it off straight away. We obviously disagree sometimes but we discuss everything and respect each other's views. Whilst we were still at the RCA we got the odd external commission. We were young and inexperienced and neither of us would have had the confidence to take these projects on individually. We have never worked independently since. We sit on either side of a table and talk about a project and one of us starts to sketch. The other looks at the drawing upside down and sees something that is completely different. It's a back-and-forth process. It's very rarely that you can say that an idea came from one or the other of us because, by the time a project is finished, it's so much a part of both of us.

The designer and educator Bruce Mau wrote in the introduction to your recent monograph that 'Edward and Jay use industry as craft'. Can you explain?

He has recognized the fact that we consider industrial processes, take the best from them and work with them in a slower, craftlike way. Take the Iris Table (opposite page, right), for example: the components had to be machined from solid aluminium and individually anodized, and we hijacked that industrial finishing technique. We found a company that was prepared to stop making hi-fi fronts for a couple of weeks and instead produce multicoloured iridescent pieces of aluminium for us. We arrested industry for a moment and reappropriated it as craft.

Bottom left: Loop low table for Isokon Plus (1998)

Bottom right: Planform Array V, 'Ascent' exhibition, Haunch of Venison, London (2011)

You talk a lot about 'hidden design' when referring to your work. Please can you explain what you mean by this?

This relates to our 'Ascent' exhibition at the Haunch of Venison in London. We have always been inspired by nautical and aeronautical design and fluid dynamics. Hidden design relates to the undesigned parts of structures that move. There is something about the way outlines are made and volumes are created in a lightweight way: skeletons that are then skinned with metal or fabric. For the exhibition we played with this reference in a series of objects with similar shapes that created a dialogue between solid, empty and translucent.

Would you say there is a BarberOsgerby style?

Our main aim is to make objects that are understandable and that people are comfortable with and want to keep forever. Our work resonates emotionally yet it is quite geometric and simple. That comes from the fact that we don't use elaborate computer programs to design but begin with the sketch.

Can you briefly describe two of the pivotal projects of your studio?

The Loop Table (below left) is the most important single piece that we've ever done, because it captured the moment when we moved from architecture to objects. At the time we were working in the Trellick Tower, Ernö Goldfinger's modernist masterpiece, and the cantilevers and rounded corners in that building influenced us. The Loop Table is the product that introduced us to Cappellini and made our name. That was a pivotal moment.

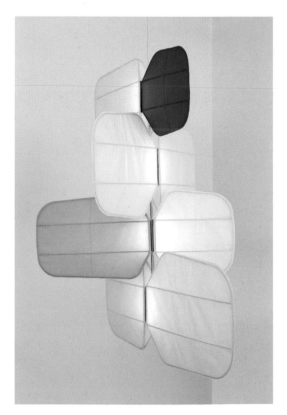

The Tip Ton chair (page 52) is another important project for us. It's our first piece for Vitra and was the result of in-depth research into the benefits of a forward tilt function in seating designed for schools. The Tip Ton tilts forward towards a table or desk, where it then remains in place. The movement between two sitting positions increases muscular activity in the stomach and back regions, which increases the flow of oxygen around the body and in turn aids concentration. This movement is unique to a simple, solid plastic chair. The Tip Ton is also light, it stacks, is incredibly durable and 100% recyclable. We've just kitted out our first school and it's working very well.

The Olympic Torch (below) is one of the most visible design briefs in the world. How onerous was the commission?

We entered the competition for the design of the torch as soon as it was announced. The torch is the iconic symbol of the games and will pass on as a legacy. It is also an incredibly complicated piece of industrial design. From over 1,000 entries, our concept was chosen: a three-sided design perforated with 8,000 holes to represent the motto of the games (Faster, Higher, Stronger) and the number of people who will carry it. It is one of those incredible things that you only have the chance to do once in a lifetime. It was very onerous; we had to create something that represented the nation. It's the first opportunity we've had to design an object that everyone recognizes.

How do you balance your conceptual and studio work?

We are always making sketches and saving them. 'Ascent' was essentially the realisation of five years of sketches made on the edges of drawings for other products. Most of what we do feels conceptual to us. A design doesn't start off in a pragmatic way but as a series of discussions and doodles.

You have three companies: BarberOsgerby, Universal Studio, and Map, which cover product design, architecture, and design consultancy respectively. How does one practice affect the other?

We are involved across all three, but at BarberOsgerby we're involved with everything from the concept onwards. The work emanating from Universal Design Studio and Map is far more a collaboration between ourselves and some of the most talented designers and architects in the world. Working across so many different kinds of project and scales, from architecture to microelectronics, fascinates us and keeps our spirit fresh.

When design historians look back at the last twenty years, will they consider it to have been an exciting period?

That's been an incredibly exciting time for design and production. In the 1990s there were only a handful of manufacturing companies making avant-garde furniture. Now you go to Milan and you are bombarded with hundreds of them. China now leads the world in manufacturing. That's changed everything – the speed of production and the need for innovation. There have been some really interesting developments in terms of computer software and technology, such as 3D printing. Also, designers are now making objects that are not functional. That's quite a turning point. Before you either had artists and sculptors or designers, but now there is a middle ground, which we have crossed with the 'Ascent' pieces (opposite page, bottom right). We never thought we would, but in the end it made sense for us.

Left: Olympic Torch for London Organising Committee of the Olympic and Paralympic Games (2012)

Right: Iris Table for Established & Sons LIMITED gallery, London (2008)

**Rotating bookcase,
Book Tower**
Samuel Chan
European oak veneer
H (tower I): 150cm (59in)
W (tower I): 45cm (17¾in)
D (tower I): 45cm (17¾in)
H (tower II): 100cm (39in)
W (tower II): 45cm (17¾in)
D (tower II): 45cm (17¾in)
H (tower III): 50cm (19in)
W (tower III): 49cm (19¼in)
D (tower III): 49cm (19¼in)
Linteloo, The Netherlands
www.linteloo.com

**Modular storage system,
Brace (The Black & Black
Collection)**
Nendo
Powder-coated steel
H: 30cm (11¾in)
W: 50cm (19in)
D: 28cm (11in)
K%, Singapore
www.kpercent.com

**Modular shelving
unit, Staccato**
Atelier Oï
Natural oak
H: 191.5cm (75in)
W: 22.8 + 20.4cm per element
(9 + 7⅞in per element)
D: 42.3cm (16½in)
Röthlisberger Kollektion,
Switzerland
www.roethlisberger.ch

**Modular storage
system, Dice**
Stefan Diez
Kvadrat fabrics, painted MDF
Various dimensions
Schönbuch GmbH, Germany
www.schoenbuch.com

Storage container/ seat, cBox

Gianmarco Blini
Steel, upholstery
H: 47.5cm (18⅞in)
W: 45cm (17¾in)
D: 45cm (17¾in)
Dieffebi SpA, Italy
www.dieffebi.com

Bookshelf, Stix

Benninghoff & Bond
Lacquered MDF, iron
H: 105cm (41in)
W: 35cm (13¾in)
L: 242cm (95in)
Covo srl, Italy
www.covo.it

Storage shelf, Times Square

Cluesson Koivisto Rune
Laquered wood (MDF)
H (small): 89.8cm (35in)
H (large): 195.4cm (76in)
W (small): 81.6cm (32in)
W (large): 183.2cm (72in)
D (small): 29cm (11⅜in)
D (large): 38cm (15in)
David Design, Sweden
www.daviddesignfurniture.se

Modular shelf system, Stacked

JDS Architects
Painted MDF, wood
Small box: 21.8 x 43.6cm
(8⅝ x 17⅜in)
Medium box: 43.6 x 43.6cm
(17⅜ x 17⅜in)
Large box: 65.4 x 43.6cm
(25 x 17⅜in)
D: 35cm (13¾in)
Muuto, Denmark
www.muuto.com

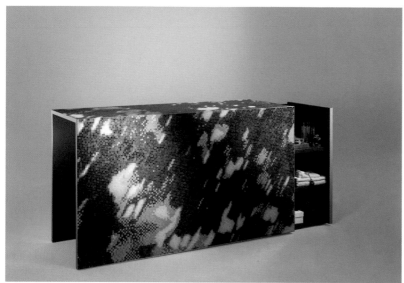

Cabinet, Summer Trees Commode (Digital Memories Collection)
Tord Boontje
Bisazza glass mosaic, lacquered wood, steel
H: 101cm (40in)
L: 180cm (70in)
D: 63cm (24in)
Bisazza, Italy
www.bisazza.com

Chest, Altdeutsche Blanket Chest
Studio Job
Solid pine, hand-painted artwork
H: 78cm (30in)
W: 120cm (47in)
D: 55cm (21in)
Moooi, The Netherlands
www.moooi.com

Children's storage, Flapjack Storage
Sebastian Bergne
Certified FSC beech plywood with laminate faces and water-based varnish
H: 70cm (27in)
W: 84.5cm (33in)
D: 29cm (11⅜in)
The Collection, France
www.buysebastianbergne.com
www.thecollection.fr

Cabinet, Job Cabinet
Studio Job
Powder-coated metal sheets
H: 180cm (70in)
W: 70cm (27in)
D: 50cm (19in)
Lensvelt b.v., The Netherlands
www.lensvelt.nl

Cabinet, Collect 2011
Sara Larsson
MDF, solid wood
H: 119cm (47in)
W: 64cm (25in)
D: 30cm (11¾in)
A2 designers AB, Sweden
www.a2designers.se

Bookcase, Forest
Nendo
White painted conglomerate
wooden structure
H: 200cm (78in)
W: 100cm (39in)
D: 40cm (15¾in)
Driade, Italy
www.driade.com

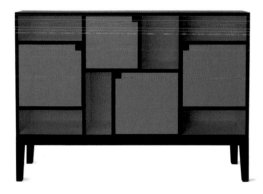

Cabinet, Flip
Håkan Johansson/Zweed
Laminated black MDF,
stained solid birch
H: 87cm (34in)
W: 118cm (46in)
D: 34cm (13⅜in)
Zweed, Sweden
www.zweed.se

Bookshelf, Industry
Benjamin Hubert
Painted metal, natural
and painted pine, metal
in Corten finish
H: 186cm (73in)
W: 153cm (60in)
D: 40cm (15¾in)
Casamania, Italy
www.casamania.it

4.

KITCHENS
AND
BATHROOMS

Gas hob, P755SG (yellow)
Marc Newson
Cast-iron panstands,
vertical flame burners,
silver compontents
W: 75cm (29in)
L: 75cm (29in)
Smeg SpA, Italy
www.smeg.com

Modular kitchen, Tetrix
Michael Young
Matt coloured glass, glossy
tempered glass, grey quartz
H (rectangular module):
36cm (14⅛in)
W (rectangular module):
60cm (23in)
Scavolini SpA, Italy
www.scavolini.com

Cooker hood, Bubble
Stefano Giovannoni
Technopolymer
H: 59.8cm (23in)
W: 59.8cm (23in)
D: 32cm (12⅝in)
Elica, Italy
www.elica.com

Modular kitchen, Cube
Claesson Koivisto Rune
Wood
H: 87 (34in)
D: 64cm (25in)
Grattarola srl, Italy
www.grattarola.it

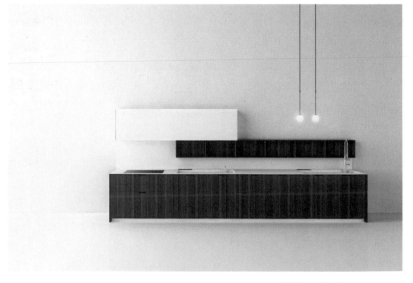

Kitchen, Aprile
Piero Lissoni
Wood, Corian®
Various dimensions
Boffi SpA, Italy
www.boffi.com

Modular kitchen, Menu 04
Paola Navone
Matt Maya silver bilaminate,
melamine panel with
metal mesh, steel-finish
aluminium frame

H (bases): 72cm (28in)
H (unit with storage doors):
183.2cm (72in)
Bontempi Cucine, Italy
www.bontempi.it

Modular kitchen, Menu 05
Paola Navone
Bilaminate door with ABS
border on four sides, vertical
wood grain, horizontal
tranché finish
H (bases): 72cm (28in)
H (tall units): 204cm (80in)
Bontempi Cucine, Italy
www.bontempi.it

Kitchen, Concrete Kitchen
Martin Steininger
Concrete
Made to order
steininger.designers, Austria
www.steininger-designers.at

Kitchen, Liquida Frame
Giovannoni Design
HPL laminate
H: 215cm (84in)
L: 390cm (154in)
D: 94cm (37in)
Veneta Cucine SpA, Italy
www.venetacucine.com

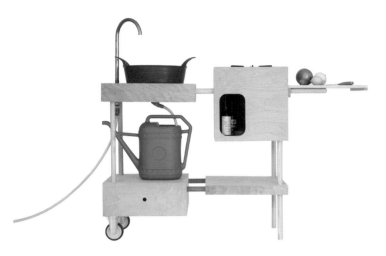

DIY outdoor kitchen project with downloadable assembly instructions, Mobile Outdoor Kitchen
Nina Tolstrup
Plywood
H: 90cm (35in)
W: 50cm (19in)
L: 100cm (39in)
Studiomama, UK
www.studiomama.com

Kitchen, Pampa
Alfredo Häberli
Wood, metal
Various dimensions
Schiffini Mobili Cucine SpA, Italy
www.schiffini.it

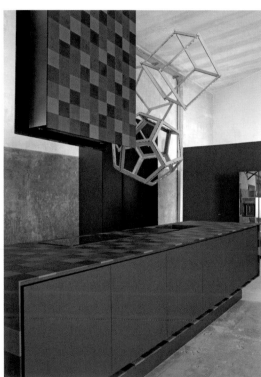

Kitchen, Eco
Alessio Bassan
PaperStone®
H: 80cm (31in)
W (max): 360cm (141in)
Key Cucine (brand of di Sbabo Cucine srl), Italy
www.keysbabo.com

Kitchen, Board
Arosio Design
High-gloss lacquer finish, Corian®
Various dimensions
Snaidero, Italy
www.snaidero.it

**Ovens, FP610SG (yellow),
FP610SBL (blue),
FP610SV (green)**
Marc Newson
Glass, stainless steel
H: 60cm (23in)
W: 60cm (23in)
D: 55cm (21in)
Smeg Sp.A, Italy
www.smeg.com

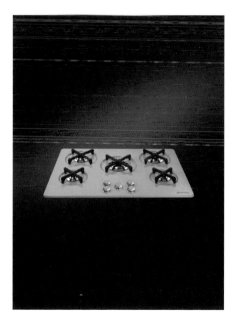

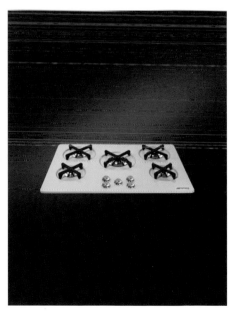

**Gas hobs, P755SG (yellow),
P755SBL (blue),
P755SV (green)**
Marc Newson
Cast-iron panstands,
vertical flame burners,
silver compontents
W: 75cm (29in)
L: 75cm (29in)
Smeg SpA, Italy
www.smeg.com

Kitchen, Liquida (Flipper)
Giovannoni Design
Glossy PET
H: 229cm (90in)
W: 345cm (136in)
D: 104cm (41in)
Veneta Cucine SpA, Italy
www.venetacucine.com

**Kitchen system,
Bulthaup b3**
Herbert Schultes/Bulthaup
design team
Laminate, solid walnut
H: 91cm (35in)
L: 362cm (143in)
D: 65cm (25in)
Bulthaup GmbH & Co KG,
Germany
www.bulthaup.com

Kitchen sink, Starck K
Philippe Starck
Impact-resistant ceramic
W: 90 or 100cm (35 or 39in)
D: 51cm (20in)
Duravit, Germany
www.duravit.com

**Free-standing kitchen
units, W range**
Jean-Michel Wilmotte
Lacquered sheet metal,
screen-printed grey
tempered glass
Various dimensions
La Cornue, France
www.lacornue.com

Kitchen, Library Kitchen
Philippe Starck
Wood veneer, white lacquer, chrome
H: 73 or 93cm (28 or 36in)
W: 93.4cm (36in)
L: 259.8 or 323.8cm (102 or 127in)
Warendorf, Germany
www.warendorf.eu

Modular kitchen, k20
Norbert Wangen
Corian®
Various dimensions
Boffi SpA, Italy

**Kitchen faucet,
Paola and the Kitchen**
Paola Navone
Chromed brass, painted die-cast metal
H: 40.1cm (15¾in)
Diam: 6cm (2⅜in)
Mamoli Robinetteria SpA, Italy
www.mamoli.com

Kitchen island, DC10
Vincenzo De Cotiis
Burnished brass
H (top included): 93.5cm (37in)
H (top excluded): 86.5cm (34in)
W: 70.4cm (27in)
L (1): 439.6cm (173in)
L (2): 259.6 (102in)
Rossana RB srl, Italy
www.rossana.it

Pot and pans, Foodwear
Rodolfo Dordoni
Wonder plus finished
stainless steel
H (pot): 11.5cm (4½in)
Diam (pot): 26cm (10¼in)
knIndustrie srl, Italy
www.knindustrie.it

Cookware, Ellie Krieger Cookware
Scott Henderson
Stainless steel, silicon
H: 10cm (4in)
Diam: 51cm (20in)
Tefal, France
www.tefal.com

Measuring cups, Ellie Krieger Cookware
Scott Henderson
Polypropylene
W (largest size):
11cm (4⅜in)
L (largest size):
16.5cm (6½in)
Tefal, France
www.tefal.com

Electric kettle, Ettore 11175
Ettore Sottsass
Plastic, stainless steel, silicone
H: 26cm (10¼in)
W: 25cm (9⅞in)
D: 16.3cm (6¼in)
Bodum, Denmark
www.bodum.com

Kitchen tools, Enjoy spatulas
Sebastian Bergne
Recycled PET
H: 4cm (1⅝in)
W: 6cm (2⅜in)
L: 30cm (11¾in)
Tefal, France
www.tefal.com
www.buysebastianbergne.com

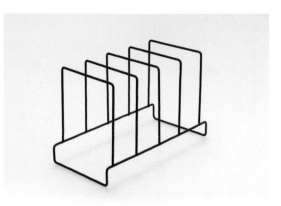

**Basket, Wire
Basket Round**
Naoto Fukasawa
Steel coated with epoxy resin
H: 6.7cm (2⅝in)
Diam: 20.2cm (7⅞in)
Plus Minus Zero Co., Ltd.,
Japan
www.plusminuszero.jp

**Toast stand, Wire
Toast Stand**
Naoto Fukasawa
Steel coated with epoxy resin
H: 8.5cm (3⅜in)
W: 15cm (5⅞in)
D: 7.4cm (2⅞in)
Plus Minus Zero Co., Ltd.,
Japan
www.plusminuszero.jp

**Water bottle opener,
Water=Life**
Arik Levy
Styrene acrylonitrile (SAN)
H: 3cm (1⅛in)
W: 7cm (2¾in)
L: 10cm (3⅞in)
Fratelli Guzzini SpA, Italy
www.fratelliguzzini.com

Chopping board, Chop
Patrick Jouin
Bamboo wood
H: 6cm (2⅜in)
W: 22cm (8⅝in)
D: 22cm (8⅝in)
Alessi SpA, Italy
www.alessi.com

Bread bin, Loaf
Established & Sons
Beech plywood
H: 19cm (7½in)
Diam: 35.5cm (14⅛in)
Established & Sons, UK
www.establishedandsons.com

Single-lever basin mixer, Kawa
Karim Rashid
Chrome-plated brass
H: 14.4cm (5¾in)
L: 18.1cm (7⅛in)
Cisal Rubinetteria, Italy
www.cisal.it

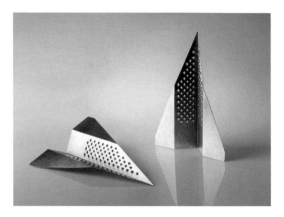

Grater, Pippo
Liviana Osti
Stainless steel
H: 3.5cm (1⅜in)
W: 25cm (9⅞in)
D: 17.5cm (6⅞in)
Paola C., Italy
www.paolac.com

Pan, Boomerang Wok
Nikolaï Carels
Aluminium, bakelite,
stainless steel
H: 12.5cm (4⅞in)
W: 48.7cm (19¼in)
D: 32cm (12⅝in)
Royal VKB, The Netherlands
www.royalvkb.com

Kitchen and serving ware, Seasons
nownao (Nao Tamura)
Silicone
H (small leaf): 5.2cm (2in)
W (small leaf): 19.2cm (7½in)
L (small leaf): 18.7cm (7¼in)
H (medium leaf):
7.3cm (2⅞in)
W (medium leaf):
31.3cm (12¼in)
L (medium leaf):
21.5cm (8⅝in)
Covo, Italy
www.covo.it

Espresso coffee maker, Moka Alessi
Alessandro Mendini
Aluminium casting,
thermoplastic resin
H: 16.4cm (6½in)
Diam: 9.6cm (3¾in)
Alessi SpA, Italy
www.alessi.com

Trivet, Rainbow Trivet
Ding3000
Nylon
H: 1.4cm (½in)
L: 18.7cm (7½in)
Normann Copenhagen, Denmark
www.normann-copenhagen.com

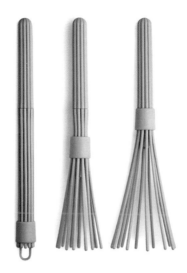

Whisk, Beater
Ding3000
Nylon
H: 28.5cm (11⅜in)
Diam: 2cm (¾in)
Normann Copenhagen, Denmark
www.normann-copenhagen.com

Whisk
LucidiPevere
Bamboo, plastic
H: 30.7cm (12¼in)
W: 10cm (3⅞in)
Normann Copenhagen, Denmark
www.normann-copenhagen.com

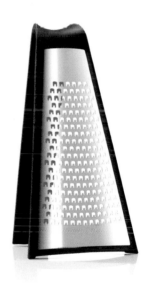

Cookware, Shiba
Naoto Fukasawa
Metal, wood
H (frying pan): 7.5cm (3in)
Diam (frying pan):
24cm (9½in)
H (saucepans): 12cm (4¾in)
Diam (large saucepan):
18cm (7⅛in)
Diam (small saucepan):
15cm (5⅞in)
Alessi SpA, Italy
www.alessi.com

**Grater, Eva Solo
XO Grater**
Tools
Stainless steel, PA66 nylon
with 10% fibreglass, silicone
H: 18cm (7⅛in)
W: 11.5cm (4½in)
L: 10cm (3⅞in)
Eva Solo, Denmark
www.evasolo.com

Richard Hutten

You made your name with a series of products called No Sign of Design (below). Could you describe the concept?

This was my graduation project. In 1991, Bořek Šípek was the number-one design star. I couldn't relate to his work at all. It's what I call 'decoration'. I thought up the concept of 'No Sign of Design' as a statement against this style. Today they would be called 'Super Normal'. It was a good idea and still relevant.

You say that design is a thinking process and that form follows concept. Could you expand on this?

For me, form is a by-product and not a goal in itself. The most important part of a design is the idea. I always want to add something new and surprising. A good design has to tell a story and be interesting in some way or another. The form then follows naturally.

You call yourself a cultural designer. What do you mean by this?

I'm an artist and I make art. My medium is not painting, nor is it sculpture; it's design. I want to tell stories and show my vision of the world through my work. That's why I call myself a cultural designer. My aim is not only profit. Obviously it's nice if some of my products are produced hundreds of thousands of times, people make their living from them and consumers can enjoy them. That's what I want. That's why I'm a designer, but it's just a nice side effect.

How do you balance the commercial and the conceptual in your work?

I never compromise on my vision. I concentrate on making good designs, and others produce and sell them. To come up with an idea that adds something to the existing and is context driven is the starting point, not whether it's commercial. I have always worked as a team with my clients. We have the same goal – to make the best product possible. Sometimes one has to push the boundaries of what is

achievable in order to innovate. In my experience, the end result has never been far away from my initial idea.

It appears that in your work you disguise high tech in the aesthetics of low tech. Is this a fair assessment?

As a designer I have a lot of knowledge about materials and techniques but I don't want to bother the user with this. For example, the Dumbo mug (opposite page, top) looks cute and makes people smile but it is actually very hard to make. I don't want to say, 'Look how high tech this is.' My aim is to make things that people want to have, enjoy and, most importantly, keep.

In your opinion, what does it mean to be an ecologically responsible designer?

Many products that have Cradle-to-Cradle certification look a bit 'eco', like brown mud. If something is visual pollution, it doesn't matter if you can recycle it or not because no one wants it. Take the Dumbo mug again: it's fairly 'green' because it's made from one material that can be shredded and reused, but it's also sustainable because you can't destroy it. It lasts a long time. I make objects that people want to keep, that increase in value as they get older and will get handed down from one generation to another. That's the highest form of sustainability. I'm art director of Gispen, which was voted the most green company in the Netherlands in 2011. The idea of Cradle-to-Cradle is important to their philosophy, but we go one step further. We follow the rules of green design but make furniture that is sexy and attractive.

What motivated you to sign over the Richard Hutten collection to Gispen in 2008?

Gispen is ninety-five years old and Holland's most well known furniture brand. They started out making domestic products but over the years had moved exclusively to office furniture. When they invited me to be their main designer I advised them to return to their roots and proposed that they take over my collection. I'm happy because I can now fully focus on designing; I don't have to deal with production or distribution. It's a very good collaboration

Right: No Sign of Design
table and chairs (1991)

You are the art director of Gispen and NgispeN, the domestic furniture label. What is it like to be sitting on the other side of the table?

It's exciting to create a vision for a brand. There are so many out there that it's very hard to establish an identity and stand out in the field when you develop a new one, such as NgispeN. I'm commissioning work from people I admire, who are also my friends and whom I've known for a long time. Some I have to 'coach' more than others, but each relationship is different and exciting.

In 2010 your mini book stamp (below) – a postal stamp that is also an eight-page book – went on sale, and in the following year you were awarded the Van Speijk Innovation Award for its design. How did the collaboration with Royal TNT Dutch come about?

I had previously worked with the Royal Dutch Post designing premium gifts for their most important clients and at that time pressed them to allow me to create a stamp, but as I'm not a graphic designer they were reluctant. At one point they invited twenty designers to come up with a celebratory stamp, including one industrial designer – me. I had the idea of making the stamp an actual book, which they loved, and I was commissioned. Then the Dutch post was asked to create a stamp to celebrate the seventy-fifth anniversary of the annual 'Book Week' (boekenweek). Of course they wanted to use my idea for this. The book can be detached from the stamp and the typeface is large enough to read with the naked eye. It has a 500-word text by the author Joost Zwagermans, an ISBN, and, as it also has a colophon, I had the opportunity of adding my name as designer. It was very successful.

Do you consider design can contribute to social change?

We can't change the world, but designers have a big responsibility to contribute to people's lives and make them better. I consider sustainability and durability, but my concern is to add to the quality of life. I take joy from my work and want to give joy to others whilst respecting the planet. I think in a very small way I can make a difference.

Top: Dumbo mug, Richard Hutten Collection available through NgispeN (2001)

Bottom: Mini book stamp for Royal TNT Dutch (2010)

**Shower/hammam,
Ananda**
Doshi Levien
Cabinet and benches:
HardLite
Showerwall: HardLite or
white Carrara marble
Made to order
Glass Idromassaggio srl, Italy
www.glassidromassaggio.com

**Single-lever basin
mixer, Gentle**
Matteo Thun and Partner
Polished chrome
H (mixer): 10.5cm (4⅛in)
Diam (hole): 3.5cm (1⅜in)
Dornbracht, Germany
www.dornbracht.com

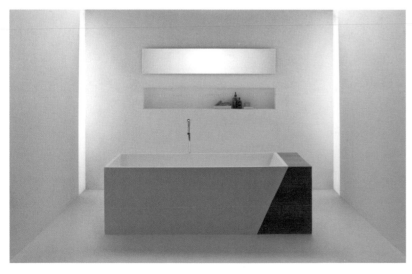

**Bath, Latis Bath with
Timber End**
Thomas Coward
American oak, acrylic cast
solid surface
H: 60cm (23in)
W: 75cm (29in)
L: 180cm (70in)
Omvivo, Australia
www.omvivo.com

**Washbasin, Le Washbasin
(Neorest Series)**
TOTO
Hybrid epoxy resin
LED lights
H: 10.9cm (4⅜in)
W: 75.5cm (29in)
D: 45cm (17¾in)
TOTO, Japan
www.eu.toto.com

Bathtub, The Hayon Collection
Jaime Hayon
White metacrylic bathtub
with high-gloss white
varnished wooden frame,
beech storage lid
H: 51cm (20in)
W: 100cm (39in)
L: 204.5cm (80in)
Bisazza Bagno, Italy
www.bisazzabagno.com

**Unit with washbasin,
The Hayon Collection**
Jaime Hayon
24kt gold hand-painted
ceramic washbasin, stainless-
steel magnifying mirror
H (washbasin): 14cm (5½in)
W (washbasin): 65.5cm (26in)
D (washbasin): 47cm (18½in)
Bisazza Bagno, Italy
www.bisazzabagno.com

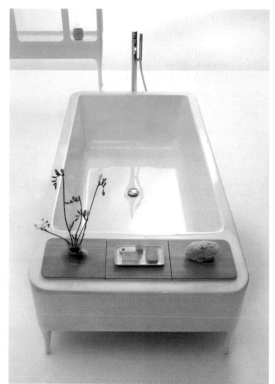

**Unit with washbasins,
The Hayon Collection**
Jaime Hayon
High-gloss copper aluminium
frame, black Marquina
marble top and shelves,
mirror, black ceramic
washbasin
H (washbasin): 12cm (4¾in)
W (washbasin): 58cm (22in)
D (washbasin): 48cm (18⅞in)
Bisazza Bagno, Italy
www.bisazzabagno.com

Bathtub, Talamo
Domenico De Palo
Cristalplant
H: 67cm (26in)
W: 100cm (39in)
L: 200cm (78in)
Antonio Lupi Design SpA,
Italy
www.antoniolupi.it

Washbasin, Kalla
Marc Sadler
High-resistance and
hygienic elastomer
H: 17cm (6¾in)
W: 80cm (31in)
D: 40cm (15¾in)
Karol srl, Italy
www.karol.it

Washbasin, Vol
Victor Carrasco
Cristalplant
H: 90cm (35in)
L: 60cm (23in)
D: 40cm (15¾in)
Boffi SpA, Italy
www.boffi.com

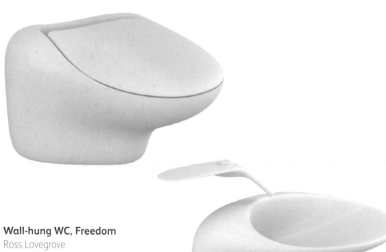

Wall-hung WC, Freedom
Ross Lovegrove
Vitreous China
W: 50cm (19in)
D: 54cm (21in)
VitrA, Turkey
www.vitra.com.tr

**Wall-hung washbasin and
faucet, Freedom**
Ross Lovegrove
Fine fire clay
W: 79.5cm (31in)
D: 48.5cm (19¼in)
VitrA, Turkey
www.vitra.com.tr

**Washlet toilet with
remote control,
Giovannoni Washlet**
Stefano Giovannoni
Ceramic with a special
CeFiONtect glaze
H: 61.6cm (24in)
W: 43.6cm (17⅜in)
D: 54.8cm (21in)
TOTO, Japan
www.eu.toto.com

Bathtub
Thomas Linssen
American white oak,
composite of marble
and polyester
H: 84cm (33in)
H (rim): 59cm (23in)
W: 85cm (33in)
L: 190cm (74in)
Studio Thol, The Netherlands
www.studiothol.nl

**Free-standing single-lever
bath/shower mixer with
diverter and shower set,
Isystick**
Matteo Thun and
Antonio Rodriguez
Painted brass
H (max): 94.5cm (37in)
Diam (base): 8cm (3⅛in)
Zucchetti Rubinetteria SpA,
Italy
www.zucchettidesign.it

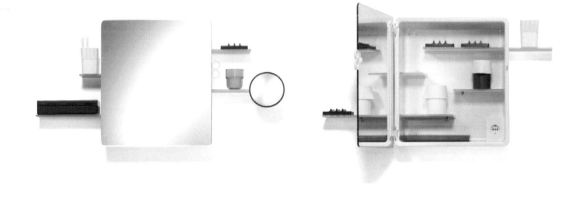

**Mirror cabinet with
bathroom accessories and
electric socket, Kali**
Doshi Levien
ASA plastic, glass, mirror
H: 58cm (22in)
W (body): 54.5cm (21in)
W (total): 113cm (44in)
D: 18cm (7⅛in)
Authentics GmbH, Germany
www.authentics.de

Bathtub, Vieques
Patricia Urquiola
Steel
H: 60cm (23in)
L: 170cm (66in)
D: 72cm (28in)
Agape, Italy
www.agapedesign.it

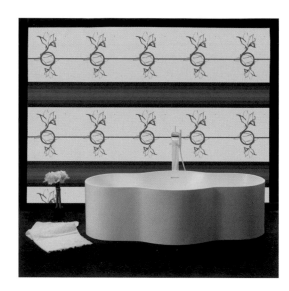

Bathtub, Chapel
Alain Berteau
Dupont Corian®
W: 95cm (37in)
L: 180cm (70in)
Aquamass, Belgium
www.aquamass.com

Bathtub, Navale
Xavier Lust
Corian®
H: 52cm (20in)
W: 80cm (31in)
L: 180cm (70in)
Aquamass, Belgium
www.aquamass.com

Bathtub, Ofurò
Matteo Thun and
Antonio Rodriguez
Larch wood
H: 60cm (23in)
W: 80cm (31in)
L: 140cm (55in)
Rapsel SpA, Italy
www.rapsel.it

**Bathtub, Ottocento
(Memory Collection)**
Benedini Associati
Cristalplant
H: 59.5cm (23in)
W: 79cm (31in)
L: 178cm (70in)
Agape srl, Italy
www.agapedesign.it

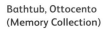

Bathtub, Amarcord
Marco Merendi
Copper, lacquered inside
H: 75cm (29in)
W: 68cm (26in)
L: 150cm (59in)
Rapsel SpA, Italy
www.rapsel.it

Bathtub, Morphing Bathroom Collection
Ludovica and Roberto Palomba
Cristalplant
H: 56cm (22in)
W: 80cm (31in)
L: 180cm (70in)
Kos, Italy
www.zucchettikos.it

Bathtub, Sartoriale Maxi
Carlo Colombo
Cristalplant
H: 55cm (21in)
W: 140cm (55in)
L: 200cm (78in)
Antoniolupi Design SpA, Italy
www.antoniolupi.it

Bathtub, Paiova Monolith
Eoos
Acrylic
W: 100cm (39in)
L: 170cm (66in)
Duravit, Germany
www.duravit.com

**Wall-mounted electronic
basin mixer, Axor Citterio
Electronic Basin Mixer**
Antonio Citterio
Solid brass with
chrome plating
L: 16cm (6¼in)
Axor – Hansgrohe, Germany
www.hansgrohe.com

**Bathroom wastebasket
with pedal, Moby**
Babled & Co.
100% recyclable
thermoplastic resins
H: 26cm (10¼in)
W: 23cm (9in)
D: 28cm (11in)
Gedy SpA, Italy
www.gedy.com

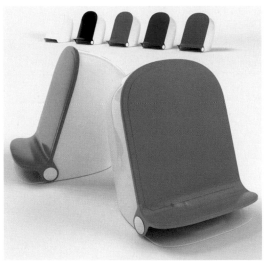

**Washbasin counter,
Counter D (The Nendo
Collection)**
Nendo
Larch wood with chrome
brass digital basin mixer
H: 90cm (35in)
W: 120cm (47in)
D: 60cm (23in)
Bisazza, Italy
www.bisazza.it

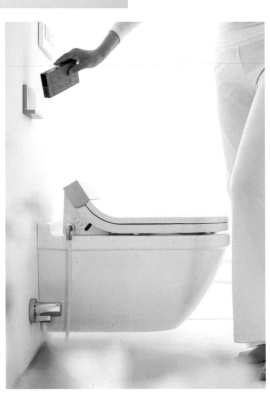

**Shower-toilet with remote
control, SensoWash Starck**
Philippe Starck
Ceramic, acrylic
H (lid closed): 42cm (16½in)
W: 37cm (14⅝in)
D: 62cm (24in)
Duravit, Germany
www.duravit.com
Due to legislation in different
countries, this product is not
available worldwide.

Washbasin, Roll
Nendo
Ceramic
Diam: 44cm (17⅜in)
Ceramica Flaminia, Italy
www.ceramicaflaminia.it

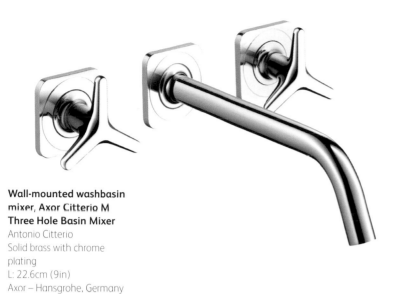

Wall-mounted washbasin mixer, Axor Citterio M Three Hole Basin Mixer
Antonio Citterio
Solid brass with chrome plating
L: 22.6cm (9in)
Axor – Hansgrohe, Germany
www.hansgrohe-int.com

Washbasin, Pool
Martí Guixé
Lacquered ceramic, stainless steel
H: 45cm (17¾in)
W: 30cm (11¾in)
L: 80cm (31in)
D: 32cm (12⅝in)
Azzurra Sanitari in Ceramica SpA, Italy
www.azzurraceramica.it

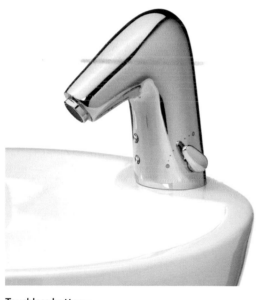

Touchless battery-operated washbasin faucet with temperature-adjustment handle, Il Bagno Alessi by Oras
Stefano Giovannoni
Chrome-plated corrosion-resistant material (DZR-brass), 6V battery
H: 14.7cm (5⅞in)
Diam: 6cm (2⅜in)
Oras Group, Finland
www.oras.com

Bathroom sink, Axor Bouroullec
Ronan and Erwan Bouroullec
Chrome-plated brass, mineral resin, polyester resin, ABS
L: 66.6cm (26in)
W: 48cm (18⅞in)
Axor – Hansgrohe, Germany
www.hansgrohe-int.com

5.
TABLEWARE

Vase, Simbiosi
Emmanuel Babled
Handblown Murano glass,
Carrara marble
H: 57.5cm (22in)
L: 42.5cm (16⅞in)
D: 39.5cm (15¾in)
Venini SpA, Italy
www.venini.com

Vases and bowls, Eye
Sebastian Bergne
Iznik quartz ceramics,
Swarovski elements
H (large vase):
35cm (13¾in)
Diam (large vase):
38cm (15in)
Gaia & Gino, Turkey
www.gaiagino.com

Tray, Marble 4420
Monica Förster and
Björn Kusoffsky
Laminated textile
Diam: 49cm (19¼in)
Svenskt Tenn, Sweden
www.svenskttenn.se

Glithero's Blueware collection of vases pays homage to
the Dutch heritage of van Gameren, bringing to mind the
iconic colouring of Delftware. Weeds taken from the streets
of London are pressed, dried and delicately composed on
the surface of a vase, which is then exposed to UV light as
it rotates on a spit. This causes it to change colour, whilst
leaving a crisp white silhouette of the plants once they have
been removed. The vase is then dipped into a special acid to
produce a deep Prussian blue that contrasts starkly with the
ghostly image of the plants.

Vase, Blueware vase
Glithero
Earthenware ceramics, glazed
inside, cyanotype
H: 42cm (16½in)
Diam: 23cm (9in)
Glithero, UK
www.studioglithero.com

Vase, Blow Away Vase
Front
Royal Blue Delft porcelain
H: 30.5cm (12¼in)
Moooi, The Netherlands
www.moooi.com

Mark Vaarwerk works with a variety of discarded plastics, and his most recent pieces derive from unexpanded polystyrene containers. He researched the chemical properties of different plastics to understand how and why they behave as they do and the many ways they can be manipulated. For these bowls Mark created a template to trace the desired shape onto the polystyrene. Three segments were then placed in an airtight container, which was slowly filled with acetone vapor. The acetone acts as a solvent, softening the plastic and gradually deflating the polystyrene beads, reducing the material to around half or one-third of its original size; as it shrinks it gets more dense and pliable. The segments were then bonded together using a glue-like paste made by dissolving scraps of the unexpanded polystyrene in acetone before being shaped on a plaster dome into a vessel. After the solvent has evaporated and the vessel has hardened, the final stage is to apply a coating. The green and black bowls were spray-painted, but the white version was hand-painted using a glaze made from the keys from a computer keyboard – the ABS plastic was dissolved, again in acetone, and applied with a brush. Vaarwerk's experimentation knows no limits. He has gone so far as to create a glaze from cigarette butts, which are actually a plastic – cellulose acetate. This he uses to colour smaller polystyrene shapes to create brooches.

Bowls, Unexpanded Polystyrene Vessels

Mark Vaarwerk
Unexpanded polystyrene
H: 3cm (1⅛in)
Diam (large green): 16cm (6¼in)
Diam (medium white): 14cm (5½in)
Diam (small black): 12cm (4¾in)
Mark Vaarwerk, Australia
www.vaarwerk.com

Basket, Peneira Collection

Fernando and Humberto Campana
18/10 stainless-steel mesh, natural fibre
H: 12.5cm (4⅞in)
Diam: 35cm (13¾in)
Alessi SpA, Italy
www.alessi.com

Vessel consisting of three individual containers, Stacking Vessel

Pia Wüstenberg
Ceramic, studio glass, wood
H: 50cm (19in)
Diam: 23cm (9in)
Utopia and Utility,
UK and Finland
www.utopiaandutility.eu

Collection of jars/vases, Natura Jars

Héctor Serrano
100% recycled glass, cork
H (tallest vase): 32.1cm (12⅝in)
Diam (tallest vase): 13.4cm (5⅜in)
La Mediterranea, Spain
www.lamediterranea.com

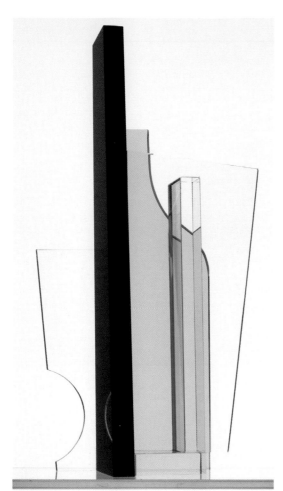

**Vase, Cubist Vase
(Absinthe)**
Constantin and
Laurene Boym
Crystal
H: 26cm (10¼in)
W: 15cm (5⅞in)
D: 10cm (3⅞in)
Boym Partners Inc., USA
www.boym.com

**Vases, containers
and low cupboard,
Truciolari Collection**
Lorenzo Damiani
Chipboard panels
Various dimensions
Lorenzo Damiani, Italy
www.lorenzodamiani.net

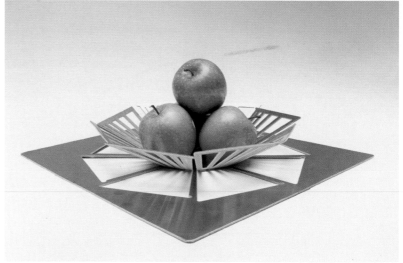

Fruit bowl, Gills Bowl
Bettina Nissen
Laser-cut steel
H: 7cm (2¾in)
W: 30cm (11¾in)
D: 30cm (11¾in)
Bettina Nissen Design, UK
www.bettinanissen.com

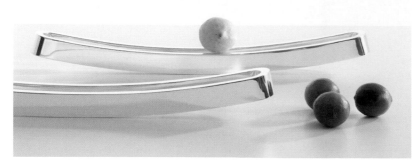

**Fruit holder
centrepiece, TIP**
Asif Khan
Sterling silver 925/1000
H: 7.2cm (2⅞in)
W: 6cm (2⅜in)
L: 60cm (23in)
Sawaya & Moroni SpA, Italy
www.sawayamoroni.com

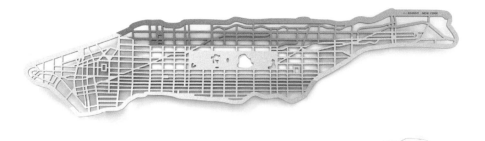

Bowls, Metrobowl New York and Amsterdam
Frederik Roijé
Cast aluminium
H (New York): 5cm (2in)
W (New York): 23cm (9in)
L (New York): 90cm (35in)
H (Amsterdam): 8cm (3⅛in)
W (Amsterdam): 35cm (13¾in)
L (Amsterdam): 48cm (18⅞in)
Frederik Roijé,
The Netherlands
www.roije.com

Vase, Cardboard Vase
Paolo Ulian
Borosilicate glass
H: 35cm (13¾in)
Diam: 20cm (7⅞in)
Skitsch, Italy
www.skitsch.it

Vase, Othilie
Kari Håkonsen
Blown glass
H. 50cm (19in)
Diam: 20cm (7⅞in)
Kari Håkonsen/Klart glass,
Norway
www.klartglass.no

Plate installation, Supermodel
Phoebe Richardson and
Paul Bishop
Fine English bone china
Diam: 25, 20 and 15cm
(10, 8 and 6in)
The New English, UK
www.thenewenglish.co.uk

Mug, teacup with saucer and coffee cup with saucer, Paper Porcelain
Scholten & Baijings
Porcelain
H (mug): 10cm (3⅞in)
Diam (mug): 7cm (2¾in)
Hay, Denmark
www.hay.dk

Coffee cup with saucer, Vela
Luca Nichetto
Ceramic
H (cup): 6.5cm (2⅝in)
W (saucer): 10cm (3⅞in)
Bosa Ceramiche, Italy
www.bosatrade.com

Table set, Dressed
Marcel Wanders
Porcelain, glass, metal
Diam (mug): 8cm (3⅛in)
Alessi SpA, Italy
www.alessi.com

Table set, Lilli Primavera
Licia Martelli
Hand made ceramic
Diam (plate): 26cm (10¼in)
Licia Martelli-Ceramiche
Libere!, Italy
www.liciamartelli.com

Teacup and saucer, Mosaic
Jasper Conran
Fine bone china
H (teacup): 5.5cm (2¼in)
W (teacup): 13cm (5⅛in)
L (teacup): 11cm (4⅜in)
H (saucer): 2cm (¾in)
Diam (saucer): 16cm (6¼in)
Wedgwood, UK
www.wedgwood.co.uk

Teapot and cups, Metae
Marre Moerel
Earthenware ceramic
H (teapot): 14cm (5½in)
W (teapot): 10cm (4in)
L (teapot): 13cm (5in)
H (cup): 6.5cm (2½in)
Diam (cup): 8.5cm (3⅓in)
Marre Moerel Design Studio,
Spain
www.marremoerel.com

Set of plates, Flying City Tableware
Carsten Höller
Porcelain
Diam: 16, 21 and 25cm
(6¼, 8¼ and 9⅞in)
Porzellan Manufaktur
Nymphenburg, Germany
www.nymphenburg.com

Plate, Black Widow
Insideout
Fine English bone china
Diam: 25.4cm (10in)
The New English, UK
www.thenewenglish.co.uk
www.colette.fr

Table set, Haphazard Harmony
Maarten Baas
Ivory porcelain
H (teapot): 18.5cm (7¼in)
Diam (large plate):
30cm (11¾in)
Skitsch, Italy
www.skitsch.it

Reflect brings life back to orphaned antique saucers, meticulously selected from dealers across Britain. The bone china teacups are hand-painted with platinum, giving them a highly reflective surface. The mirrored cups reflect the patterned saucers, uniting them as a perfect pair.

**Teacup and saucer,
Reflect**
Richard Brendon
Bone china, platinum gilding
H: 8.5cm (3¼in)
W: 15cm (5⅞in)
D: 15cm (5⅞in)
Richard Brendon, UK
www.richardbrendon.com

**Table setting,
Table-Palette**
Kiki van Eijk
Glassware: Royal
Leerdam Crystal
Silverware: Koninklijke van
Kempen & Begeer
Textiles: Audax Textile
Museum Tilburg
Studio Kiki van Eijk,
The Netherlands
www.kikiworld.nl (ceramics)
www.textielmuseum.nl
(tablecloth)
www.leerdamkristal.nl
(glassware)
www.royalvkb.com (cutlery)

Tableware, Delfts Blauw
Douwe Egberts in
collaboration with
Piet Hein Eek
Ceramics
Various dimensions
Piet Hein Eek,
The Netherlands
www.pietheineek.nl

Tableware, Re-purposed Ceramics
Piet Hein Eek
Ceramics
Various dimensions
Piet Hein Eek,
The Netherlands
www.pietheineek.nl

Cups, M-Set
Van Eijk & Van der Lubbe
Porcelain with transfer
H (cup): 6cm (2⅜in)
W (cup): 9cm (3½in)
Diam (dish): 14cm (5½in)
Usuals, The Netherlands
www.usuals.nl

Ceramic collection, Moulding Tradition
Studio Formafantasma
Ceramic, cotton, glass
H (flask): 18cm (7⅛in)
W (flask): 12cm (4¾in)
D (flask): 8cm (3⅛in)
Studio Formafantasma,
The Netherlands
Gallery Libby Sellers, UK
www.formafantasma.com
www.libbysellers.com

**Carafe and vases,
Collection Vindobona**
Claesson Koivisto Rune
Silver and gold-plated silver
940/1000, glass
H (silver top 'Tulips'):
10cm (3⅞in)
H (silver top 'Poppies'):
5.5cm (2¼in)
H (silver top 'Lily'):
18.5cm (7¼in)

H (tumbler): 7cm (2¾in)
Diam (glass protection ring
'Crown'): 7.4cm (2⅞in)
Wiener Silber Manufactur and
J. & L. Lobmeyr, Austria
www.wienersilbermanufactur.com
www.lobmeyr.at

Vase, Butterfly
Bořek Šípek
Glas crystal
H: 42cm (16½in)
Diam: 26cm (10¼in)
Šípek Team, Czech Republic
www.boreksipek.cz

Drinking glass, Ice
Ichiro Iwasaki
Glass
H (short): 6.6cm (2⅝in)
H (tall): 11cm (4⅜in)
Diam (short): 8.3cm (3¼in)
Diam (tall): 7.6cm (3in)
Sfera srl, Italy
www.ricordi-sfera.com

**Decanter, United
Crystal Woods**
Marcel Wanders
Blown crystal
H: 29.5cm (11¾in)
Baccarat, France
www.baccarat.com

**Bordeaux wine glass,
United Crystal Woods**
Marcel Wanders
Blown crystal
H: 22.9cm (9in)
Baccarat, France
www.baccarat.com

**Vase and votive holder,
United Crystal Woods**
Marcel Wanders
Cut and engraved crystal
H: 25.5cm (10¼in)
W: 6.8cm (2⅝in)
L: 30.8cm (12¼in)
Baccarat, France
www.baccarat.com

**Vase, United
Crystal Woods**
Marcel Wanders
Blown and cut crystal,
solid brass
H: 55cm (21in)
Diam: 19.5cm (7⅝in)
Baccarat, France
www.baccarat.com

**Candlestick, United
Crystal Woods**
Marcel Wanders
Cut crystal
H: 12.6cm (4⅞in)
W: 6.8cm (2⅝in)
L: 12.8cm (5⅛in)
Baccarat, France
www.baccarat.com

**Plate, Christmas Edition
2010**
Maria Volokhova
Porcelain, inglaze decals,
overglaze decals
H: 2cm (¾in)
W: 19cm (7½in)
L: 27.5cm (11in)
Maria Volokhova, Germany
www.volokhova.com

Vase, Pebble
Kate Hume
Mouth-blown glass
H: 19cm (7½in)
W: 20cm (7⅞in)
L: 26cm (10¼in)
When Objects Work, Belgium
www.whenobjectswork.com

Bowl, Reversed Volumes
mischer'traxler studio
Ceramic plaster
H: 3–7cm (1⅛–2¾in)
Diam: 10–21cm (3⅞–8¼in)
mischer'traxler studio, Austria
www.mischertraxler.com
www.foodmarketo.com

Centrepiece, Silver Ray
Karim Rashid
Silver
H: 4.8cm (1⅞in)
Diam: 51cm (20in)
Christofle, France
www.christofle.com

Tea caddy, Chazutsu
Kaikado
Copper, brass, tin
Left to right.
H (brass double-decker):
13.6cm (5⅜in)
Diam (brass double-decker):
7.8cm (3⅛in)
H (copper double-decker):
9.5cm (3¾in)
Diam (copper double-decker):
6.5cm (2⅝in)
H (tin double-decker):
13.6cm (5⅜in)
Diam (tin double-decker):
7.8cm (3⅛in)

H (brass stackable):
5.5cm (2¼in)
Diam (brass stackable):
7.8cm (3⅛in)
H (copper stackable):
5.5cm (2¼in)
Diam (copper stackable):
7.8cm (3⅛in)
H (tin stackable):
5.5cm (2¼in)
Diam (tin stackable):
7.8cm (3⅛in)
Kaikado, Japan
www.kaikado.jp

Bowl, Timeline
Luca Nichetto
Polished brass
H: 4.8cm (1⅞in)
Diam: 8.5cm (3⅜in)
Skultuna 1607, Sweden
www.skultuna.com

Vase, Bloom
Meirav Barzilay
Coated tin
H: 27cm (10⅝in)
Diam: 17cm (6¾in)
Meirav Barzilay design
studio, Israel
www.meiravbarzilay.com

Carafes, Fortune
Mark Braun
Glass
H: 23cm (9in)
Diam: 10cm (3⅞in)
J. & L. Lobmeyr, Austria
www.lobmeyr.at

**Drinking glasses,
Trinkservice No 282**
Ted Muehling
Lead-free crystal, hand cut
and hand polished
H: 15.3, 9.8, 10.3 and 16.3cm
(6⅛, 3⅞, 4⅛ and 6½in)
Diam: 8.2, 7.5, 8.5 and 5.2cm
(3¼, 3, 3⅜ and 2in)
Lobmeyr, Austria
www.lobmeyr.at

**Glass collection,
Base Collection**
Olgoj Chorchoj
Glass
Various dimensions
Bohemia Machine Glass,
Czech Republic
www.bomma.cz

**Glass collection,
Collection 2011**
Frantisek Vizner
Glass
Various dimensions
Bohemia Machine Glass,
Czech Republic
www.bomma.cz

Series of crystal tumblers, Quarz
Max Lamb
Lead-free crystal, hand cut
and hand polished
H (small): 5.5cm (2¼in)
H (medium): 8.7cm (3½in)
H (large): 14cm (5½in)
Diam: 6cm (2⅜in)
Lobmeyr, Austria
www.lobmeyr.at

**Wine glass, Orrefors
by Karl Lagerfeld**
Karl Lagerfeld
Glass
H: 19.6cm (7⅝in)
Diam: 8.1cm (3⅛in)
Orrefors, Sweden
www.orrefors.se

Platter, Oyster Platter
Heather Gillespie
Blown glass cut and engraved
using traditional techniques
H: 20cm (7⅞in)
W: 25cm (9⅞in)
L: 52cm (20in)
D: 18cm (7⅛in)
Gillespie Glass, UK
www.gillespieglass.co.uk

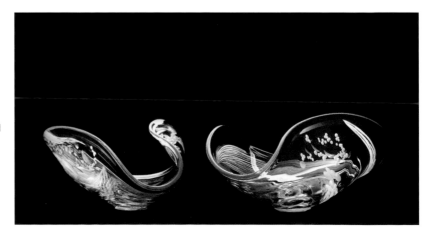

Vessel, Large Oak Vessel
Gareth Neal
Oak
H: 45cm (17¾in)
W: 20cm (7⅞in)
D: 20cm (7⅞in)
Gareth Neal Ltd, UK
www.garethneal.co.uk

Carafe, Jug
Aldo Bakker
Porcelain
H: 27cm (10⅝in)
W: 20cm (7⅞in)
D: 13cm (5⅛in)
Particles Gallery,
The Netherlands
www.particlesgallery.com

Vase, Coiled
BCXSY + Lobolile Ximba
(L) and Princess Ngonephi
Ngcobo (M) from the
Siyazama Project
Glass beads, textile,
recycled PET bottle
H (large vase):
30cm (11¾in)
Diam (large vase):
24cm (9½in)
Editions in Craft, Sweden
www.editionsincraft.com

Vase, Monoliti
Andrea Branzi
Bronze
H: 23.5cm (9½in)
W: 17cm (6¾in)
L: 35cm (13¾in)
Galleria Clio Calvi Rudy
Volpi, Italy
www.cliocalvirudyvolpi.it

**Salt and pepper
shakers, Par**
Nendo
Agglomerated cork, glass
H: 8.8cm (3½in)
Diam: 4.1cm (1⅝in)
Amorim Cork Composites, S.A,
Portugal
www.corkcomposites.amorim.com

Bowl centrepiece, Furo
Fernando Brízio
Agglomerated cork, pencils
H: 28.6cm (11⅛in)
Diam: 25.5cm (10¼in)
Amorim Cork Composites, S.A,
Portugal
www.corkcomposites.amorim.com

**Candleholder,
Woodwork Collection**
Aldo Cibic
Wood
Various dimensions
Paola C., Italy
www.paolac.com

**Set of tabletop containers,
Bakelite Borgo**
Julia Lohmann
Bakelite
H: 16.5cm (6½in)
L: 40cm (15¾in)
D: 25cm (9⅞in)
PlusDesign srl, Italy
www.plusdesigngallery.com

Storage box, Butte Tuna
Scholten & Baijings
European oak veneer with
printed illustration, coloured
veneer, beech bent wood,
clear matt lacquer
H: 16cm (6¼in)
Diam: 22cm (8⅝in)
Established & Sons, UK
www.establishedandsons.com

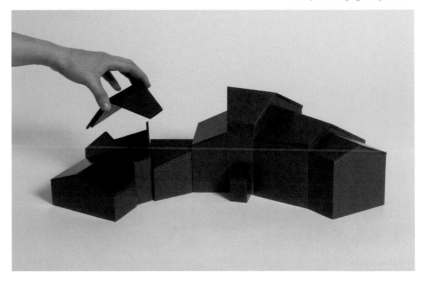

Collection of vases and glasses, Variations
Patricia Urquiola
Crystal glass
Various dimensions
Baccarat, France
www.baccarat.com

Vases, Vasi nei vasi
Michele De Lucchi with
Alberto Nason
Borosilicate glass
H: 73.5cm (29in)
Diam: 27cm (10⅝in)
Produzione Privata, Architetto
Michele De Lucchi srl, Italy
www.produzioneprivata.it

Vase and bowls, Vessel
Hanna Krüger
Mouth-blown glass
H (vase): 35cm (13¾in)
Diam (vase): 20cm (7⅞in)
H (bowls): 20cm (7⅞in)
Diam (blue bowl):
30cm (11¾in)
Diam (clear bowl):
25cm (9⅞in)
Rosenthal GmbH, Germany
www.rosenthal.de

Carafe, Belly
Aldo Cibic
Borosilicate
H: 26cm (10¼in)
Diam: 19cm (7½in)
Paola C. srl, Italy
www.paolac.com

Carafe, Water
Pieke Bergmans
Handblown glass
Unique pieces
Pieke Bergmans,
The Netherlands
www.piekebergmans.com

Bowl, Herb
Ludovica and Roberto Palomba
Murano glass
Diam: 55cm (21in)
When Objects Work, Italy
www.whenobjectswork.com

Carafe, Foxy
Aldo Cibic
Borosilicate
H: 25cm (9⅞in)
Diam: 11cm (4⅜in)
Paola C. srl, Italy
www.paolac.com

**Vase, Airvase
(Gradation and Cube)**
Torafu Architects
Cut and shaped paper
Various dimensions
Ligne Roset, France
www.ligne-roset.com

Vase, Story Vase
Front in collaboration with
members of the Siyazama
Project: Lobolile Ximba (blue),
Kishwepi Sitole (red) and
Beauty Ndlovu (black)
Traditional Czech glass
beads, glass
H: 35cm (13¾in)
Diam: 23cm (9in)
Editions in Craft,
South Africa/Sweden
www.editionsincraft.com

Designers are renowned for fusing seemingly diverse references, concepts and materials in order to realize individual and innovative projects. The advent of the designer/maker, or the designer working closely with the artisan, could be viewed as just another expression of this versatility, driven both by a need to express a personal identity and the possibility of bypassing mass production in response to a society tired of constant neutrality. However, the motivation to not only 'do good design but also do some good' is apparent in the many initiatives that aim to preserve traditional crafts and empower communities by encouraging collaboration with artists and designers, aspiring to produce something morally superior to the made-for-profit products with which we fill our homes.

In response to geopolitical change and environmental concern, there is a growing market for the designer product with a conscience, evidenced by the popularity of modest, nonprofit design schemes such as Balance (page 197), Coopa-Roca (page 269) and the FlipFlop Project (page 266), which seek to put tools in place for people in societies struggling for survival. Network organizations such as Stockholm-based Editions in Craft (EiC) merge traditional techniques and modern practice, employing local labour while developing marketing strategies that establish contacts between small-scale producers and market-related distributors. These organizations exist not to 'modernize' craft into marketable products customized for a Western market but to establish cross-cultural models of viable design by joining forces and exchanging expertise, ideas and techniques.

The Story Vases collection is a collaboration between the South African Siyazama Project and Swedish design studio

Front. The Siyazama Project was founded in 1999 to educate a group of traditional doll makers on the concerns and taboos surrounding the HIV/AIDs epidemic, while also promoting better understanding of beadwork as visual metaphoric expression and of design as a means to spread information. Today it consists of a collective of native Zulu women who sell their wares to the tourist market as their only source of income. Front, which is known for its conceptual approach to design, material and narrative, was introduced to five members of the project by EiC.

Working with beads is an important part of Zulu tradition and historically has been used to tell stories. In the past, patterns and colours that symbolized feelings and ideas were woven for lovers and friends. The Story Vases record conversations about the pasts, hopes and dreams of the Zulu women, who spelled out portions of their lives in beads that were then threaded on wire and wrapped around a wooden mould. When the beads were set, the mould was removed and the void filled by a skilled glass blower. Because the finished pieces are transparent, the glass acts as a lens, distorting, magnifying and adding emphasis to every letter. Each vase is unique and significant, but together they document the daily existence of women in rural, post-apartheid South Africa. The beauty of the project lies in the fact that, although the collection was organized to advance a social good, the end result demonstrates that nonprofit design need not always be 'rough around the edges', but can be compelling, contemporary and beautiful in its own right.

Fruit bowl, Dende Fruit Bowl
Humberto and Fernando Campana
Flexible resin, piacava
H: 20cm (7⅞in)
Diam: 40cm (15¾in)
Corsi Design Factory, Italy
www.corsidesignfactory.it

Vase, Clear Special Vase
Gaetano Pesce
Flexible resin
H: 37cm (14⅝in)
Diam: 28cm (11in)
Fish Design, Italy
www.corsidesignfactory.it

Vase, Industrial Intervention – Crystal Glass
Folkform
Hand- and machine-cut crystal glass
H: 35–40cm (13¾–15¾in)
W: 18cm (7⅛in)
D: 18cm (7⅛in)
Folkform, Sweden
www.folkform.se

Vases, Matelasse'
Patricia Urquiola
Transparent or batch-dyed polycarbonate
H: 24 or 40cm (9½ or 15¾in)
D: 30cm (11¾in)
Kartell SpA, Italy
www.kartell.it

Vases and bowls, Thom series
Sebastian Menschhorn
Lead-free crystal
H: 21.5, 29.5 and 9.5cm (8⅝, 11¾ and 3¾in)
Diam: 16.3, 11.5 and 26.5cm (6½, 4½ and 10⅝in)
Lobmeyr, Austria
www.lobmeyr.at

Bowl, Fruit Bowl
Shigeru Ban
Epoxy
Diam: 45cm (17¾in)
When Objects Work, Belgium
www.whenobjectswork.com

Teaspoon, Forest Spoon
Nendo
Stainless steel
W: 3.7cm (1½in)
L: 18cm (7⅛in)
Kobayashi industry, Japan
www.luckywood.jp

Storage containers, Potto
Established & Sons
Japanese Tokoname ceramic,
rubber, wood
H (sugar bowl): 8.5cm (3⅜in)
Diam (sugar bowl):
10.5cm (4⅛in)
H (small pot): 10cm (3⅞in)
Diam (small pot):
12.5cm (4⅞in)
H (large pot): 12cm (4¾in)
Diam (large pot):
14.5cm (5¾in)
Established & Sons, UK
www.establishedandsons.com

Plate and bowls, Blossom
Bodo Sperlein
Bone China
W (deep plate):
22cm (8⅝in)
W (desert/soup bowl):
16cm (6¼in)
W (white bowl):
11cm (4⅜in)
Nikko, Japan
www.nikko-bodosperlein.com

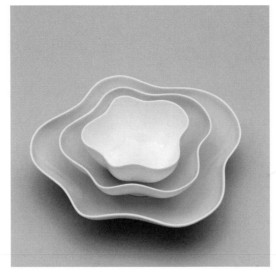

Citrus basket, Hellraiser
Karim Rashid
Steel coloured with
epoxy resin
H: 19.2cm (7½in)
W: 23.8cm (9½in)
L: 25cm (9⅞in)
Alessi SpA, Italy
www.alessi.com

**Vase cover, La Stanza
dell Scirocco**
Mario Trimarchi
Stainless steel, epoxy resin
H: 35.5cm (14⅛in)
W: 19cm (7½in)
D: 17.8cm (7⅛in)
Alessi SpA, Italy
www.alessi.com

Sarah K and Liane Rossler of Sydney-based design collective Supercyclers launched a series of products in an exhibition entitled 'The Other Hemisphere' during the 2011 Salone Internazionale del Mobile, Milan, to showcase how ordinary waste can be upcycled into objects of beauty. Supercyclers' philosophy is that recycling is a universal concern that can be approached creatively by everyone. By explaining the processes behind the products they make, they aim to inspire others to attempt their own versions. The Plastic Fantastic range of delicate, translucent bowls, cups and vases was made by gently heating cut-up plastic bags over objects that had the form K and Rossler wished to emulate. All that was necessary for this process was a heat gun and protective clothing to guard against the heat source and the low-grade toxic fumes.

Vessels, bowls and cups, Plastic Fantastic Ware
Supercyclers
Used plastic bags
H: 8–10cm (3⅛–3⅞in)
Diam: 6–12cm (2⅜–4¾in)
Plastic Fantastic, Australia
www.supercyclers.com

Collection of vases and bowls, Tribe
Arik Levy
Ceramic
H (tallest vase): 58cm (22in)
Diam (tallest vase): 19cm (7½in)
Bitossi Ceramiche, Italy
www.bitossiceramiche.it

Vase, Weight
ECAL/Decha Archjananun
Concrete, steel
H: 23cm (9in)
W: 10cm (3⅞in)
L: 13cm (5⅛in)
Specimen Editions, France
www.specimen-editions.fr

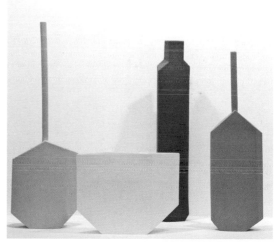

Bottles and vases, Lunare, Singolare, Solitario and Notturno
Rosaria Rattin
Clay, hand-painted with natural colours
Left to right:
H (Lunare): 89cm (35in)
W (Lunare): 32cm (12⅝in)

H (Singolare): 36cm (14⅛in)
W (Singolare): 45cm (17¾in)
H (Solitario): 85cm (33in)
W (Solitario): 18cm (7⅛in)
H (Notturno): 78cm (30in)
W (Notturno): 30cm (11¾in)
Kose srl, Italy
www.kosemilano.com

**Plates and bowls,
Fundamentals of Makkum**
Atelier NL
Earthenware
H (large bowl): 9cm (3½in)
Diam (large bowl):
22cm (8⅝in)
Koninklijke Tichelaar
Makkum, The Netherlands
www.tichelaar.nl

Centrepiece, Maru
Shigeru Ban
Cardboard
Diam (each piece):
37cm (14⅝in)
When Objects Work, Belgium
www.whenobjectswork.com

Vase, Wood Vase
Paul Loebach
Maple wood
H: 25.4cm (10in)
W: 15.2cm (6in)
D: 15.2cm (6in)
Paul Loebach, USA
www.paulloebach.com

Cup, Zen Cup
Pu Tai
Porcelain, silicone
H: 18cm (7⅛in)
Diam: 7.6cm (3in)
Think If Design Co., Ltd,
Taiwan
www.think-if.com

**Teapot, Teapot with
Wooden Saucer**
Front
Ceramic
H: 19cm (7½in)
Diam: 15.2cm (5⅞in)
Höganäs Keramik, Sweden
www.hoganaskeramik.se

Vase, The Devar
Hendzel & Hunt
Reclaimed pallet board
H. 33cm (13in)
W: 21cm (8¼in)
Hendzel + Hunt, UK
www.hendzelandhunt.com

Bowl, ZZ66A – 546
Ettore Sottsass
Ceramic
H: 20cm (7⅞in)
Diam: 25cm (9⅞in)
Bitossi Ceramiche, Italy
www.bitossiceramiche.it

**Table mat, Slice of
Briccole Slice of Venezia**
Philippe Starck
Reused briccola oak wood
H: 2.5cm (1in)
L: 24cm (9½in)
D: 24cm (9½in)
Riva Industria Mobili, Italy
www.riva1920.it

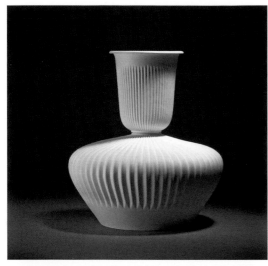

Vase, Plastic Ceramic Vase
Pili Wu
Eggshell porcelain
H: 32cm (12⅝in)
Diam: 28cm (11in)
Yii, Taiwan
HAN Gallery, Taiwan
www.yiidesign.com
www.han-gallery.com

Vase, IKEA plus 365+
Pili Wu
Glass
H: 23cm (9in)
Diam: 9cm (3½in)
Yii, Taiwan
HAN Gallery, Taiwan
www.yiidesign.com
www.han-gallery.com

Cup, Moon Rabbit
Hsiao-ying Lin
Black clay
H: 8.5cm (3⅜in)
W: 13.5cm (5⅜in)
Yii, Taiwan
HAN Gallery, Taiwan
www.yiidesign.com
www.han-gallery.com

Bowls, Lace Bowls
Ching-ting Hsu
Porcelain
H: 15cm (5⅞in)
Diam: 15cm (5⅞in)
Yii, Taiwan
HAN Gallery, Taiwan
www.yiidesign.com
www.han-gallery.com

**Cup, World Cup
(Croaking Frog)**
Idee Liu
Bamboo
H: 24cm (9½in)
Diam: 9cm (3½in)
Yii, Taiwan
HAN Gallery, Taiwan
www.yiidesign.com
www.han-gallery.com

In Taiwanese, *Yii* means 'change and transformation'. The word is made up of three characters, the first representing the central idea in Eastern philosophy: the rotation of the sun and the moon, yin and yang – the alternating and fixed laws of nature. The second depicts exquisite craft, while the third stands for ideas and creativity. It is apt, therefore, that Gijs Bakker, jewellery designer and co-founder of the Dutch collective Droog Design, chose Yii as the name for the brand he created in 2009 in collaboration with the National Taiwan Craft Research Institute (NTCRI) and the Taiwan Design Center (TDC). Since the first collection was exhibited at the Milan Triennale during the 2010 Salone Internazionale del Mobile, Bakker's vision of merging traditional craft with contemporary design in surprising ways has been received with enthusiasm by the international design media. It was a well-timed launch, coinciding with the design world's rediscovery of the value of the artisan's hand as well as the importance of the authentic and local to consumers, who are beginning to reject homogenous, global design and are increasingly demanding individuality, emotion and sensuality in the products they buy.

Bakker was first introduced to the NTCRI in 2006 when he was invited to develop a line of products for the gift shop of the National Palace Museum in Taipei with some young Taiwanese designers. His idea was to steer clear of tacky souvenirs and research ways of translating historical artefacts into contemporary objects that demonstrated traditional methods such as lacquering, carving and engraving but were also useful and had relevance in the modern world. Such was his success that three years later his expertise was sought to develop the Yii label as a means of stimulating Taiwan's foundering craft tradition. He was given the portfolios of thirty professional designers by the TDC, from which he selected fifteen. The NTCRI then chose twenty craftsmen from their enormous database, each skilled in a particular process and in working with different materials. The designers were free to choose the craft they wanted to use.

Initially, the collaboration between the professionals, the designers and Bakker was not easy. Hierarchy is extremely important in the East, and there is less of an emphasis in schools on 'thinking outside the box' – this runs contrary to Bakker's attitude towards design, which he conceives as a mentality based on individual vision in all aspects of life. Added to which, modern design colleges in Taiwan offer students an education based on an international language, with a focus on Europe and North America. The youngsters with whom he was working knew almost nothing about their native craft culture, and their design language lacked a personal identity. The coaching period, consisting of workshops and long and exhaustive Skype meetings, was intense. 'It was a continuing discussion: What are you making? What does it bring/add? What is its meaning in a global context? All those questions are always put in relation to their own identity. I discovered that the awareness of their own identity wasn't very strong and had to be encouraged,' says Bakker. 'In the final results the answers to these questions come to life.'

Bakker maintains that any similarity between Yii and Droog Design products is unintentional, but the influence of Dutch Conceptualism, subversion and in some cases even dry Dutch humour can be detected. Although the aesthetics and techniques used by Yii designers are Asian, it is in the narratives behind each of the works that this Dutch influence becomes apparent. Idee Liu's World Cups, for instance, are personal interpretations of the iconic Starbuck's logo (opposite page, bottom), while the bamboo seat of Rock Wang's Cocoon Plan sofa (page 94) will eventually disappear under silk, spun around it by silk worms. Wang's Brick Plan vase (below) nods to the Dutch, who introduced bricks to Taiwan in the seventeenth century.

Yii's first collection used only Taiwanese designers, as Bakker wanted to distance his project from what he refers to as the almost colonial way that Western designers travel to Asia to have their ideas realized by its cheap labour. However, his second outing, showcased again at the Milan Triennale and entitled 'Street Life', celebrates the fact that the brand is now strong enough to bring international designers into the fold. Along with a raft of native designers, Fernando and Humberto Campana (see page 65) and Nendo (see page 64), among others, were asked to express the culture of Taiwan through its everyday life. Recognizable elements of daily street rituals were interpreted as design objects and refined with skilled craft techniques. On the occasion of the 2011 exhibition, Bakker stated: 'The first collection was more closely linked to craftsmanship and consisted mostly, perhaps, in pieces of art, but this year it is design-led. The designers felt freer and arrived with their own ideas.'

Yii is now closed. They have moved some of their pieces to their follow up platform, the HAN Gallery in Taipei, for production. Run by the original team behind the Yii project and still under the creative direction of Bakker, the HAN Gallery will focus on both production pieces and exclusive artworks, giving 'Made in Taiwan' a new, authentic and deep meaning For further examples from both collections, see Yu-jui Chou's Bubble sofa (page 86) and Bambool and Apple stools (pages 57 and 73), Tong Ho's Lantern lamp (page 268), and Chen-hsu Liu's Bentboo stool (page 56).

Vase, Brick Plan
Rock Wang
Bricks, concrete
H (tall): 45cm (17¾in)
Diam (tall): 16cm (6¼in)
H (short): 35cm (13¾in)
Diam (short): 20cm (7⅞in)
Yii, Taiwan
HAN Gallery, Taiwan
www.yiidesign.com
www.han-gallery.com

Flatware, Paris
Tamar Ben David
Stainless steel
H (dining fork): 1.8cm (¾in)
W (dining fork): 2.4cm (1in)
L (dining fork): 19.5cm (7⅝in)
Serafino Zani, Italy
www.serafinozani.it

Cutlery set, Dressed
Marcel Wanders
18/10 stainless steel
L (knife): 21cm (8¼in)
Alessi SpA, Italy
www.alessi.com

Cutlery, Zlin
Future Systems
Thermoplastic resin
L: 17cm (6¾in)
Alessi SpA, Italy
www.alessi.com

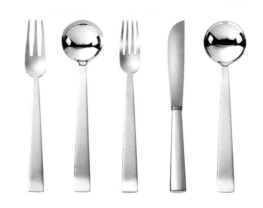

Cutlery re-edition, Cutlery No 135 (designed in 1902)
Josef Hoffmann
Silver 940/1000
L (spoon): 20.3cm (7⅞in)
L (fork): 21.4cm (8¼in)
L (knife): 23.2cm (9in)
L (pastry fork): 17.8cm (7⅛in)
L (teaspoon): 16.5cm (6½in)
Wiener Silber Manufactur, Austria
www.wienersilbermanufactur.com

Cutlery collection, Zermatt
Patrick Jouin iD
Steel
L (knife): 23cm (9in)
W (knife): 2cm (¾in)
Puiforcat, France
www.puiforcat.com

**Coffee spoons,
Il Caffe Spoons**
Left to right: Mirriam Mirri,
David Chipperfield, Wiel Arets,
Sanaa, Tom Kovak
18/10 stainless steel
Various dimensions
Alessi SpA, Italy
www.alessi.com

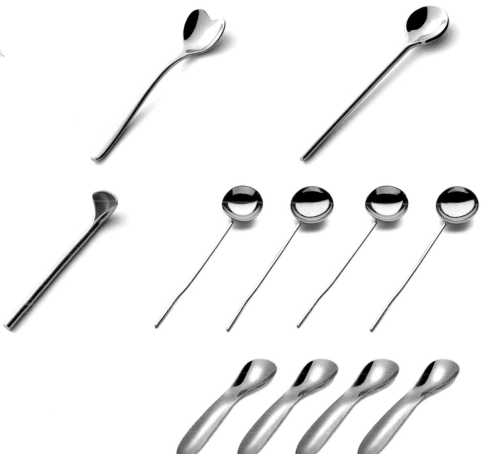

Cutlery Collection
Skitsch Studio
Stainless steel, special
colour treatment
L (spoon and fork):
21cm (8¼in)
L (knife): 24cm (9½in)
L (teaspoon): 14.5cm (5¾in)
Skitsch, Italy
www.skitsch.it

Cutlery, Dorotea
Monica Förster
Stainless steel
L (table fork): 20.4cm (7⅞in)
L (table spoon): 19.8cm (7⅞in)
L (table knife): 21.9cm (8⅝in)
L (coffee spoon): 15cm (5⅞in)
Gense, Sweden
www.gense.eu

Luca Nichetto

Research and development is something you take very seriously. What do you consider the most exciting research trends at the moment?

There are no trends in research, only needs. The most important one now is the functionality of objects both before and after their use: correct production, shipment and what happens to them once they are no longer required – as well as the need for enjoyment, of course.

You have offices in Venice and Stockholm. How would you describe the differences between Scandinavian and Italian manufacturers?

Probably Italian manufacturers are more enthusiastic and love challenges more than Swedish ones. The Swedish system is much more organized than the Italian. My private life has led me to have a stronger understanding of Scandinavia, especially Sweden, where there is a long tradition of design. A company's size and the supply network are similar to Italy, but there is a different and more developed sense of service. The emotional and instinctive element of a product is less present in Scandinavian design to allow for a greater attention to function and the quality of an object. My goal at the moment is to understand whether the truth could lie somewhere in the middle.

Your grandfather was a master glassblower on the Venetian island of Murano. Does this have an effect on how you view the relationship between craft and design?

Yes, of course. I like to learn from craftsmen and I like to put craft knowledge in my research for industrial production. This way of working is thanks to my grandfather's teaching. In the manufacture of glass you have only a second to determine whether it's worked and the object is good, otherwise it can turn out quite differently. This means that the relationship between the designer and the glass master must be really tight-knit. This is a great way to interact and a good paradigm to take into other disciplines and contexts.

You maintain you have found the perfect balance in your work, producing three types of products every year: one commercial, one for self-advertisement and one for your own personal pleasure. Do you approach each category in the same way?

The approach is basically the same, but the results are different. For the first type of product, I try to put more emphasis on the client's needs. For the second, the research for materials and production technologies is more important. Also, smaller companies may not have large distribution networks, but they can give you a strong visibility. As for the third, it's down to instinct. If I like the client and the idea being proposed, it offers the opportunity to experiment without the restrictions that apply to the first two categories.

How would you describe the evolution of your work?

I think it's quite simple: when you do something, you learn something. Evolution for me is when I use what I've learned and one project develops from another. The last one will teach me something new, and this is without end until I stop working.

How would you describe the way you work, the process you follow in designing and developing a product?

There's no unique way to create a product. There are, however, some basic steps that I always use when I receive a brief: research into that specific typology of product, making sketches and scale models, then creating a 3D computer model to check proportions and functionality. This stage is like a game of ping-pong and defines the process of making an object. I love to go to my clients with solutions rather than questions. But every project is different and sometimes these steps change.

You have often voiced the need for a more critical approach in the design media. Why do you consider this important?

It's quite simple. Not everything is good and it's important that the design media is honest about this. In magazines or blogs, or whatever, I only ever read positive comments about objects. No one says, 'In my opinion this product is not good.' Brands and designers are not gods: they can even fail... The responsibility of the media is important, and criticism, if it's honest, is constructive for everyone!

You have been quoted as saying that 'designers need to create a total concept, with a social context'. What exactly do you mean by this?

I think that designers should care about areas of everyday life that are not normally considered designed. For example, in 2011 I worked for a company that produces high-quality prosciutto. I created its brand identity and a collection of utensils (below). I was asked to design a knife and an apron, but instead I dreamed up a whole new vision for them. Prosciutto is not thought of as designed, but it can become part of the designed world and in the process be made more contemporary.

You have said that the Robo chair for Offecct (page 69) is not just a product but an educational tool, and you have used it as an example to teach your Italian clients about sustainable design. Could you elaborate on this?

The Robo project considers not only the final user. It's a total concept that takes care of the correct production methods and using good materials in a good way, as well as considering the cost of transport, both ecologically and financially speaking. The chair is shipped in a small box; this means less stock and haulage costs, and also less pollution. It takes into account use. Robo is a very strong chair and whoever buys it knows that it will last for a long time. Finally, this project bears in mind the chair's afterlife. Robo can be almost totally disassembled for disposal and recycling. In Italy there is no consciousness of where a product will end up after it's obsolete. QUALITY=TIME=LESS GARBAGE.

What do you consider to be the catalysts for design's development today?

We have different kinds of urgency in this particular moment. The most important are the threat to the environment and the current economic crisis. I think design should try to find answers to both of these problems by creating objects that are durable and sustainable. It's not easy, but we should start from this point.

Range of utensils designed for Prosciutteria King (2011)

Vase, Metropolitan
Harry Allen
Optical glass
H: 26cm (10¼in)
W: 7.5cm (3in)
L: 12.5cm (4⅞in)
Gaia & Gino, Turkey
www.gaiagino.com

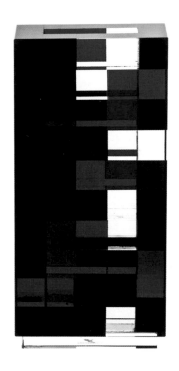

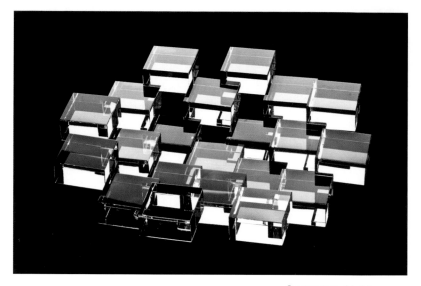

Centrepiece, Matrix
Constantin Boym
Optical glass
H: 5.2cm (2in)
W: 25cm (9⅞in)
L: 25cm (9⅞in)
Gaia & Gino, Turkey
www.gaiagino.com

Double-wall bowl, Nice
Terence Conran
18/10 stainless steel
H: 9.5cm (3¾in)
Diam: 20cm (7⅞in)
Alessi SpA, Italy
www.alessi.com

Carafe and bowl, Alfredo
Alfredo Häberli
Carafe: Glass
Bowl: Stainless steel
H (carafe): 32cm (12⅝in)
W (carafe): 9.5cm (3¾in)
H (bowl): 8.7cm (3⅜in)
Diam (bowl): 28cm (11in)
Georg Jensen A/S, Denmark
www.georgjensen.com

Vases, RGB Vases (P242)
Oscar Diaz
Glass
H: 52.6cm (20in)
Diam: 32.5cm (13in)
Oscar Diaz, UK
www.oscar-diaz.net

Vase, Lanterne Marine London
BarberOsgerby
Glass, metal
H: 60cm (23in)
Diam: 34cm (13⅜in)
Venini SpA, Italy
www.venini.com

Oil bottle, Kink Bottle
Deb Jones/Jam Factory
Glass, steel
H: 33cm (13in)
Diam (base): 9cm (3½in)
Matilda Ltd, UK
www.matilda-design.com

Venini, the largest and most successful glass furnace in Venice, celebrated its ninetieth anniversary at the 2011 Salone Internazionale del Mobile in Milan with an exhibition at the Palazzo Bagetti Valsecchi that demonstrated why the brand has become synonymous with Italian glass design for nearly a century. Against the rich setting of Renaissance paintings, ceramics, armour, sculptures and woodwork, the latest collection of pop lamps and objets d'art by the likes of Studio Job (see page 241), Fernando and Humberto Campana (see page 237), Emmanuel Babled (opposite), Edward van Vliet (see page 244) and Luca Nichetto (see page 244) shone like jewels alongside work by Alessandro Mendini, Ettore Sottsass and Vittorio Zecchin from the company's historic archive.

Paolo Venini established his eponymous firm on the small island of Murano in the Venetian lagoon in 1921. A large glass industry had existed there for centuries, but the sculptural pieces and banal objects that were being produced had become commercial and predictable. Venini was a lawyer by profession but had been born into a family of glassmakers. Having invested in an established factory with antique glass dealer Giacomo Cappellin, his visionary creative direction was liberated a couple of years later when the partnership dissolved. His idea was to adopt the French fashion houses' policy of working with avant-garde painters, architects and artists. Many of those he invited to collaborate with Venini were unschooled in the art of glass, and he encouraged them to experiment with new design concepts and techniques, whilst also ensuring that they took inspiration from the expertise of the island's artisans. In so doing, he revolutionized the way glass was created, marketed and sold. In the years that followed, each decade became associated with a different world-famous name, from architect Carlo Scarpa in the 1930s and illustrator and

caricaturist Fulvio Bianconi in the 1940s to Postmodernist Alessandro Mendini in the 1980s and, in the twenty-first century, the idiosyncratic work of the Campanas and the exquisite pieces of glass artist Emmanuel Babled. Today Venini is headed by entrepreneur Giancarlo Chimento, along with Gabriella Berti and Giuliano and Guglielmo Tabacchi, all of Italian Luxury Industries, who have extended the tradition by working not only with individual designers but also with another producer.

In 2010, the British brand Established & Sons united existing designers from its stable, including Ronan and Erwan Bouroullec (see page 252), with newcomers Konstantin Grcic (see page 12) and Michael Eden (below left) in a collaboration that combined a focus on producing innovative contemporary design with the mastery of Venini's glass manufacturing. The result, rather than being a collection of design-art pieces, was a series of functional, everyday objects that showcased Venini's vast colour palettes and world-famous techniques alongside Established & Sons' eye for modern yet sophisticated designs and elegant forms.

Michael Eden took his inspiration for the Audrey vase from Renato Giuseppe Bertelli's ultramodern 1933 reinterpretation of the portrait bust, *Continuous Profile – Head of Mussolini*. Each example is individually handblown, using both free-blowing and mould-blowing techniques – in the former, the shape is controlled by the skill of the blower, while the latter is used when more complex shapes are required. The contrast between the inside and outside forms allowed Eden to juxtapose strong and subtle colours as well as plain glass and cane or filigree decoration. These choices resulted in subtle movement and illusion – the image of the head appears to float in the space between the glass elements.

Vase, Audrey
Michael Eden
Handblown Venini glass,
marble
H: 36.5cm (14⅛in)
Diam: 37cm (14⅝in)
Established & Sons, UK
Venini SpA, Italy
www.establishedandsons.com

Vase, Murana
Fabio Novembre
Handblown Murano glass
H: 38cm (15in)
Diam: 22cm (8⅝in)
Venini, Italy
www.venini.it

Vase, Seaform
Emmanuel Babled
Handblown Murano glass
H: 41.5cm (16½in)
W: 18cm (7⅛in)
Studio Babled,
The Netherlands
www.babled.net

Vase, Simbiosi
Emmanuel Babled
Handblown Murano glass,
black Belgian marble
H: 52cm (20in)
W: 41cm (16⅛in)
Venini, Italy
www.venini.it

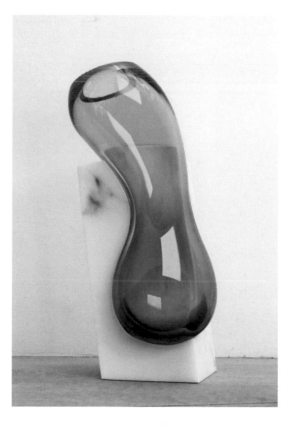

Vase, Simbiosi
Emmanuel Babled
Handblown Murano glass,
Carrara marble
H: 57.5cm (22in)
L: 42.5cm (16⅞in)
D: 39.5cm (15¾in)
Venini SpA, Italy
www.venini.com

Vase, Osmosi
Emmanuel Babled
Handblown Murano glass,
Carrara marble
H: 55cm (21in)
W: 28cm (11in)
D: 28cm (11in)
Studio Babled,
The Netherlands
www.babled.net

6.

TEXTILES AND SURFACES

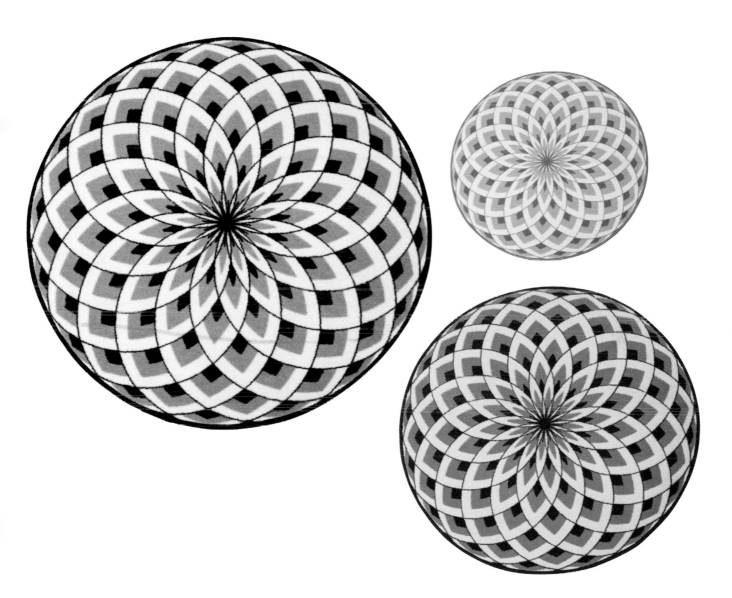

Rug, Dahlia
Claydies
100% wool
Diam: 100, 130 and 200cm
(39, 51 and 78in)
Normann Copenhagen, Denmark
www.normann-copenhagen.com

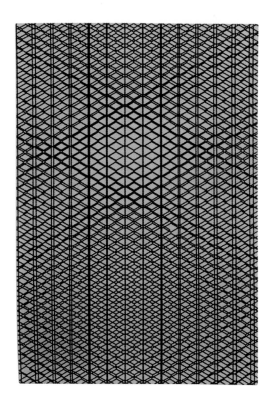

Hand-knotted rug, Breeze
Emmanuel Babled
Wool
W: 190 or 200cm (74 or 78in)
L: 240 or 300cm (94 or 118in)
I+I, Italy
www.i-and-i.it

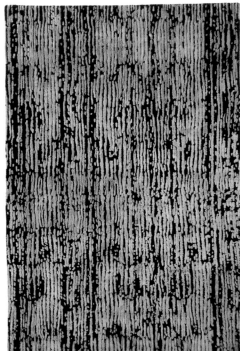

Hand-knotted carpet, Shell
Paolo Giordano
Wool, viscose
W: 170 or 200cm (66 or 78in)
L: 240 or 300cm (94 or 118in)
I+I, Italy
www.i-and-i.it

Carpet, Leaf
Setsu and Shinobu Ito
Wool, viscose
W: 170cm (66in)
L: 240cm (94in)
I+I, Italy
www.i-and-i.it

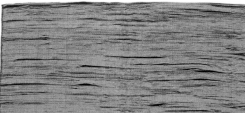

Handwoven carpet, Wavelength
Paolo Giordano and
Sangeeta Sen Davis
Cotton
W: 170 or 200cm (66 or 78in)
L: 240 or 300cm (94 or 118in)
I+I, Italy
www.i-and-i.it

**Hand-knotted carpet,
City Grid**
Emmanuel Babled
Wool, viscose
W: 170 or 200cm (66 or 78in)
L: 240 or 300cm (94 or 118in)
I+I, Italy
www.i-and-i.it

Carpet, Nani
Atelier Blink
80% wool, 20% polyamide
W: 150cm (59in)
L: 200cm (78in)
Atelier Blink, Belgium
www.atelierblink.com

Rug, Capitone
Jaime Hayon
Hand-knotted and
hand-carved wool
W: 183cm (72in)
L: 274cm (108in)
The Rug Company, UK
www.therugcompany.info

**Hand-knotted carpet,
Reflection**
Paolo Giordano
Wool, viscose
W: 170 or 200cm (66 or 78in)
L: 240 or 300cm (94 or 118in)
I+I, Italy
www.i-and-i.it

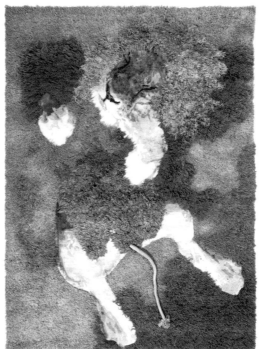

Carpet, Lion
Aldo Bakker with Duijf Brecht
Wool, canvas, bamboo silk
W: 200cm (78in)
L: 350cm (138in)
Nodus, Italy
www.nodusrug.it

Hand-knotted carpet,
Respun Silk
I+I
Recycled silk
Made to order, widths up to
400cm (157in)
I+I, Italy
www.i-and-i.it

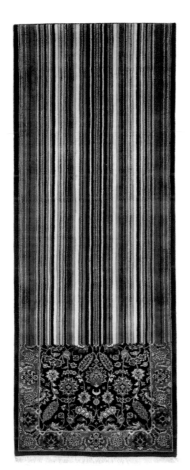

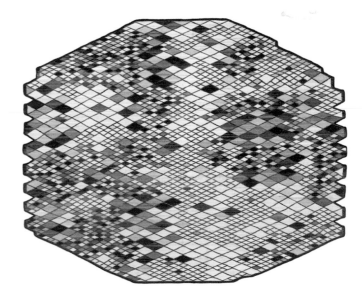

Hand-knotted runner,
Playing with Tradition
Richard Hutten
Wool, viscose
W: 80cm (31in)
L: 220cm (86in)
I+I, Italy
www.i-and-i.it

Persian rug using ancient
kilim technique, Losanges
Ronan and Erwan Bouroullec
100% hand-spun Afghan wool
W: 290, 230 or 165cm
(114, 90 or 65in)
L: 410, 300 or 245cm
(161, 118 or 96in)
Nanimarquina, Spain
www.nanimarquina.com

**Pouffes, Frank, Ernest
and Henry**
Donna Wilson
Knitted wool
Diam (Frank): 80cm (31in)
Diam (Ernest): 60cm (23in)
Diam (Henry): 40cm (15¾in)
SCP, UK
www.scp.co.uk

**Hand-knotted rug,
Textured Daisy**
Tania Johnson
Tibetan wool and Chinese
silk, hand-knotted in Nepal
Made to order, bespoke sizes
Tania Johnson Design,
UK and USA
www.taniajohnsondesign.com

Carpet, Colour
Scholten & Baijings
100% New Zealand wool
W: 170cm (66in)
L: 240cm (94in)
Hay, Denmark
www.hay.dk

Pouffes and rugs, Mangas
Patricia Urquiola
100% virgin wool
H (large pouffe):
43cm (16⅞in)
W (large pouffe):
80cm (31in)
L (large pouffe):
136cm (54in)
Gandia Blasco SA, Spain
www.gan-rugs.com

**Self-adhesive
wall tiles, Flock**
Monika Piatkowski
100% wool felt
H: 26cm (10¼in)
W: 19cm (7½in)
D: 0.3cm (⅛in)
Hive, UK
www.hivespace.com

**Metal rug/tapestry,
Yachiyo**
Philippe Malouin
Galvanized steel, nickel
H: 1cm (⅜in)
W: 150cm (59in)
Philippe Malouin Studio, UK
www.philippemalouin.com

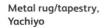

Hand-knotted rug, Blur
Tania Johnson
Tibetan wool and Chinese
silk, hand-knotted in Nepal
Made to order, bespoke sizes
Tania Johnson Design,
UK and USA
www.taniajohnsondesign.com

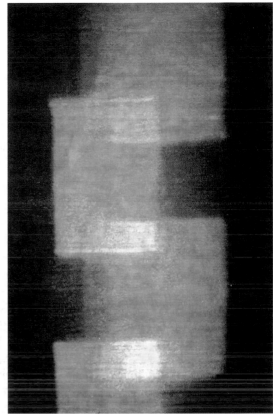

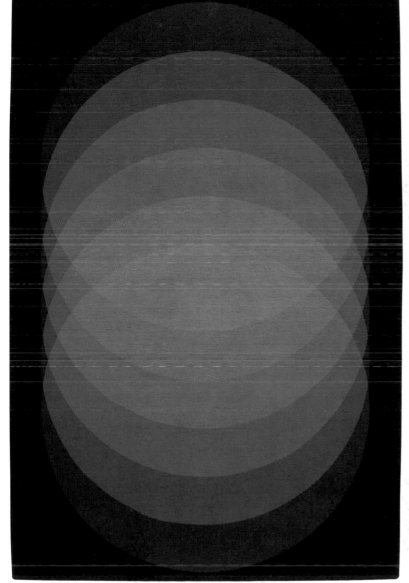

Rug, Tube
Tom Dixon
Hand-knotted Tibetan wool
W: 183cm (72in)
L: 274cm (108in)
The Rug Company, UK
www.therugcompany.info

Rug, Step
Tom Dixon
Hand-knotted Tibetan wool
W: 183cm (72in)
L: 274cm (108in)
The Rug Company, UK
www.therugcompany.info

Rug, Do-Lo-Rez
Ron Arad
100% wool
W: 184cm (72in)
L: 276cm (109in)
Nanimarquina, Spain
www.nanimarquina.com

Carpet, Baroccabilly
Nigel Coates
Wool
W: 160cm (63in)
L: 260cm (102in)
Nigel Coates Ltd, UK
www.nigelcoates.com

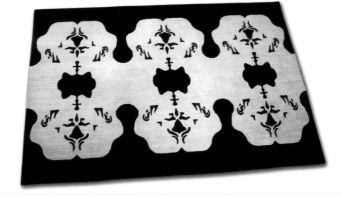

Textile (upholstery), Elements
Studio Tord Boontje
Wool
W: 140cm (55in)
Kvadrat, Denmark
www.kvadrat.dk

Hand-tufted carpet, Rose Lace Carpet
Kiki van Eijk
100% New Zealand wool
W: 170cm (66in)
L: 240cm (94in)
Skitsch, Italy
www.skitsch.it

Wallpaper, Portraits
Giovanni Pagani
Vinyl wallpaper
H: 300cm (118in)
W: 47cm (18½in)
Wall&Decò, Italy
www.wallanddeco.com

Wallpaper, Skulls
Giovanni Pagani
Vinyl wallpaper
H: 300cm (118in)
W: 47cm (18½in)
Wall&Decò, Italy
www.wallanddeco.com

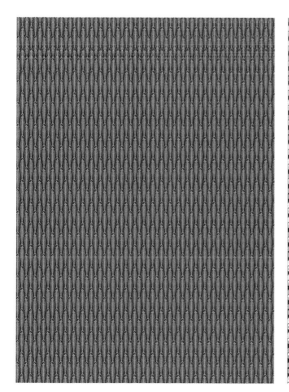

**Laminates, Fishbone
and Paesemio (Parade
Collection)**
Giulio Iacchetti
Plastic laminates with
digital printing
Abet Laminati, Italy
www.abet-laminati.it

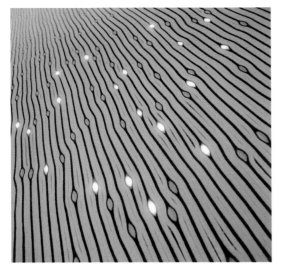

Carpet, CELL+LED
Erik Mantel and
Yvonne Laurysen
100% pure new wool felt
7.2W Power LED
H: 0.8cm (⅜in)
Lama Concept,
The Netherlands
www.lamaconcept.nl

Rug, Ros(a)e
Paola Lenti and m-ar
New Zealand wool
Made to order
Paola Lenti srl, Italy
www.paolalenti.com

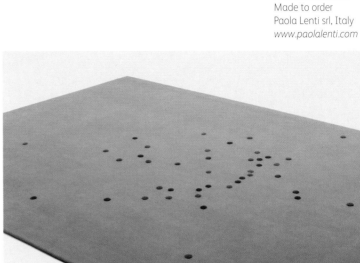

**Carpet, Panton Carpet
Grande 1965**
Verner Panton
100% New Zealand wool
Diam: 220cm (86in)
Verpan, Denmark
www.verpan.com

Rug, Round Diamond
Emma Elizabeth
100% New Zealand wool,
viscose
Diam: 250cm (98in)
Emma Elizabeth Designs,
Australia
Designer Rugs, Australia
www.emmaelizabethdesigns.com
www.designerrugs.com.au

Balance is the second collection in the ongoing Origin project by Eindhoven-based design partnership BCXSY. Origin researches crafts from a wide variety of backgrounds and disciplines – the first series included Join, a trio of modern screens in hinoki cypress wood inspired by the ancient Japanese art of Tategu carpentry (page 305). Balance consists of seven rugs created in collaboration with Lakiya Negev Weaving, a collective of female artisans, and Sidreh, a nonprofit organization focusing on representing, empowering and improving the socioeconomic situation of Bedouin women living in Israel's Negev Desert. Each piece is woven on native ground looms from local wool that has been dyed by hand. Dutch-Israeli Boaz Cohen and Sayaka Yamamoto, a jewellery designer from Tokyo, are partners in life and founded their concept-led practice in 2007, and have since gained

media attention for their thought-provoking explorations and translations of traditional techniques. Following a visit to the Negev, they reflected: 'Throughout our time in these villages, we were continually overwhelmed by the positive attitudes of the women we encountered. We became increasingly inspired by the choice they have made to focus on their optimistic progress, rather than their more obvious hardships. Balance is our response to this optimism, that in the midst of adversity and misfortune there is a lasting element of proportion and beauty.' Working within the confines of the Bedouin weaving practice, which allows only long, narrow strips of material to be produced, the designers have cut and repositioned the textiles into nontraditional and innovative silhouettes, suitable for use within a contemporary interior. In so doing, they have found a modern context for an ancient native craft.

Rug, Origin part II:
Balance
BCXSY
100% sheep wool
Various dimensions
Sidreh, Israel
www.lakiya.org
www.bcxsy.com

Outdoor carpet, Loop
Michaela Schleypen
Polypropylene with
latex backing
W: 200cm (78in)
L: 300cm (118in)
Dedon GmbH, Germany
www.dedon.de

Rug, Perished Persian
Studio Job
100% wool
W: 250cm (98in)
L: 350cm (138in)
Nodus, Italy
www.nodusrug.it

Rug, Patine Brown
Brad Davis and Janis Provisor
100% silk, hand-knotted
L: 270 or 400cm
(106 or 157in)
W: 220 or 300cm
(87 or 118in)
Hermès (La Maison), France
www.hermes.com

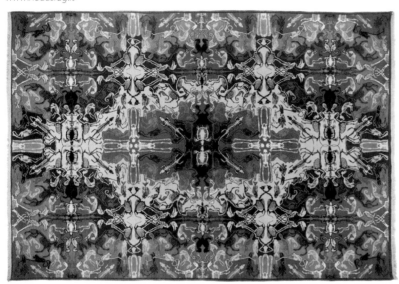

Printed rug, Dag&Natt
Petra Lundblad-Fridén
100% wool woven on a
linen warp
L: 300 and 240cm
(118 and 94in)
W: 195 and 160cm
(76 and 63in)
Kasthall, Sweden
www.kasthall.se

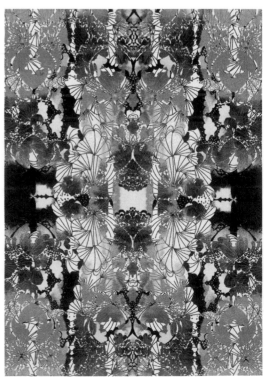

Furnishing fabric, SO'H
Henri d'Origny
50% horsehair, 50% cotton
W: 70cm (27in)
Hermès (La Maison), France
www.hermes.com

Rug, Volcano
Klaus Haapaniemi and
Mia Wallenius
100% pure New Zealand wool
Diam: 240cm (94in)
Established & Sons, UK
www.establishedandsons.com

**Carpet, Fata Morgana
TJ One**
Marcel Wanders
Printed nylon threads

L: 300cm (118in)
W: 200cm (78in)
Moooi, The Netherlands
www.moooi.com

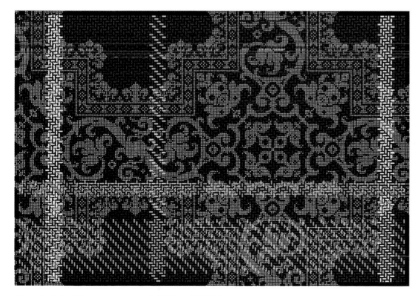

Rug, Giverny 40, 25
Perrine Vigneron
100% pure new wool
H (Giverny 40): 4cm (1⅝in)
H (Giverny 25): 2.5cm (1in)
W: 450cm (177in)
L: Various (unlimited)
Danskina rugs from Kvadrat,
The Netherlands/Denmark
www.danskina.com

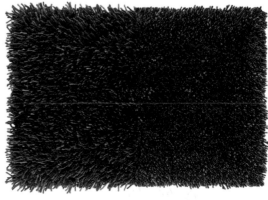

Rug, Reborn
Rapee Leelasiri
Sisal, fabric
Diam: 80–300cm (31–118in)
All Art Craft Co., Ltd.,
Thailand
www.rapeeleela.com

Carpet, Firmship Carpet
Studio Job
Printed nylon threads
Diam: 350cm (138in)
Moooi, The Netherlands
www.moooi.com

Rug, Moroccan Garden
Michaela Schleypen
100% viscose on cotton
canvas weave (handmade)
H: 0.8cm (⅜in)
L: 250cm (98in)
W: 200cm (78in)
Floor to Heaven, Germany
www.floortoheaven.com

Rug, Woodheart Pure Shine
Michaela Schleypen
100% viscose on cotton
canvas weave (handmade)
H: 0.8cm (⅜in)
Diam: 200cm (78in)
Floor to Heaven, Germany
www.floortoheaven.com

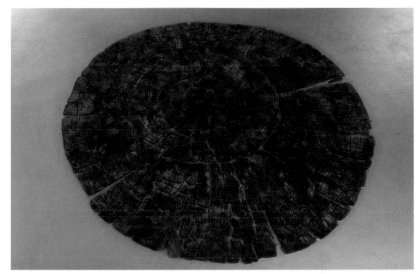

Rug, Circus
Fernando and Humberto
Campana
Hemp and rag dolls
Diam: 200cm (78in)
Nodus, Italy
www.nodusrug.it

Carpet, Fata Morgana TJ Two
Marcel Wanders
Printed nylon threads
Diam: 350cm (138in)
Moooi, The Netherlands
www.moooi.com

Hand-knotted rug, Barbed Wire
Studio Job
Silk, wool
Diam: 220cm (86in)
Nodus, Italy
www.nodusrug.it

**Carpet, Flowers from
Canevas Collection**
Charlotte Lancelot
100% wool
W: 170cm (66in)
L: 240cm (94in)
Gandia Blasco, Spain
www.gandiablasco.com

Carpet, Rooster
Fernando and
Humberto Campana
100% wool
W: 122cm (48in)
L: 188cm (74in)
Nodus, Italy
www.nodusrug.it

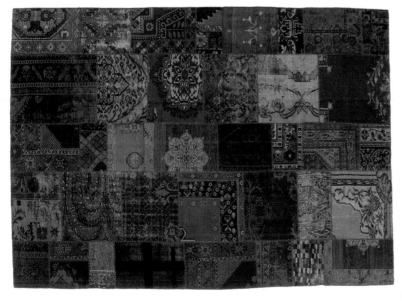

Carpet, Carpet Reloaded
Golran Development Team
Vintage carpets
L: 349cm (137in)
W: 258cm (102in)
Carpet Reloaded by Golran,
Italy
www.carpetreloaded.com
www.golran.com

**Three-dimensional textile
art, Puzzle**
Penelope Jordan
Felt
L: 145cm (57in)
W: 85cm (33in)
Penelope Jordan Textile Art,
UK
www.penelopejordan.com

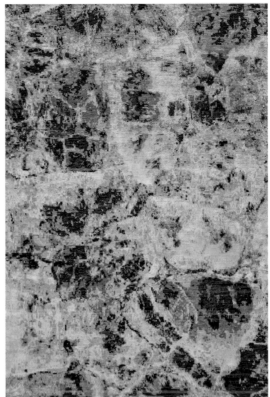

Carpet, Emerald
Jan Kath and Dimo Feldmann
Tibetan highland wool,
1st choice Chinese silk
H: 0.9cm (⅜in)
W: 250cm (98in)
L: 300cm (118in)
Jan Kath Design GmbH,
Germany
www.jan-kath.com

Rug, Industrial Pure
Miinu
Pure new wool
Unique pieces (similar pieces
will be available in similar
sizes, but each is unique)
Miinu, Germany
www.miinu.de

Area rug, SG Suave
kymo Design Department
100% polyester with 100%
cotton backing
L: 60cm (23in)
W: 60cm (23in)
kymo, Germany
www.kymo.de

**Area rug, Fabric (Flat)
Superdots**
Eva Langhans
88% polyester,
12% polyurethane
L: 60cm (23in)
W: 60cm (23in)
kymo, Germany
www.kymo.de

Hand-knotted carpet, Popclassic Polka Dots
Paolo Giordano
Wool
L: 275cm (108in)
W: 165cm (65in)
I+I, Italy
www.i-and-i.it

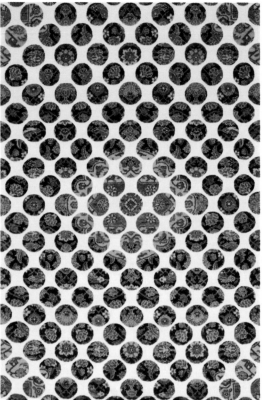

Rug, Trenzas
Gandia Blasco
100% new wool
W: 170 or 200cm (66 or 78in)
L: 240 or 300cm (94 or 118in)
Gandia Blasco SA, Spain
www.gan-rugs.com

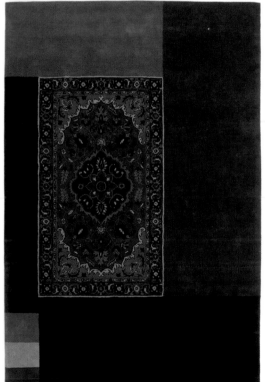

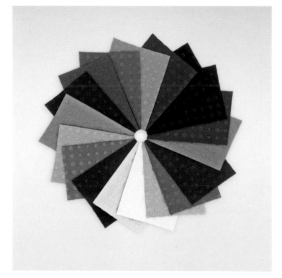

Rug, Extended
Martí Guixé
100% wool
L: 300 (118in)
W: 200 (78in)
Nanimarquina, Spain
www.nanimarquina.com

Upholstery fabric, Highfield 2
Alfredo Häberli
Trevira CS
Made to order
Kvadrat, Denmark
www.kvadrat.dk

Rug, Eros
Sofie Lachaert and
Luc d'Hanis
100% banana silk
L: 350cm (138in)
W: 250cm (98in)
Nodus, Italy
www.nodusrug.it

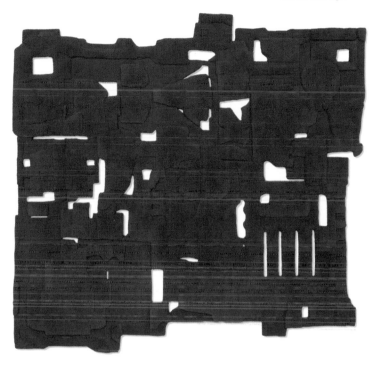

Rug, Sao Paulo
Fernando and Humberto
Campana
100% wool
L: 300cm (118in)
W: 289cm (114in)
Nodus, Italy
www.nodusrug.it

Rug, Parquet Rug
Ora-Ito
Wool
L: 70, 120 and 240cm
(27, 47 and 94in)
W: 90,100 and 170cm
(35, 39 and 66in)
Stepevi, Turkey
www.stepevi.com

Draped Delusion formed part of a master's degree project by Swedish textile designer Ulrika Hägglöf at the Kontstfack University College of Arts, Crafts and Design in Stockholm, and has since been exhibited both in Sweden and the UK to much acclaim. Now available made to order, the trompe l'oeil fabric creates a dialogue between the two-dimensional and the three-dimensional in a hanging that challenges our perception of surface patterning and depth. Hägglöf started by photographing folded textiles, then manipulated the images in Adobe Photoshop by reducing the scale of the greys to create a graphic and repeatable pattern. She then adjusted the weave structures to achieve a gradation in colour from light to dark. The information was fed into an industrial Jacquard loom, which allowed Hägglöf to control each thread individually to achieve her desired effect.

Jaquard-woven upholstery fabric, Draped Delusion
Ulrika Hägglöf
100% wool
W: 149cm (59in)
Ulrika Hägglöf, Sweden
www.ulrikahagglof.se

Furnishing fabric, Bibliothèque
Hugo Gryckar
100% cotton
W: 140cm (55in)
Hermès (La Maison), France
www.hermes.com

Furnishing fabric, Finish
Jean-Louis Clerc
100% cotton
W: 140cm (55in)
Hermès (La Maison), France
www.hermes.com

**Fabric, Mumbai
(The Tracery Collection)**
Robert A.M. Stern
53% cotton, 37% nylon,
10% post-consumer
recycled polyester
W: 137cm (54in)
CF Stinson, USA
www.cfstinson.com

**Fabric, Seville
(The Tracery Collection)**
Robert A.M. Stern
38% post-industrial recycled
polyester, 33% polyester,
29% post-consumer
recycled polyester
W: 137cm (54in)
CF Stinson, USA
www.cfstinson.com

**Fabric, Algiers
(The Tracery Collection)**
Robert A.M. Stern
77% post-consumer
recycled polyester, 23%
solution-dyed nylon
W: 137cm (54in)
CF Stinson, USA
www.cfstinson.com

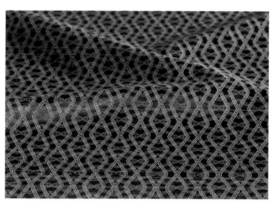

Textile, 100 Years
Studio Tord Boontje
Trevira CS
W: 145cm (57in)
Kvadrat, Denmark
www.kvadrat.dk

Curtain fabric, Dentelle
Creation Baumann
21% viscose 29% polyester
W: 145cm (57in)
Creation Baumann,
Switzerland
www.creationbaumann.com

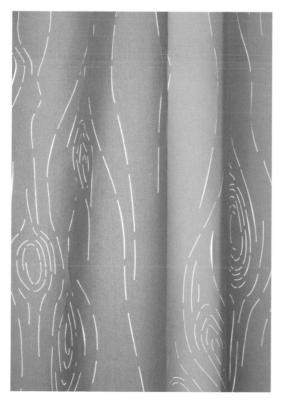

**Flooring system,
Profile Hex**
Marcel Wanders
Liquid resin, hand-cast
polymer
Senso, The Netherlands
www.sensovloeren.nl

**Flooring system,
Delicate Round**
Marcel Wanders
Liquid resin, hand-cast
polymer
Senso, The Netherlands
www.sensovloeren.nl

**Wallpaper, Stone
Angel Wallpaper**
Young & Battaglia
Fabric-backed paper
W: 50cm (19in)
L: 250cm (98in)
Mineheart, UK
www.mineheart.com

Wall and floor tiles, Azulej
Patricia Urquiola
Glazed porcelain stoneware
W: 20cm (7⅞in)
L: 20cm (7⅞in)
Ceramiche Mutina srl, Italy
www.mutina.it

Wallpaper, Knitted Room
Chae Young Kim
Digitally printed nonwoven
wallpaper
H: 1000cm (393in)
W: 46.5cm (18½in)
Tapeten Agentur, Germany
www.chaeyoungkim.com

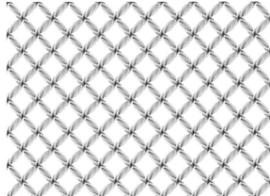

Chae Young Kim's work explores the boundaries between
digital and analogue by applying two-dimensional vector
graphics to everyday objects, from textiles to ceramics.
The Knitted Room prints blur reality, illusion, art and design.
Despite the appearance of having been photographed
or hand-drawn, the delicate and intricate patterns of the
wallpapers were created by a computer graphic technique
using scripts and numbers, with the detail added by
manipulating carefully drawn vector lines one by one.
The result has a tactile quality that imitates the warmth
of knitted material.

Jaime Hayon

Would you say that your early involvement in the world of skateboard and graffiti cultures has had a direct influence on the work you do today?

Skateboarding was very important to me as it introduced me to creativity. It's about finding your own language and developing a personal style. In that sense, there is a very strong parallel to design. The graphic element also captured my interest.

You trained as a designer but have been quoted as saying you are an artist at heart. To what extent is this true?

I tend to reject labels. I consider myself a creator. Creativity is my driving force, and this can have results that tend towards either art or design. I don't think about it when I'm working. I just develop an idea until it comes to life. The fact is I do things that are functional, and sometimes not functional. I like the opportunity to work on both.

Would you say your work has evolved over the years?

The evolution is very clear. Although there is a common trait from the start of my career to my most recent work, I feel there is a growing tendency towards the essential quality of shape. I've become more 'minimal', appreciating that substance doesn't come from more, but from better. As one faces fresh challenges and learns about different subjects and materials, the work gradually transforms as these new disciplines merge with other themes. I find the learning curve is dynamic and interactive.

Is there a particular commission or collaboration from which you've learned the most?

That's tough to answer as all new projects face different challenges. Working in product design, on art installations and interiors, it is very interesting for me to see how experimentation in each area crosses over and affects the others. When I consider the work I've done over the past years, it's like watching an unfolding story of small obsessions taking different shapes and translating into various languages.

You often collaborate with craftsmen and involve yourself in production processes. How important is it for you to be hands-on?

Each day I feel more strongly that being in contact with how things are made is essential to my work. Collaborating with artisans, understanding and being involved in the crafting process, is indispensable. I like to get my hands dirty whenever I can. I believe in learning by doing.

What is it that attracts you to a commission?

Several things can attract me to a commission. The first is personal empathy. I need to work with people I like, or else the process would be very tedious. It also has to be a challenge, a project on which I can make a very real contribution and that will allow me to grow. It needs to make me dream. This is a personal element, a gut feeling. I need to be enthusiastic; otherwise, I would prefer not to engage.

You have described your style as 'Mediterranean Digital Baroque'. What do you mean by this?

'Mediterranean Digital Baroque' was the title of my first installation in 2003. The phrase has obviously stuck, as it has become a definition of my style for almost ten years now. Although it was a great name for an exhibition, it doesn't identify my work. I don't think I will ever come up with a definition, but if I had to describe my style I would say that it is organic with a passion for shapes that are feminine and sophisticated. It values long-lasting materials and also pays homage to the past, but in a contemporary way. There is passion, humor and a very personal language. I love quality and challenge and the conservation of a craft tradition in an iPhonic speed era.

In your monograph you write that you use experimentation and artistic research as a platform to create commercially viable products. Can you expand on this?

My creative process relies on an interaction between experimentation, artistic research and a more industrial

Top right: 'Mediterranean Digital Baroque' exhibition, David Gill Galleries, London (2003)

'Mon Cirque' travelling exhibition (ongoing)

21st International Biennial Interieur, Kortrijk, Belgium (2008)

approach There are many examples of this. For example, if you consider the Hayon Collection for Bisazza Bagno (page 143), you can see that the cacti I designed for the 'Mediterranean Digital Baroque' installation (opposite page, top right) inspired the shapes that I used. Similarly, the idea for the legs of the Tudor Chair for Established & Sons were based on those of a baseball table I created for the International Biennial Interieur, Kortrijk, 2008 (above). I use experimentation to give initial form to concepts and these often influence the commercial pieces I create for brands.

In 2010 you took over the Directorship of Madrid's Istituto Europeo di Design's Master of European Design Labs programme. What message do you want to convey to your students?

I wanted to become involved in teaching as I felt it would be a mutually beneficial experience for both my students and me. There is much to be said for the traditional approach to teaching industrial design, but for the main part it is focused on technical aspects and neglects the importance of creativity and the development of a personal language. In directing the Masters, it is my intention to bring attention to what I feel matters most and will become a valuable tool for a designer. We run workshops by great designers from all over Europe and try to create a window where the students can see and appreciate what is happening in design today (not only in the past). We aim to bring them closer to the manufacturing experience by collaborating with outstanding craftsmen in the production of their pieces. This gives an understanding of the entire process from the initial idea to the development of a prototype. I think all these things matter tremendously and it's the best aid we can offer to future designers.

You have said that it's a very interesting moment for design. Why?

It's a very interesting moment for most things. We live in a time of hybrids, when everything influences everything else. Communication has created new channels for interaction and this is visible in art and design as well as in life itself. It's a very dynamic time with stimuli coming from all directions. Learning to take them in without losing a personal voice is quite tricky. Younger generations need to think about the conservation of techniques and quality whilst challenging the existing possibilities. With passion and patience there is much to do!

Coating, Piega
Jacopo Cecchi
Fibre-reinforced ceramic-
coated solution for
indoor use
H: 60cm (23in)
W: 60cm (23in)
D: 4cm (1⅝in)
3D SURFACE srl, Italy
www.3dsurface.it

Coating, Caos
Jacopo Cecchi
Fibre-reinforced ceramic-
coated solution for indoor
and outdoor use

H: 42cm (16½in)
W: 60cm (23in)
D: 6.5cm (2½in)
3D SURFACE srl, Italy
www.3dsurface.it

**Decorative tiles, Karma,
Kink and Ubiquity (Karim
for ALLOY Collection)**
Karim Rashid
Brushed stainless steel
Left to right:
L (Karma): 6cm (2⅜in)
D (Karma): 4cm (1⅝in)
L (Kink): 5cm (2in)
D (Kink): 5cm (2in)
L (Ubiquity): 5cm (2in)
D (Ubiquity): 4cm (1⅝in)
W (all): 0.16cm (⅛in)
ALLOY, Australia
www.alloydesign.com.au

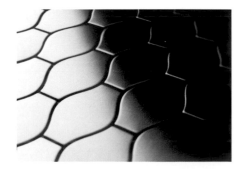

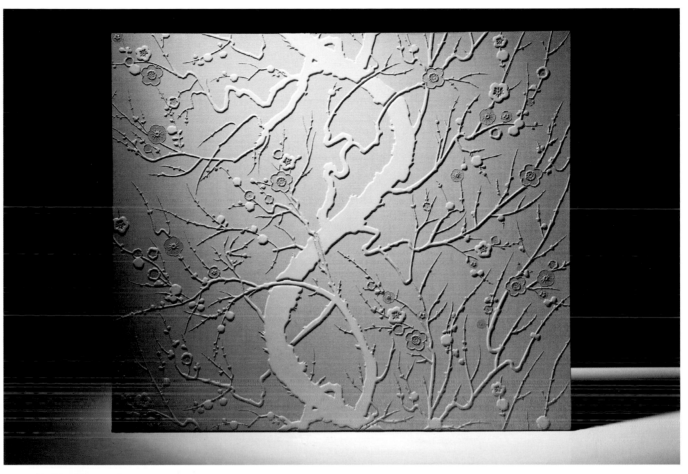

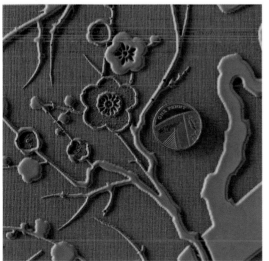

Eric Barrett made a name for himself with Concrete Blonde, a company that he founded in 2001 with the aim of creating contemporary design using concrete. Recognizing its adaptability and potential, Barrett created the Textural-Walled-Paper collection of cast panels embossed with traditional wallpaper prints, demonstrating the hidden beauty of the industrial material. Ten years later he joined forces with inventor Mark Dale to form Graphic Relief Ltd. Together they have developed a new technique for digitally printing onto concrete sheets. Two-dimensional artwork is reinterpreted and manipulated in Adobe Photoshop to form files of three-dimensional textures and graphic effects. This information is used to make moulds into which the concrete is poured, achieving a wide range of surface designs, including photo-quality images. The panels are cast in sizes up to 2 by 1.2 metres (6 feet 7 inches by 3 feet 11 inches), suitable for building facades and exterior and interior cladding, as well as floor and wall tiles. The process is currently being developed for use with a variety of materials.

Interior and exterior cladding, Spring Blossom
Graphic Relief in collaboration with Timorous Beasties
Glass-reinforced concrete and steel-reinforced concrete
Made to order up to
200 x 120cm (78 x 47in)
Graphic Relief Ltd, UK
www.graphicrelief.co.uk

Andrea Hegedűs's panels combine artistic design, handicraft and industrial technology. The plate-glass-laminated textile panels can be produced at any size and used in a variety of ways, from outdoor–indoor partitions, sliding doors, room dividers, shower walls and bar counters to stand-alone sculptures. The glass serves to conserve and fix the textile within, but it also sharpens and enlarges its appearance, giving a dynamic effect to Hegedűs's designs. She uses different materials and motifs as well as surface techniques including embroidery and cutouts. The panels can be adjusted according to customers' preferences, resulting in translucent, light-filtering versions and dense, opaque ones.

Glass textile room divider
Andrea Hegedűs
Tulle, spangle, cotton
W: 300cm (118in)
L: 340cm (133in)
Rakosy Glass, Hungary
www.glasstextile.eu
www.hegedusandrea.hu

Wall covering/tiles, Cuscini (Soft Marble Collection)
Ron Gilad
Marble
W (module): 30cm (11¾in)
L (module): 30cm (11¾in)
Salvatori, Italy
www.salvatori.it

Textile, Point
Paul Smith
97% rayon, 3% nylon
W: 135cm (53in)
Maharam, USA
www.maharam.com

Fabric, Visiona
Nya Nordiska Design Team
60% polyester,
40% metal fibre
W: 300cm
Nya Nordiska Textiles GmbH,
Germany
www.nya.com

**Digitally printed
wall installation,
Hand Tinted Rose**
Paul Smith
48% cellulose, 35% latex,
17% nylon
Scalable and repeatable
Maharam, USA
www.maharam.com

**Wall covering, From
Object to Space Collection**
Atelier Oï
Vinyl on cotton backing
W: 100cm (39in)
Vescom, The Netherlands
www.vescom.com

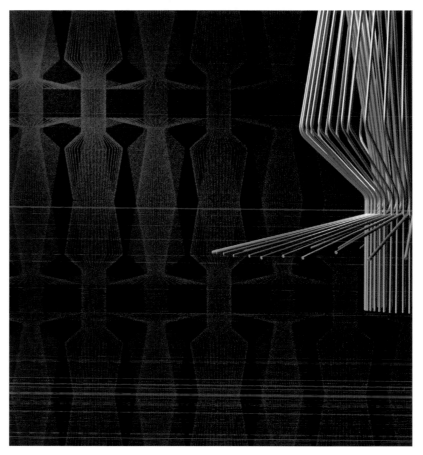

**Fabric, Allium
(Botanic Collection)**
Lori Weitzner
Digitally printed semi-sheer
airy linen mix
W: 135cm (53in)
Sahco, Germany
www.sahco.com

Wallpaper, Forest Muses
Marcel Wanders
Expanded nonwoven flock
L (roll): 1000cm (393in)
Graham & Brown, UK
www.grahambrown.com

Wallpaper, Key Muses
Marcel Wanders
Expanded nonwoven flock
L (roll): 1000cm (393in)
Graham & Brown, UK
www.grahambrown.com

Wallpaper, Rose Beds
Marcel Wanders
Expanded nonwoven flock
L (roll): 1000cm (393in)
Graham & Brown, UK
www.grahambrown.com

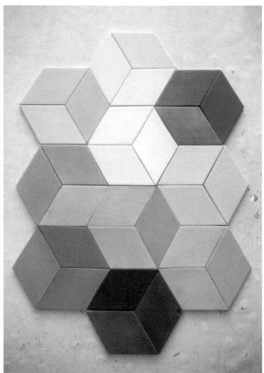

Wall and floor tiles, Tex
Raw Edges
Mixture of clays as an
extruded and glazed
porcelain stoneware
W: 11.5cm (4½in)
L: 20cm (7⅞in)
Ceramiche Mutina srl, Italy
www.mutina.it

**Mosaic pattern,
Hearts & Robots Black**
Bisazza Design Studio
Bisazza glass and
gold mosaic with
Swarovski crystals
Bisazza, Italy
www.bisazza.com

Acoustic panels, Layer
Arik Levy
Fabric, upholstery
with technical foam
soundproofing
H (panel 90): 90cm (35in)
W (panel 90): 90cm (35in)
H (panel 130): 75cm (29in)
W (panel 130): 130cm (51in)
H (panel 180): 60cm (23in)
W (panel 180): 180cm (70in)
D: 3cm (1⅛in)
Viccarbe, Spain
www.viccarbe.com

Wall and floor tiles, Terraviva
Massimilano Adami
Grès Porcelain stoneware
H: 60cm (23in)
W: 60cm (23in)
Refin, Italy
www.refin.it

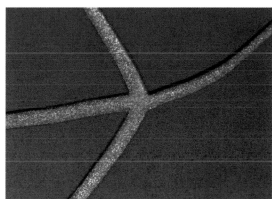

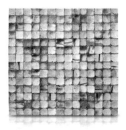

Despite being the largest economy in South East Asia, Indonesia is dogged by unemployment, and around 30 million people live below the poverty line. Agriculture has for centuries been the country's largest industry. Cocomosaic's aim is to create eco-friendly products whilst improving the grassroots economy by supporting local communities. Their tiles are made from coconut-shell chips, a natural, abundant and fully sustainable national resource, only a small percentage of which had previously been exploited commercially in the production of charcoal. Each member of the highly skilled workforce hand-assembles the coconut-chip tiles, of which they make around 250 square metres (2,700 square feet) per month. This eco-friendly business provides employment for forty individuals, including disabled people, whom Cocomosaic actively seeks to include on its team. The company has also set up tree-planting programmes to further its environmental and ethical commitment.

Tiles, Cocomosaic tiles
Cocomosaic
Coconut shell
L: 42cm (16½in)
W: 42cm (16½in)
Cocomosaic, Indonesia
www.cocomosaic.com

7.
LIGHTING

**Pendant lamp,
Spinning Light**
Benjamin Hubert
Spun aluminium
Max 60W 12V E27
low energy
H: 34cm (13⅜in)
Diam: 40cm (15¾in)
& Tradition, Denmark
www.andtradition.com

LED Light, Dropled
Simon Brünner
Aluminium, chrome
LED
H (glass ball): 5 or 10cm
(2 or 3⅞in)
neuesLicht, Germany
www.neuesLicht.de

Floor lamp, Emperor
Neri & Hu
Bamboo rattan, aluminium,
glass, Zamac, steel
Max 60W G9 halogen
H: 180cm (70in)
Diam: 53cm (20in)
Moooi, The Netherlands
www.moooi.com

Lamp, Mask
Stefano Giovannoni
3D pressed-oak
veneer, chrome
LED
H: 75cm (29in)
W: 32.5cm (13in)
D: 19cm (7½in)
Moooi, The Netherlands
www.moooi.com

Table lamp, Lolita
Nika Zupanc
Injection-moulded ABS,
polyurethane
Max 25W E14, type B (Europe)
Max 40W E12, type B (USA)
H: 78cm (30in)
Diam: 37cm (14⅝in)
Moooi, The Netherlands
www.moooi.com

Lighting object, Explosion
Camo Lin
Bamboo, glass tube, cast
aluminium, plastic
Cold Cathode Light Kit
H: 56cm (22in)
L: 66cm (26in)
D: 50cm (19in)
Yii, Taiwan
HAN Gallery, Taiwan
www.yiidesign.com
www.han-gallery.com

**Lamp with clamp,
Sempé w103c**
Inga Sempé
Hand-spun aluminium,
steel, cast iron
1.8W LED
H: 48cm (18⅞in)
Diam: 28cm (11in)
Wästberg, Sweden
www.wastberg.com

Task lamp, W101
Claesson Koivisto Rune
DuraPulp, cast-iron base
1–5W LED
H: 50cm (19⅝in)
W: 11cm (4⅜in)
D: 39cm (15⅜in)
Wästberg, Sweden
www.wastberg.com

In a statement issued to coincide with the launch of the W101 lamp by Swedish lighting brand Wästberg during the 2010 Milan Salone Internazionale del Mobile, its designers, Claesson Koivisto Rune, declared, 'We dare anyone to manufacture a more ecological electric lamp.' In the face of the growing environmental crisis, designers are increasingly developing products that minimize the use of nonrenewable resources and have fewer negative effects on the environment, applying advanced technology to responsible production. The W101 is CKR's second collaboration with Södra, a Swedish forestry company that harvests sustainable wood. In its search for new markets, this forward-looking enterprise developed DuraPulp, a mix of wood pulp and polylactide (PLA), a thermoplastic made from corn or sugarcane that is fully biodegradable, as pliable as plastic and incredibly strong. Depending on the geometry of the part, a sheet of DuraPulp

that is just 1.8 centimetres (¾ inch) thick can support a person's weight. CKR's first experiment with the material was the prize-winning children's chair Parupu.

Following this success, CKR approached Marcus Wästberg, who was at first sceptical about mixing paper and electrical wiring. However, by suggesting the use of custom-designed, low-voltage, state-of-the-art warm-white LEDs, the designers managed to overcome his misgivings. The result of the collaboration is an elegant task light with a sculptural, origami-like shape that helps to ensure rigidity. Four thin, uninsulated copper wires are laid between the layers of DuraPulp, and a heavy supply base makes the lamp stable and houses the power source for the lights. Built for easy disassembly once these technical elements are removed, the rest of the lamp can be safely thrown onto the compost heap.

Table lamp, Binic
Ionna Vautrin
Polycarbonate, ABS
12W fluorescent
H: 20cm (7⅞in)
W: 14cm (5½in)
D: 14cm (5½in)
Foscarini srl, Italy
www.foscarini.com

Table lamp, Gamete
Xavier Lust
Polyamide
Max 40W 210–230V G9
halogen
H: 34.7cm (13¾in)
W: 26.3cm (10¼in)
D: 14.6cm (5⅞in)
MGX by Materialise, Belgium
www.mgxbymaterialise.com

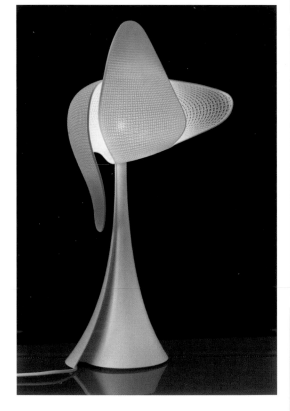

Pendant lamp, Coroa
Emmanuel Babled
Lacquered metal, double-
face mirror PMMA or
opaque white
16 x max 25W E14
Diam: 90cm (35in)
Oluce srl, Italy
www.oluce.com

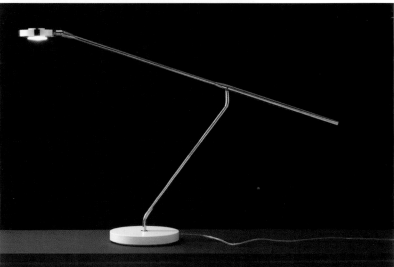

**Adjustable table
lamp, Lutz**
Lutz Pankow
Metal
Max 8W LED
H (max): 60cm (23in)
W (max): 90cm (35in)
Oluce srl, Italy
www.oluce.com

Wall lamp, Cadmo Parete
Karim Rashid
Injection-moulded
thermoplastic, optic
aluminium
CFL
H: 54cm (21in)
Diam: 13cm (5⅛in)
Artemide SpA, Italy
www.artemide.com

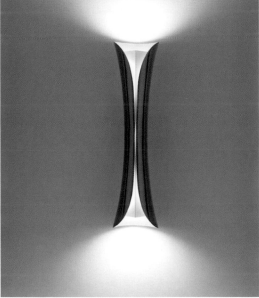

Pendant lamp, Can Can
Marcel Wanders
Injection-moulded PMMA,
polycarbonate
Max 105W E27 HSGSA/
Max 30W E27 CFL FBT
H: 36cm (14⅛in)
Diam: 34.7cm (13¾in)
Flos SpA, Italy
www.flos.com

**Energy-saving desk lamp,
Kelvin LED Green Mode**
Antonio Citterio with
Toan Nguyen
Aluminium
30 x 4W TOP LED (2700K,
324 lm, CRI 80)

H: 43.5cm (17⅜in)
W (base): 16cm (6¼in)
L: 58.1cm (22in)
Flos SpA, Italy
www.flos.com

**Ceiling/wall lamp,
Veli Prisma**
Adriano Rachele
Lentiflex
2 x 15W E27 FBT
H: 20cm (7⅞in)
Diam: 53cm (20in)
Slamp SpA, Italy
www.slamp.com

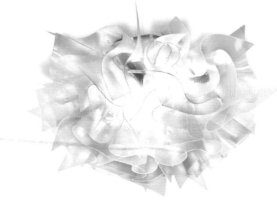

Wall/ceiling lamp, Droplet
Ross Lovegrove
Painted aluminium
Halogen with mains voltage/
metal halide
H: 34cm (13⅜in)
Diam: 60cm (23in)
Artemide SpA, Italy
www.artemide.com

**Adjustable table
lamp, Puk**
Siw Matzen
Metal
Max 75W E27
H: 71.5cm (28in)
Diam: 22cm (8⅝in)
Anta Leuchten GmbH,
Germany
www.anta.de

Floor lamp, Vader
Luca Nichetto
Ceramic
E27 low-energy dimmable
H: 48.8cm (19¼in)
W: 50.6cm (20in)
D: 34cm (13⅜in)
David Design, Sweden
www.daviddesignfurniture.se

**Pendant lamp,
Cosmic Leaf**
Ross Lovegrove
Chromed steel, transparent
methacrylate
Low-voltage halogen/
metal halide
H: 192cm (76in)
Diam: 22cm (8⅝in)
Artemide SpA, Italy
www.artemide.com

Pendant lamp, Morgana
Stefano Papi
Polycarbonate
75W G9 HSGST/C/UB
H: 58cm (22in)
Diam: 45cm (17¾in)
Slamp SpA, Italy
www.slamp.com

**Series of pendant
lamps, Void**
Tom Dixon
Solid metal (brass, copper
and stainless steel)
Max 33W G9 halogen
clear (Europe)
Max 25W G9 halogen
frosted (USA)
H: 15.5cm (6⅛in)
Diam: 30cm (11¾in)
Tom Dixon, UK
www.tomdixon.net

**Pendant lamp,
Andromeda**
Ross Lovegrove
Steel with painted finish, hard
polyurethane foam, mirror
8 x 1.1W LED
H: 27cm (10⅝in)
W: 80cm (31in)
D: 46cm (18⅛in)
Yamagiwa, Japan
www.yamagiwa-lighting.com

Table lamp, Candy Light
Jaime Hayon
Copper-coloured ceramic,
luminous red crystal
dimmer-switch button,
crystal lampshade
2 x 40W G9 halogen (max
electric power of lamps 80W)
H: 51cm (20in)
Diam: 23cm (9in)
Baccarat, France
www.baccarat.fr

**Chandelier, Old
Lampshade-Lamp**
Piet Hein Eek
Old lampshades
62 x 15W clear
H: 300cm (118in)
Diam: 200cm (78in)
Piet Hein Eek,
The Netherlands
www.pietheineek.nl

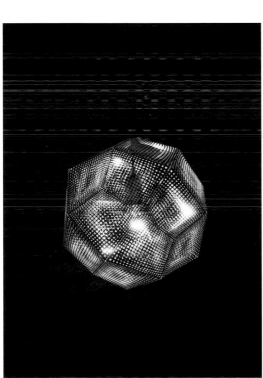

Pendant lamp, Etch
Tom Dixon
Digitally etched brass sheets
Can be used with any
standard fitting
H: 27.5cm (11in)
Diam: 30cm (11¾in)
Tom Dixon, UK
www.tomdixon.net

**Table lamp with 360°
rotating shade, Golconda**
Luca Nichetto
Sprayed aluminium,
plastic diffuser
Max 100W 110/120V or
220/240V E27
H: 63cm (24in)
Diam: 45cm (17¾in)
Established & Sons, UK
www.establishedandsons.com

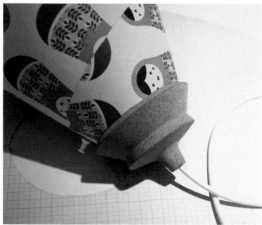

Lamp, Pinha
Raw Edges
Cork lampshell, Dupont
Tyvek® lampshade
Cold light bulb
H: 11cm (4⅜in)
Diam: 13cm (5⅛in)
Amorim Cork Composites, S.A,
Portugal
www.corkcomposites.amorim.com

Cork is one of Portugal's most important resources – it sustains about 800,000 hectares (2 million acres) of forest in the south of the country alone and is exported all over the world. Its largest producer, Amorim, has joined forces with ExperimentaDesign, Lisbon's design biennial, to form Materia, a brand established to highlight the design potential of this flexible, sustainable material. Cork – the outer bark of the cork oak tree – is the perfect environmentally friendly, renewable substance. It can be harvested from the same tree for about two hundred years with minimal impact on the ecosystem. It is elastic, compressible, impermeable to liquids and gases, resistant yet lightweight and buoyant. Despite these qualifications, however, the extent of its potential is often overlooked both from a technical aspect and in terms of aesthetics. The Materia project, spearheaded by the co-founder of ExperimentaDesign, Guta Moura Goedes, invited ten top Portuguese and international designers – project coordinator Filipe Alarcão (see page 299), Fernando Brizio (see page 167), Miguel Vieira Baptista, Daniel Caramelo,

Studio Pedrita and Marco Sousa Santos, all from Portugal, along with Inga Sempé (see page 118), Nendo (see page 167), BIG-GAME and Raw Edges (above) – to interpret the material in their own distinct ways, taking advantage of its physical and mechanical characteristics whilst playing with its visual and sensory qualities. 'Cork is enjoying a renaissance,' says Amorim's chairman, Antonio Amorim. 'There is a new understanding of its potential for many applications and recognition of the added value it brings to the products in which it is used.'

The Pinha lamp by Raw Edges uses the low thermal conductivity of cork to its advantage by including a three-tiered cork surround, or 'lampshell', for the light source. This can be handled in perfect safety, and a printed-paper shade, selected from among different patterns and drawings, can be attached with ease. The direction and range of the light can be adjusted by pinning the shade at different places on the surround, thereby altering the mood and ambience in a room.

Desk light, Heavy
Benjamin Hubert
Cast concrete, wood
Max. 40W G9 halogen
H: 46cm (18⅛in)
W: 20cm (7⅞in)
D: 30cm (11¾in)
Decode, UK
www.decodelondon.com

Pendant lamp, Float
Benjamin Hubert
Cork
60W
H: 20, 30 or 40cm
(7⅞, 11¾ or 15¾in)
Diam: 25, 40 or 60cm
(9⅞, 15¾, 23in)
Benjamin Hubert Studio, UK
www.benjaminhubert.co.uk

Pendant lamp, Swell
Paul Cocksedge
Pyrex glass, aluminium
Max 35W 12V GY6.35 HSG
H (max): 150cm (59in)
Diam: 14cm (5½in)
Yamagiwa, Japan
www.yamagiwa-lighting.com

Table lamp, Pipe
Luca Nichetto
Sand blasted pyrex® glass,
polycarbonate, powder-
coated aluminium, powder-
coated steel
Max 100W 220/240V E27
H (small version): 37.5cm (15in)

Diam (small version):
11.5cm (4½in)
H (large version):
43.5cm (17⅜in)
Diam (large version):
17cm (6¾in)
Established & Sons, UK
www.establishedandsons.com

Task light, Crane
Benjamin Hubert
Industrial steel, aluminium
LED
H: 60cm (23in)
W: 50cm (19in)
Örsjö Belysning AB, Sweden
www.orsjo.com

Task light, Edge
Amanda Levete
Stainless steel
OLED
H: 28.5cm (11⅜in)
L: 50cm (19in)
D: 37cm (14⅝in)
Established & Sons, UK
www.establishedandsons.com

Lighting, ToFU
Tokujin Yoshioka
Methacrylate (PMMA),
aluminium
10W 12V G4 halogen
H: 29.5cm (11¾in)
W: 36.5cm (14⅝in)
D: 7.6cm (3in)
Yamagiwa, Japan
www.yamagiwa-lighting.com

**Pendant lamp,
Spinning Light**
Benjamin Hubert
Spun aluminium
Max 60W 12V E27
low energy
H: 34cm (13⅜in)
Diam: 40cm (15¾in)
& Tradition, Denmark
www.andtradition.com

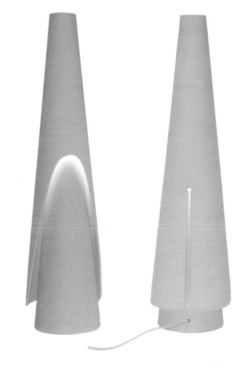

Table/floor lamp, Monja
Marre Moerel
Earthenware ceramics
Max 14W (=75W) E27
energy-saving fluorescent,
warm white
H: 68cm (27in)
W: 5.5cm (2½in)
L: 14.5cm (5½in)
Marre Moerel Design Studio,
Spain
www.marremoerel.com

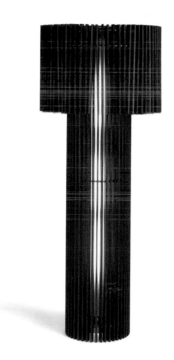

Floor lamp, Wood Lamp
Fernando and Humberto
Campana
Wood, metal
220/240V
H: 177cm (70in)
Diam: 75cm (29in)
Skitsch, Italy
www.skitsch.it

Pendant lamp, Plass
Luca Nichetto
Polycarbonate
6 x 60W + 1 x 100W halogen
H (max): 500cm (196in)
Diam: 75cm (29in)
Foscarini srl, Italy
www.foscarini.com

Floor lamp, Mayuhana II
Toyo Ito
Fibreglass, aluminium
Max 20W E27 FBA
H: 226.5cm (89in)
W: 43cm (16⅞in)
D: 205cm (80in)
Yamagiwa, Japan
www.yamagiwa-lighting.com

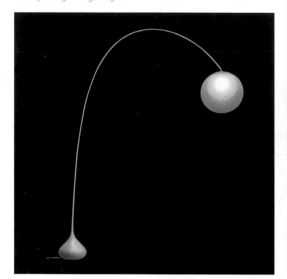

Pendant lamp, Dew
Emmanuel Babled
Glass diffuser, die-cast
aluminium
4W Power LED
Diam: 11cm (4⅜in)
Kundalini srl, Italy
www.kundalini.it

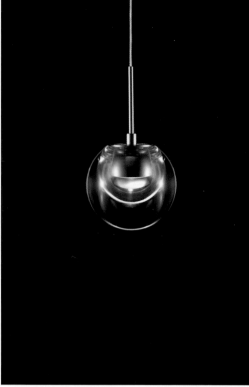

**Pendant lamp,
Silly-Kon**
Ingo Maurer and Team
Silicone, plastic, metal
Max 75W 230/125V E27
energy-saving halogen
W: 15cm (5⅞in)
L: 200cm (78in)
Ingo Maurer GmbH,
Germany
www.ingo-maurer.com

Pendant lamp, Clover
Brodie Neill
Moulded polyurethane,
aluminium
2 x max 205W B15D
H: 25cm (9⅞in)
Diam: 70cm (27in)
Kundalini srl, Italy
www.kundalini.it

Table lamp, Unmetro
Marco Merendi
Metal
3W 220/240V LED,
24VDC power supply
Diam (base): 20cm (7⅞in)
Davide Groppi, Italy
www.davidegroppi.com

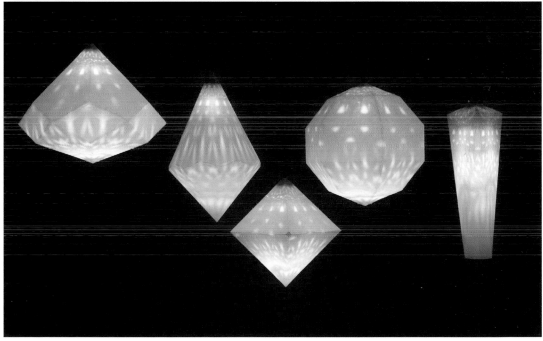

Light, Amplify
fuseproject
Paper shade, crystal
LED
H (second lamp from left):
65cm (25in)
W (second lamp from left):
40cm (15¾in)
Swarovski, Austria
www.swarovski.com

For nearly a decade now, Swarovski, the iconic purveyor of crystals, has been showcasing its expertise in a series of annual exhibitions held alongside the Salone Internazionale del Mobile in Milan. In these shows, called the Crystal Palace, designers such as Ron Arad, Tokujin Yoshioka, Gaetano Pesce, Paul Cocksedge and Ross Lovegrove have displayed spectacular one-off chandeliers as part of, according to Swarovski, 'a revolutionary project that has aimed to create signature interpretations of light and design using the emotive medium of cut crystal'.

Amplify is fuseproject's Yves Béhar's fourth collaboration with Swarovski in a Crystal Palace installation. His past works were large-scale lighting sculptures, but this time his aim was to bring the notion of accessibility and sustainability to crystal

lighting. He says: 'It is a pursuit in our work to try and achieve the maximum effect with the minimum amount of materials and energy: we want to create consciously and conscientiously, and yet there is a need for beauty. So the challenge is to rethink how to achieve the magical effect of many crystals on a chandelier. Can we amplify a single crystal and create an entire chandelier?' His winning formula is '1 crystal + 1 low-energy LED light + a faceted paper shade = AMPLIFY'. For the show, Behar and his fuseproject team designed a variety of different crystalline-shaped lamps, each crafted to maximize the refractions caused by a single light source hitting one gemstone and then being duplicated on the inner surfaces of a recycled-paper shade. The effect emulates the beautiful reflections and rainbow colour bursts of crystals. Each of the lantern shapes is now in production from Swarovski.

Pendant lamp, Vertigo
Constance Guisset
Polyurethane, fibreglass
15–20W (=75–100W)
220–240V E27 energy saver
H: 17cm (6¾in)
Diam: 200cm (78in)
Petite Friture, France
www.petitefriture.com

**Floor lamp
(reintroduction), Van
Severen w111**
Maarten Van Severen
Aluminium
LED
H: 122cm (48in)
L: 60cm (23in)
Wästberg, Sweden
www.wastberg.com

Pendant and table lamps, Vapeur
Inga Sempé
Lacquered metal, Tyvek®
23W energy saver
H (suspension lamp): 52cm (20in)
L (suspension lamp): 55cm (21in)
W (suspension lamp): 40cm (15¾in)
H (small table lamp): 63cm (24in)
L (small table lamp): 54cm (21in)
W (small table lamp): 35cm (13¾in)
H (large table lamp): 85cm (33in)
L (large table lamp): 71cm (28in)
W (large table lamp): 52cm (20in)
Moustache, France
www.moustache.fr

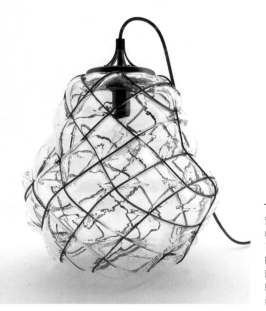

Table lamp, Lantern Table
Stephen Burks
Glass, brass
75W Edison
H: 49cm (19in)
Diam: 39cm (15⅜in)
MatterMade, USA
www.mattermatters.com

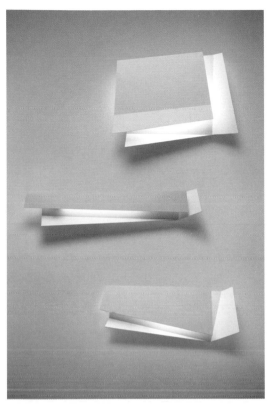

Wall lamp, Flap
Marco Zito
Lacquered aluminium
2 x 18W or 1 x 40W
fluorescent
H (Flap 1): 46cm (18⅛in)
L (Flap 1): 58cm (22in)
H (Flap 2): 28cm (11in)
L (Flap 2): 66cm (26in)
H (Flap 3): 17cm (6¾in)
L (Flap 3): 82cm (32in)
D: 10cm (3⅞in)
Foscarini srl, Italy
www.foscarini.com

Chandelier, Esperança
Fernando and Humberto
Campana
Glass, metal
3 x max 40W G9 halogen
H: 100cm (39in)
Diam: 60cm (23in)
Venini SpA, Italy
www.venini.com

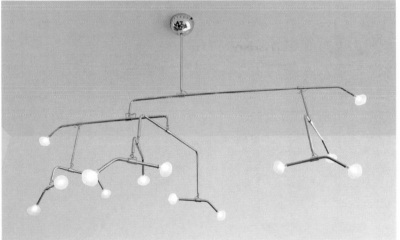

Pendant lamp, Fireworks
Xavier Lust
Chromed steel, opaline
blown glass
Up to 13 x max 20W 12V G4
halogen
H: 135cm (53in)
W: 180cm (70in)
D: 115cm (45in)
Driade, Italy
www.driade.com

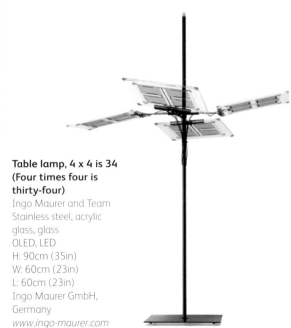

**Table lamp, 4 x 4 is 34
(Four times four is
thirty-four)**
Ingo Maurer and Team
Stainless steel, acrylic
glass, glass
OLED, LED
H: 90cm (35in)
W: 60cm (23in)
L: 60cm (23in)
Ingo Maurer GmbH,
Germany
www.ingo-maurer.com

Task light, Anglepoise TypeC
Kenneth Grange
Glass, anodized aluminium, stainless steel
LED
H: 54cm (21in)
Diam (base): 17.8cm (7⅛in)
Anglepoise, UK
www.anglepoise.com

Pendant lamp, Etch Light Web
Tom Dixon
Copper-anodized aluminium with digital photo-acid etching
Halogen or LED
Diam: 65cm (25in)
Tom Dixon, UK
www.tomdixon.net

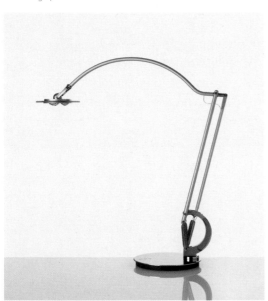

Table and floor lamps, 96 Molecules
Ofir Zucker and Albi Serfaty in collaboration with origami artist Ilan Garibi
Paper, untreated mahogany
LED
H (table lamp): 21cm (8¼in)
Diam (table lamp): 30cm (11¾in)
H (floor lamp): 89cm (35in)
Diam (floor lamp): 35cm (13¾in)
Aqua Creations, Israel
www.aquagallery.com

Lamps, Raft (Cats) and Raft (Dogs)
Stuart Haygarth
Found ceramic figurines, spun aluminium dish, Corian® base
4 x low energy, warm white
H: 127cm (50in)
Diam (base): 86cm (33in)
Stuart Haygarth, UK
www.stuarthaygarth.com

**Table lamp with
adjustable arms and
head, Grifo**
Ross Lovegrove
Painted die-cast aluminium,
painted extruded aluminium
13W LED
H: 54.3cm (21in)
W: 59.7cm (23in)
Artemide SpA, Italy
www.artemide.com

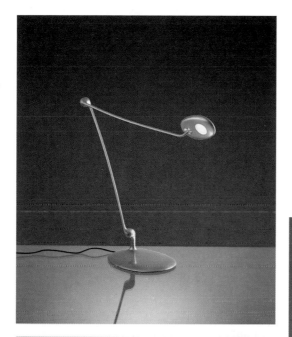

**Ceiling lamp, Cosmic
Rotation riflessa**
Ross Lovegrove
Aluminium, injection-moulded
opal methacrylate
2 x 87W G24q-5 TC-DEL Fluo
H: 29cm (11⅜in)
Diam: 76cm (29in)
Artemide SpA, Italy
www.artemide.com

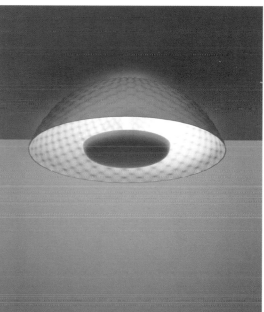

Table lamp, Halo
Karim Rashid
Metal, silicone rubber
LED 8W
H: 53cm (20in)
W: 35cm (13¾in)
Diam (base): 16cm (6¼in)
Artemide SpA, Italy
www.artemide.com

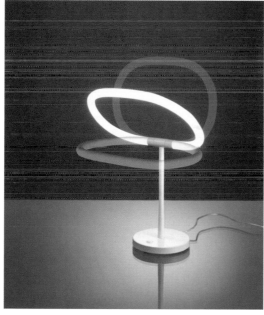

**Table lamp with
adjustable arms and
head, Lotek**
Javier Mariscal
Painted steel, painted
aluminium, anodized
aluminium
13W LED
H: 62cm (24in)
W: 62cm (24in)
W (base): 18cm (7⅛in)
Artemide SpA, Italy
www.artemide.com

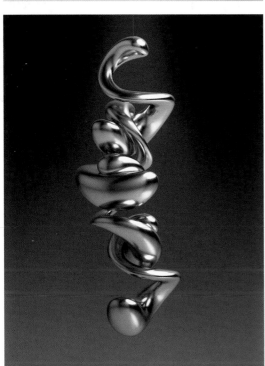

**Pendant lamp,
Twiggy Lamp**
Tomoko Azumi
Steel, paper
25W E17
H: 30cm (11¾in)
Diam: 12cm (4¾in)
Maxray, Japan
Sfera srl, Italy
www.ricordi-sfera.com

Pendant lamps, Bloom
Ferruccio Laviani
Transparent polycarbonate,
batch-dyed technopolymer
thermoplastic
9 x 33W 220–240V G9
halogen
H (large version):
35cm (13¾in)
D (large version):
53cm (20in)
H (small version):
19cm (7½in)
D (small version):
28cm (11in)
Kartell SpA, Italy
www.kartell.it

**Lighting, Johnny B.
Butterfly**
Ingo Maurer and Team
Hand-made insect models
Bulb with white Teflon shade
H: 25cm (9⅞in)
Ingo Maurer GmbH,
Germany
www.ingo-maurer.com

**Ceiling lamp (single or
multiple modules), Nearco**
Karim Rashid
Rotationally moulded
polyethylene
Max 100W G53 QR-LP111
halogen/70W G8.5 HIR-CE111
metal halide
H: (single element):
66cm (26in)
Artemide SpA, Italy
www.artemide.com

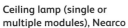

Floor/table lamp, Amanita
Fernando and Humberto Campana
Rattan
2 x max 20W 220–230V
H: 60cm (23in)
Diam: 50cm (19in)
Alessi SpA, Italy
www.alessi.com

Table light, Behive
Werner Aisslinger
ABS, polycarbonate
150W E27 halogen/20W
E27 fluorescent/150W E26
medium type T10 shielded
frosted halogen/23W E26
medium fluorescent
H: 40cm (15¾in)
Diam: 39.5cm (15¾in)
Foscarini srl, Italy
www.foscarini.com

Lamp, A Piece of Forest
Modern Times
DuraPulp (composite of
PLA and selected wood
pulp) by Södra
LED
H: 200cm (78in)
W: 90cm (35in)
D: 7cm (2¾in)
Modern Times, Sweden
www.modern-times.se

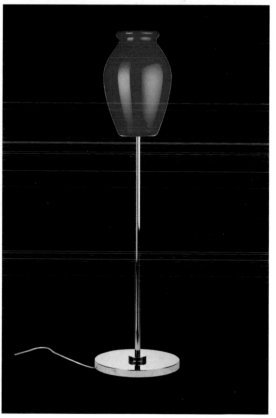

Floor lamp sculpture, Vase Lamp
Studio Job
Handblown glass, metal
18W G9 halogen
H: 119 (47in)
Diam: 30 (11¾in)
Venini SpA, Italy
www.venini.com

Benjamin Hubert

How did your career start?

I started my career after university when I began to work for large industrial design consultancies such as DCA and Seymourpowell, etc. I worked for these companies for around four years across consumer electronics and medical and transport design as well as interiors, collaborating with multinational brands. Once I began to design for myself, I filled my evenings and weekends creating prototypes and concepts. Eventually the studio output was in such high demand that the decision to quit the day job was not difficult.

You have produced an amazing body of work in a short period of time. How do you account for your early professional and media recognition?

I work really hard and instil this ethos into the studio. The work is our passion, so we live and breathe it. We also try and talk to the right people and make engaging products that can be marketed through our core message of 'simplicity, materiality and process'.

What steps are you taking to build on this success?

We are now becoming more selective with our partners and look for experts in production technology or service, whether it's the brand or the factory. In that way we can really start to push innovation and research with very capable collaborators. The projects are therefore also becoming a little longer and in-depth. Right now we are working on some interesting new processes that give benefits such as greater strength to weight ratio, sustainability, interactivity, etc.

You say that the inspiration behind your work is led by process and materials, rather than form or even function.

Yes this is the way we like to work. We do a lot of research into new materials and constructions sometimes before we find an application for them. It frees us to really analyse the properties and push things as far as we can and then find the appropriate product. However, we do also believe in great functionality and usability, and often these considerations go hand in hand with the materials research. In our working process, form follows. It has an appropriateness and simplicity that lets the materials and function speak for themselves.

A good example of this is the Maritime chair (page 45), for which we found an interesting construction technique normally used in the shipbuilding industry, where a series of ribs increases the strength of a thin material. I applied this logic to the chair and allowed the construction to also become the design language.

You often use raw and tactile materials. How do you seek to elevate their design credentials away from craft?

We like to play with the consumer's perception of quality, application and context. Some of the materials we use are very normal but employed in very precise specifications.

For example, concrete is ubiquitous but generally used in architecture. By creating a process of casting it with a thin section and using it as a lighting product (as in the Heavy desk light, page 230), people's ideas of the value and beauty of the material are challenged. Another example is Loom (opposite page), where we used a 3D woven nylon normally used in the bedding industry. Through our research into lighting we discovered it has great diffusion qualities. Or take the pressed

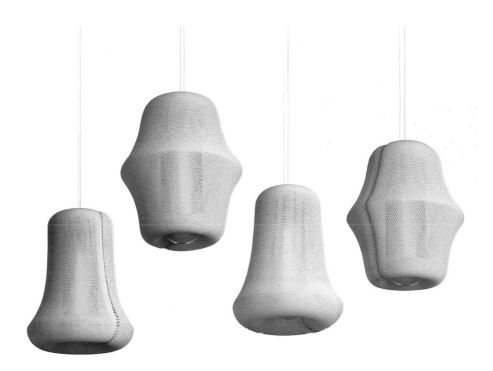

felt used in the automotive industry. By creating large shells with acoustic benefits in the Pod chair (page 48), we again challenged its expected application.

You maintain that creating a narrative saves design from being stereotypical or formulaic.

We try to tell a story with our work: A story of materials, inspiration and the semantics of function. We believe this will create designs that people can relate to and that have a lasting value – products that have been designed for the right reasons.

You frequently collaborate with skilled artisans. What have you learned from the experience?

Working with an expert in a material or process gives you the ability to gain a true understanding of its properties. Being armed with this knowledge allows us to push things forward and challenge the conventions.

The definition of sustainable design is difficult and contradictory. What is your understanding of the term?

Sustainability is a formula. You need to have the elements in balance to have a truly sustainable product. For example, it's important that an object has longevity, that it does not respond to trends, but that it is also made with quality and functionality so that it will last and generations will be able to use it. It's also important to consider a product's carbon footprint, the impact of the materials used and the production process, as well as how it is transported around the world. But if it does not have the values of longevity then all the other credentials are in vain.

What do you consider to be the catalysts for design's development today?

The catalysts are the benefits. Can we improve functionality? Can we make products stronger and with less material? Can we reduce a product's carbon footprint? There are many valuable benefits that should be considered when introducing new products to the world, which the designer should always keep as the main focus of a project. In essence, the quality of the question should be the catalyst.

When design historians look back over the first decade of the present century, will they consider it to have been an exciting period?

Yes, with all the new technology, societal change, globalization, etc., it's a very stimulating period in which we live. And the role of the designer is becoming ever more important because of it.

Loom pendant lamp for Zero (2011)

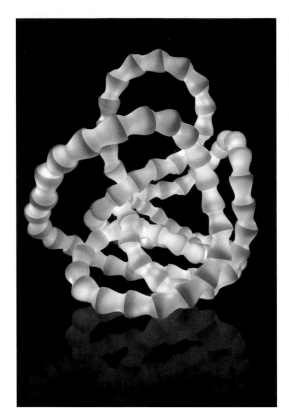

**Modular table
lamp, Abyss**
Osko & Deichmann
Injection-moulded opal
polycarbonate
High-voltage LED strip
Diam: 110cm (43in)
Kundalini, Italy
www.kundalini.it

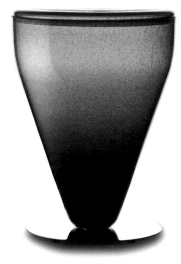

Light sculpture, Argo
Luca Nichetto
Handblown glass, metal
1.5W LED
H: 38.5cm (15⅜in)
Diam: 40cm (15¾in)
Venini SpA, Italy
www.venini.com

Ceiling lamp, Galata
Edward van Vliet
Handblown glass, metal
20W E27
H: 72cm (28in)
Diam: 30cm (11¾in)
Venini SpA, Italy
www.venini.com

**Table lamp,
Satelight/Altaïr**
Emmanuel Babled
Plexiglas
LED
H: 38.5cm (15⅜in)
W: 26.5cm (10⅝in)
L: 65cm (25in)
Emmanuel Babled Studio,
The Netherlands
www.babled.net

Pendant lamp, Rorrim
Ross Lovegrove
Italian handblown glass
24W E27 Osram Circline/
25W E27 Philips Circular
H: 27cm (10⅝in)
Diam: 45cm (17¾in)
Yamagiwa, Japan
www.yamagiwa-lighting.com

Pendant lamps, Calabash
Komplot Design
Aluminium with chrome lacquer
Max 25W E27 (small)
Max 40W E27 (medium)
Max 100W E27 (large)
H (small): 21cm (8 in)
Diam (small): 15.8cm (6¼in)
H (medium): 30.5cm (12¼in)
Diam (medium): 22.4cm (8⅝in)
H (large): 48.5cm (19¼in)
Diam (large): 34cm (13⅜in)
Lightyears A/S, Denmark
www.lightyears.dk

**Table lamp with
tray, Piani**
Ronan and Erwan Bouroullec
Plastic
14 x 5W TOP LED (2700K,
336 lm, CRI 90)
H: 20cm (7⅞in)
L: 26.4cm (10¼in)
D: 18.3cm (7¼in)
Flos SpA, Italy
www.flos.com

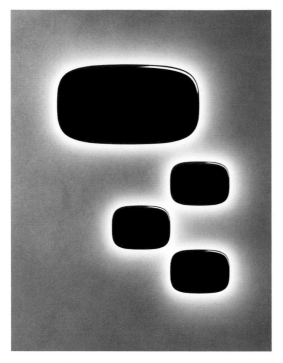

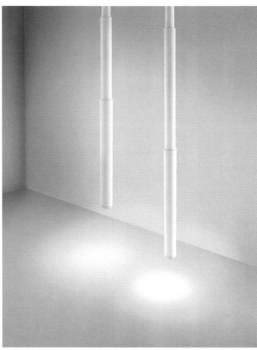

Extendable pendant lamp, Micro Telescopic
Jean Nouvel
Aluminium
13W Power LED
3-element lamp:
H (min): 94cm (37in)
H (max): 155cm (61in)
Diam (min) 4cm (1⅝in)
Diam (max): 6cm (2⅜in)
4-element lamp:
H (min): 109cm (43in)
H (max): 220cm (86in)
Diam (min): 4cm (1⅝in)
Diam (max): 6cm (2⅜in)
Pallucco srl, Italy
www.pallucco.com

Wall lamp, Tivu
Jozeph Forakis
Polycarbonate
2 x 18W fluorescent/
1 x 20W halogen
H (large version):
23cm (9in)
L (large version):
40.5cm (16⅛in)
D (large version): 8cm (3⅛in)
H (small version): 13cm (5⅛in)
D (small version): 6cm (2⅜in)
Foscarini srl, Italy
www.foscarini.com

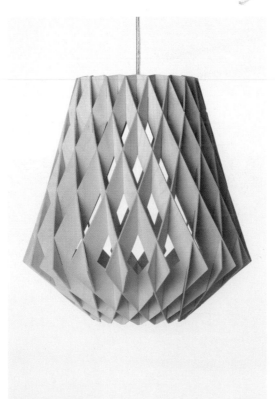

Pendant lamp, Pilke 36
Tuukka Halonen
Birch plywood
Max 40W energy saver
H: 38cm (15in)
Diam: 36cm (14⅛in)
Showroom Finland Oy,
Finland
www.showroomfinland.fi

Floor lamp, Tress Stilo
Marc Sadler
Compound material on
lacquered glass fibre base
100W 220/240V halogen/
75W 120V halogen
H: 185cm (72in)
Diam: 15cm (5⅞in)
Foscarini srl, Italy
www.foscarini.com

Light shades, Koura and Kina (Grow Range)
David Trubridge
Bamboo plywood, nylon push-in clips
LED or CFL recommended
H (Koura): 96, 160, 200 or 240cm (37, 63, 78 or 94in)
Diam (Koura): 55, 95, 110 or 140cm (21, 37, 43 or 55in)
H (Kina): 37, 42 or 70cm (14⅝, 16½, 27in)
Diam (Kina): 80, 100 or 160cm (31, 39 or 63in)
David Trubridge Ltd, New Zealand
www.davidtrubridge.com

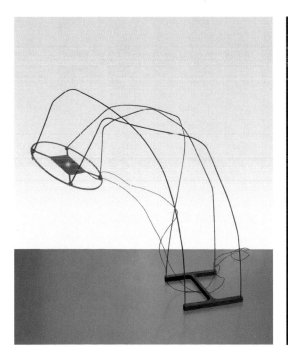

Table lamp, Filmografica
Martí Guixé
Metal
LED
H (max): 60cm (23in)
Diam: 26cm (10¼in)
Danese Milano, Italy
www.danesemilano.com

Pendant lamp, Fly-Fly
Ludovica and Roberto Palomba
Polycarbonate
300W halogen
H: 24cm (9½in)
L: 80cm (31in)
D: 66cm (26in)
Foscarini srl, Italy
www.foscarini.com

Many have mourned the slow death of the incandescent light bulb since its manufacture began to be phased out in 2009 by the European Union for environmental reasons. The CFLs being pushed on consumers today may use 80 per cent less energy and last eight times as long as their conventional predecessors, but the light they shed simply doesn't compare, casting a ghoulish pale over our lives, while their gas-filled tubes are awkward in appearance. Facing the inevitable but recognizing the drawbacks, today's lighting designers are looking at ways to make the dreaded more palatable. The Plumen 001 bulb, designed by Samuel Wilkinson for British product-design company Hulger, is one such innovative concept and earned the accolade of Brit Insurance Design of the Year in 2011. At the prize-giving, Stephen Bayley, chair of the jury, enthused, 'The Plumen light bulb is a good example of the ordinary thing done extraordinarily well, bringing a small measure of delight to an everyday object.'

Interviewed for *Architonic* online magazine, Wilkinson says, 'Low-energy lighting had a bad reputation as being something that you were forced to use, rather than through pure desire. The standard incandescent bulb has a simple beauty, but the standard CFLs appear as if designed by an engineer, lacking the "soul" of the original. So there was a clear opportunity to really add value.' In collaboration with Hulger, Wilkinson examined the usual CFL manufacturing processes in order to radically change the shape of the bulb and create a warmer, more yellow glow. He wanted an aesthetic that at first appeared random but, when viewed from different angles, took on a more rational and recognizable form. The Plumen is both poetic and seductive, and its fluorescent tubes were designed to echo and pay homage to its antecedent.

Wilkinson subsequently worked with the recently founded British design brand Decode to create the Vessel collection, a series of three handblown glass shades that are cut on individual slants to focus on the different faces of the Plumen. Illuminated, the glass tint mutes the light without hiding the shape of the bulb, producing an unexpected irregular reflection that appears holographic.

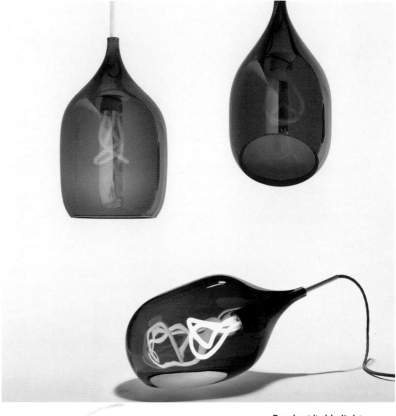

**Pendant/table light,
Vessel Series 01-03**
Samuel Wilkinson
Mouthblown glass
Plumen 001 bulb E27/ES
H: 42cm (16½in)
Diam: 24cm (9½in)
Decode, UK
www.decodelondon.com

**Energy-saving light bulb,
Plumen 001**
Hulger/Samuel Wilkinson
Glass, plastic, electronics,
phosphor, gases
H: 19.2cm (7½in)
W: 10cm (3⅞in)
D: 10cm (3⅞in)
Hulger, UK
www.hulger.com

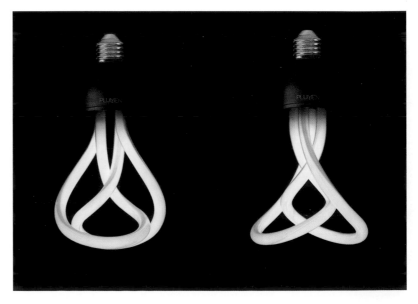

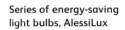

**Series of energy-saving
light bulbs, AlessiLux**
Giovanni Alessi Anghini and
Gabriele Chiave (Abatjour
and Flame)
Frederic Gooris (Paraffina,
Polaris, Tam Tam, U2Mi2,
Vienna)
5.5 or 7.5W LED
Left to right: Abatjour, Flame,
Paraffina, Polaris, Tam Tam,
U2Mi2, Vienna
H (Abatjour): 12.4cm (4⅞in)
D (Abatjour): 7.4cm (2⅞in)
H (Flame): 11.3cm (4⅜in)
D (Flame): 7.5cm (3in)

H (Paraffina): 12.2cm (4¾in)
D (Paraffina): 6.3cm (2½in)
H (Polaris): 11.4cm (4½in)
D (Polaris): 7.5cm (3in)
H (Tam Tam): 13cm (5⅛in)
D (Tam Tam): 6.3cm (2½in)
H (U2Mi2): 13.3cm (5⅜in)
D (U2Mi2): 7.2cm (2⅞in)
H (Vienna): 11.9cm (4¾in)
D (Vienna): 7cm (2¾in)
Alessi SpA, Italy
Foreverlamp Europe BV,
The Netherlands
www.alessi.com
www.foreverlamp.eu

Alessi is known worldwide for its designer kitchen utensils,
but sees its future turning towards more innovative and
experimental products. The AlessiLux range is the latest in
the company's exploration of different fields of production
that its CEO, Alberto Alessi, sees as 'Alessi-able'. A group of
young designers (Giovanni Alessi Anghini, Gabriele Chiave
and Frederic Gooris) was asked to create lamp/bulb hybrids
to celebrate the advantages of using LEDs over incandescent
light bulbs. LED technology significantly reduces carbon
dioxide emissions thanks to its low energy consumption, but,
as well as its green credentials, it also offers extraordinary
design possibilities. LEDs enable the creation of small,
vibration-free light sources that generate little heat and can
safely be touched. Alberto Alessi sums up the results of the
project: 'The topic brought us towards a kind of evaporation
of the boundaries between light bulbs and lamps in a most
natural way; actually, some of the projects are probably closer
to a real lamp than to a simple bulb. I think that the new
operation with Foreverlamp [the producers and distributors of
AlessiLux] is going to blaze a trail for a revolutionary story in
the world of lighting: it's as if hiding those boring, anonymous
and often truly ugly light bulbs will no longer be necessary.'

**Pendant light,
Filament Lamp**
Scott, Rich & Victoria
Glass
CCFL
H: 42cm (16½in)
Diam: 15.5cm (6⅛in)
Northern Lighting, Norway
www.northernlighting.no

**Pendant lamp,
Slingerlamp**
Richard Hutten
Laser-cut steel
Energy saver
H: 35cm (13¾in)
Diam: 59cm (23in)
NgispeN, The Netherlands
www.ngispen.com

**12-light chandelier,
Marie Coquine**
Philippe Starck
Crystal, umbrella with
chestnut wood handle,
white pleated taffeta
Zénith lampshades
12 x max 40W E14 CEI/
E12 UL, JETRO incandescent
H: 110cm (43in)
Diam: 140cm (55in)
Baccarat, France
www.baccarat.fr

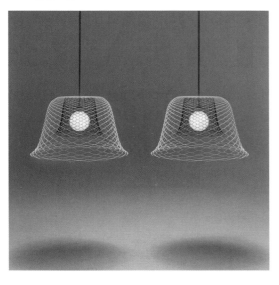

Floor lamp, Yumi
Shigeru Ban
Composite material
coated with carbon fibre,
lacquered metal
18W LED
H: 210cm (82in)
L (arch from base to LED
board): 230cm (90in)
Diam (base): 50cm (19in)
FontanaArte SpA, Italy
www.fontanaarte.it

16-light chandelier, Ellipse
Arik Levy
Frosted crystal, polished
stainless steel wiring, white
pleated taffeta Zenith
lampshades
16 x max 40W E14 CEI/
E12 UL, JETRO incandescent
2 x max 25W G9 halogen
H: 98cm (38in)
Diam: 81 to 117cm
(31 to 46in)
Baccarat, France
www.baccarat.fr

Lamp, Metropolis
Lladró
Porcelain
G9 halogen
H: 35cm (13¾in)
W: 15cm (5⅞in)
D: 15cm (5⅞in)
Lladró, Spain
www.lladro.com

LED tea lights,
Ambiance Accessories
LED Tea Lights
Philips Design
Glass
LED
H: 6.2cm (2½in)
Diam: 6cm (2⅜in)
Philips, The Netherlands
www.philips.com

Lamp, The Clown Lamp
Jaime Hayon
Porcelain
100W E27
H: 60cm (23in)
Diam: 35cm (13¾in)
Lladró, Spain
www.lladro.com

Double-sided lamp, Sfera
Michele De Lucchi
Crystal, brushed nickel-
plated brass
Max 40W G9 halogen
H: 53cm (20in)
Diam: 30cm (11¾in)
Baccarat, France
www.baccarat.fr

Fernando Prado, head designer for São Paulo–based lighting manufacturer Lumini, believes in creating an element of surprise in his work. Rather than opting for expensive technical solutions, he employs simple mechanical elements that invite users to interact with his lamps to alter ambience. This hand-crafted aluminium pendant light, Bossa, was created in response to Prado's recognizing the difficulty of designing lights for use over glass-topped dining tables, which require a light source that does not glare uncomfortably. His solution has a reflector in front of the compact fluorescent bulb that can be moved up and down by gently pulling the lampshade. As the reflector moves, the light effect changes from downlighting to uplighting, adjusting the atmosphere in the room in an ingeniously effortless way.

Pendant lamp, Bossa 26w
Fernando Prado
Aluminium
26W TC-TEL GX24q-3
H: 45cm (17¾in)
Diam: 75cm (29in)
Lumini, Brazil
www.lumini.com.br

Lamp, Lighthouse
Ronan and Erwan Bouroullec
Venini Murano glass,
marble, aluminium
Halogen
H: 70cm (27in)
D: 37cm (14⅝in)
Established & Sons, UK
Venini SpA, Italy
www.establishedandsons.com

**Pendant lamp,
Goccia Prisma**
Stefano Papi
Lentiflex
24W E27 FBG
H: 43cm (16⅞in)
Diam: 30cm (11¾in)
Slamp SpA, Italy
www.slamp.com

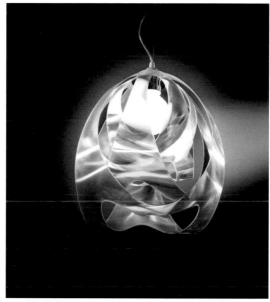

Modular lighting, Halo
Martin Azúa
Methacrylate, lacquer
13W 24V LED strip
Various sizes depending
on layout of modules
Vibia, Spain
www.vibia.es

**Indoor/outdoor wall art/
lighting, Origami**
Ramón Esteve
Polycarbonate, lacquer
17.2W 24V LED strip
Various sizes depending
on layout of modules
Vibia, Spain
www.vibia.es

Pendant lamp, Rhythm
Arik Levy
Polycarbonate, lacquer
3.2W 24V LED strip
Various sizes depending
on layout of modules
Vibia, Spain
www.vibia.es

Nendo

You maintain that the starting point in all your work is isolating and shaping the small, happy moments hidden in everyday life and forming them into a design that's easy to understand subliminally. Can you describe exactly what you mean?

We see our job as being able to give people small '!' moments, where '!' indicates a change in their emotions: joy, anger, grief, pleasure... We want to reconstitute everyday experiences by collecting and reshaping them into objects or spaces that can be easily understood. We would like the people who have encountered Nendo's designs to feel these small moments instinctively. Two recent interior projects illustrate what I mean. The Puma House (below), a showroom in Tokyo for sneaker brand Puma, features timber stairs that wrap around the space's concrete columns to form display shelves. They are not there to be climbed but form a compositional element that gives the space a special character but were inspired by my observation of people going up and down stairs at a train station. I thought, 'That's neat.' Similarly, the Indulgi boutique (opposite page) is full of fake doors that act to break

up sight lines in a long narrow space in Kyoto. They have an organizational function, but we also recognized that walls create an over-strong sense of pressure so we just decided to add fake ones to those already existing to give the interior a surreal atmosphere.

Would you say that growing up in Toronto and studying architecture at Waseda University in Tokyo has had a direct effect on either the Nendo aesthetic or the way you work?

I moved to Japan after spending ten years of my childhood in Canada. It was inspirational for me to see and experience normal, everyday life in Japan. I think I still look on Japan in the same way as a foreigner, and that could be the origin of my way of thinking when I design. Studying architecture gave me the opportunity of learning how to reason in a logical way.

You often mention that Tokyo is an inspiration to you. In which way?

In many ways Japan is still a very traditional society, but there are a few areas, and design is one of them, where a forward-looking impulse is very strong. I tend to get most of my ideas when I'm in Tokyo. After all, it's the place where I've spent the major part of my life so far. One thing I love about the city is the noise. I feel comfortable with it when I'm designing and it helps to inspire me.

Giulio Cappellini has said of your work, 'I see a spirit of lightness. That's the pure spirit of Japan.' How much do you agree with this statement?

There is no denying the fact, even though I'm not really conscious of it.

You are both an architect and a product designer. Does the way you work change depending on the project you are undertaking?

No, not really, as the concept and the story are always the most important elements for me. The way I work and the process I follow in every product and space I design is basically the same.

You have been quoted as saying that you don't consider sustainability when designing a product, but that this consideration should come afterwards. Can you explain what you mean by this?

When I design I don't usually put an emphasis on sustainability or the idea of eco-consciousness, as I believe that those factors should be regarded as conditions set by the client in the same way as the schedule or the budget.

You are incredibly prolific. How do you maintain this level of output? How would you describe the way you work, the process you follow in designing and developing a product, and the relationship you have with your design team?

All my life I've been thinking of design – 24 hours a day and 365 days a year. There are about thirty people in my office

working in product, graphic or interior design [architecture] teams, as well as staff that take care of the everyday running of the office. Once I have the initial thought or concept for a new design, based on my development of a narrative for that project, I share my ideas with my chief directors and then they direct the members of the design team. The process is one of repetition and trial and error.

Do you think there has been an evolution in your work from the first projects to the present day?

Every day and every moment is a new challenge and an evolution for me.

What do you consider to be the designer's role today?

I think that designers fulfil various roles in society today, but we believe that our responsibility is to give people those small '!' moments that I think make our days so interesting and rich. We want the people who have experienced our designs to feel these intuitively. That's Nendo's job.

Ettore Sottsass was quoted in the 1960s as saying, 'For me design is a way of discussing society, politics, eroticism, food and even design. At the end, it is a way of building up a possible figurative utopia or metaphor about life.' Do you agree with this?

Yes, I would agree with that statement. There are so many ways to describe design and Sottsass's notion might be one of them.

Opposite page, bottom:
The Puma House
showroom, Tokyo (2011)

Indulgi boutique, Kyoto
(2011)

Pendant lamp, Bubble
Missoni Home Studio
Curved steel rod, fabric
Mains-connected light source
H: 48cm (18⅞in)
Diam: 60cm (23in)
H: 72cm (28in)
Diam: 90cm (35in)
Missoni Home by T&J Vestor
SpA, Italy
www.missonihome.com

Pendant lamp, Pin-Up
Richard Hutten
Powder-coated stainless steel
E27
H: 20, 25, 30 or 35cm
(7⅞, 9⅞, 11¾ or 13¾in)
Diam: 40, 50, 60 or 70cm
(15¾, 19, 23 or 27in)
Brand Van Egmond B.V.,
The Netherlands
www.brandvanegmond.com

**Adjustable floor lamp,
Position Floor Lamp**
Rooms
Solid maple wood
20W E27 CFL spot
H: 155cm (61in)
W: 140cm (55in)
D: 42cm (16½in)
Moooi, The Netherlands
www.moooi.com

**Table lamp,
Ikea PS Svarva**
Front
Cotton, solid beech, steel
11W E27
H: 70cm (27in)
Diam: 43cm (16⅞in)
Ikea, Sweden
www.ikea.com

**Pendant lamp,
Falling Water**
Tobias Grau
Anodized aluminium
14W LED
Diam: 8cm (3⅛in)
Tobias Grau GmbH, Germany
www.tobias-grau.com

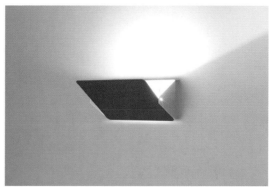

Wall lamp, Applique à volet pivotant (re-edition)
Charlotte Perriand
White metal, epoxy-coated aluminium
48W R7S halogen
H: 16.5cm (6½in)
W: 12.5cm (4⅞in)
D: 7cm (2¾in)
Nemo (Divisione luci di Cassina SpA), Italy
www.nemo.cassina.it

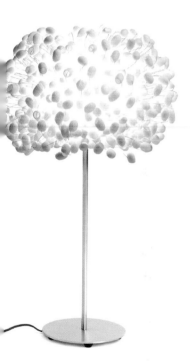

Table lamp, My Chrysalis
Angus Hutcheson
Silk cocoon, stainless steel
E27 low energy
H: 70cm (27in)
W: 32cm (12⅝in)
D: 32cm (12⅝in)
Ango, Thailand
www.angoworld.com

Wall lamp, Mysterio
Diesel
Plastic polymer, glass
G9 halogen
Diam: 30cm (11¾in)
Foscarini srl, Italy
www.foscarini.com
http://diesel.foscarini.com

Pendant lamp, Maki
Nendo
Lacquered aluminium
4W GU10 LED/35W halogen
H: 30cm (11¾in)
Diam: 9cm (3½in)
Foscarini srl, Italy
www.foscarini.com

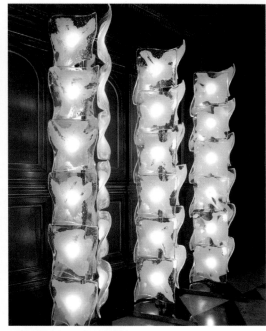

Floor lamp, Veliero
Tadao Ando
Handblown Murano glass
LED
H: 160cm (63in)
W: 47cm (18½in)
Venini, Italy
www.venini.it

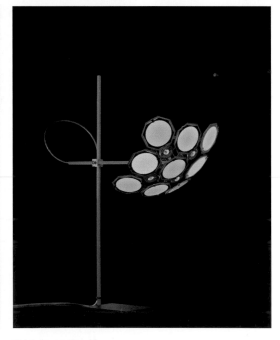

Pendant lamp, Troag
Luca Nichetto
Wood
24W/54W/80W fluorescent
L (small): 125cm (49in)
L (medium): 185cm (72in)
L (large): 215cm (84in)
Foscarini srl, Italy
www.foscarini.com

Table lamp, Double T-Future
Ingo Maurer and Team
Aluminium, steel
OLED, LED
H: 80cm (31in)
W: 30cm (11¾in)
L: 70cm (27in)
Ingo Maurer GmbH, Germany
www.ingo-maurer.com

**System of dimmable
pendant lamps,
Sempé w103s6p**
Inga Sempé
Steel, cast iron, aluminium
1–6W LED (per shade)
H: 24.3cm (9½in)
W: 139.7cm (55in)
L: 147.2cm (58in)
Wästberg, Sweden
www.wastberg.com

Desk lamp, Led Biolite
Makio Hasuike
Extruded aluminium, resin
LED
H (max): 54cm (21in)
W: 16cm (6¼in)
D (max): 50cm (19in)
Yamagiwa, Japan
www.yamagiwa-lighting.com

**Table and floor
lamps, Pipe**
Diesel
Wire frame with fabric cover
Table lamp: 1 x fluorescent
Floor lamps: 2 x E27 halogen
H (table lamp): 52cm (20in)
Diam (table lamp):
50cm (19in)
H (floor lamp, medium):
148cm (58in)
Diam (floor lamp, medium):
73cm (28in)
H (floor lamp, large):
187cm (74in)
Diam (floor lamp, large):
58cm (22in)
Foscarini srl, Italy
www.foscarini.com
diesel.foscarini.com

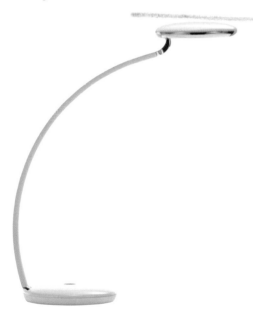

Lamp, Lampalumina
Ronan and Erwan Bouroullec
Alumina ceramic
LED
H: 80cm (31in)
L: 20cm (7⅞in)
Bitossi by Flavia srl, Italy
www.bitossiceramiche.it

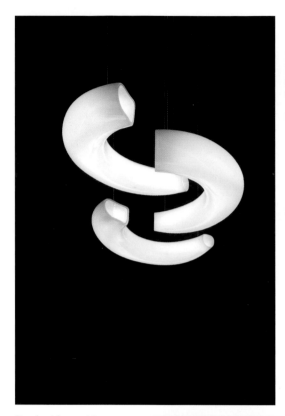

Pendant lamp, Regatta
Thomas Malmberg
Sail cloth
23W 230V E27 low energy
Diam: 50 or 70 cm
(19 or 27in)
Thomas Malmberg Design,
Sweden
www.thomasmalmberg.com

Table lamp, Denq
Toshiyuki Kita
Opaline opaque blown glass,
lacquered metal
Max 150W E27
H: 42cm (16½in)
Diam: 30cm (11¾in)
Oluce srl, Italy
www.oluce.com

Pendant lamp, Moony
Massimiliano Fuksas
Glass
LED strip
H: 7cm (2¾in)
L: 60cm (23in)
D: 36cm (14⅛in)
La Murrina SpA, Italy
www.lamurrina.com

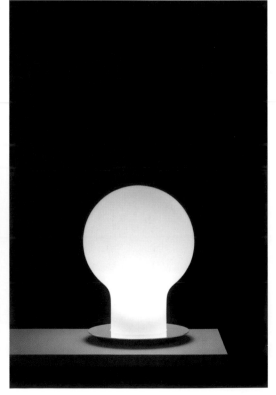

**Indoor/outdoor
lamp/seat, Pill-Low**
Francesco Rota
White polyethylene
with cover in outdoor
washable fabric
Max 25W E27 fluorescent
H: 32cm (12⅝in)
Diam: 57cm (22in)
Oluce srl, Italy
www.oluce.com

Indoor/outdoor wall lamp, Ecran In & Out
Inga Sempé
Polycarbonate
8W LED, warm white
D: 14.5cm (5¾in)
Diam: 18.5cm (7¼in)
Luceplan SpA, Italy
www.luceplan.com

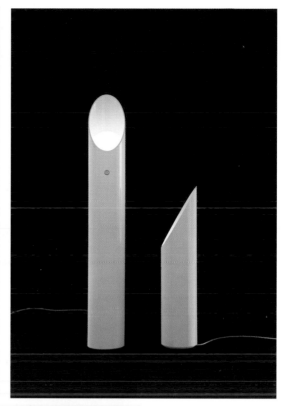

Modular pendant lamp, Honeycomb
Habits Studio
Polycarbonate
3 x 8W LED, warm white
3 x 30W 12V halogen
H (module): 8cm (3⅛in)
Luceplan SpA, Italy
www.luceplan.com

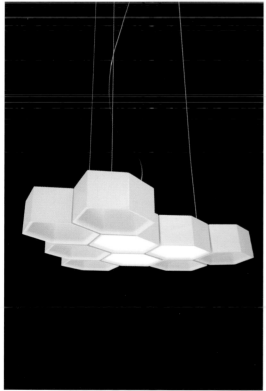

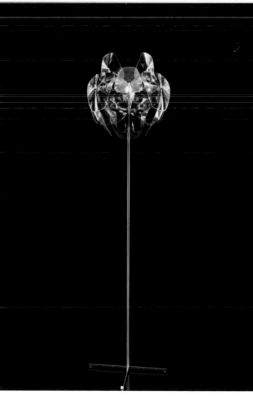

Floor and table lamp, Beth
Carlo Colombo
Aluminium, satined antiglare glass lens, metal
Table lamp: Max 100W E27
Floor lamp: Max 150W E27
H (table lamp): 75cm (29in)
H (floor lamp): 120cm (47in)
Diam: 17cm (6¾in)
Oluce srl, Italy
www.oluce.com

Floor lamp, Hope
Francisco Gomez Paz and Paolo Rizzatto
Polished stainless steel, transparent polycarbonate
105W E27 energy saver/ max 250W halogen
H: 184cm (72in)
Diam: 51cm (20in)
Luceplan SpA, Italy
www.luceplan.com

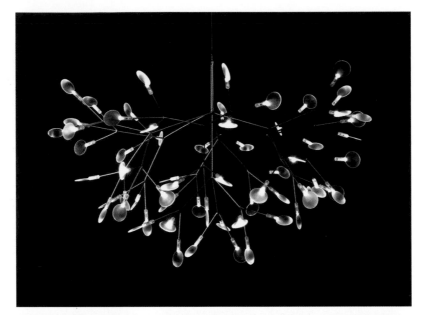

Ceiling lamp, Heracleum
Bertjan Pot
Metal wire, polycarbonate
lenses
LED
H: 65cm (25in)
Diam: 98cm (38in)
Moooi, The Netherlands
www.moooi.com

**Pendant lamp,
Faretto Double**
Nigel Coates
Cristalflex, polycarbonate
2 x 75W E27 HSGST/C/UB
H: 31cm (12¼in)
W: 72cm (28in)
D: 39cm (15⅜in)
Slamp SpA, Italy
www.slamp.com

**Ceiling lamp, LED Net
Circle Soffitto**
Michele De Lucchi and
Alberto Nason
Aluminium, methacrylate
17 x LED (39W total)
Diam: 65cm (25in)
Artemide SpA, Italy
www.artemide.com

Pendant lamp, Gio'
Angeletti Ruzza Design
Aluminium, polycarbonate
LED
H (max): 250cm (98in)
Diam: 48cm (18⅞in)
Nemo (Divisione luci di
Cassina SpA), Italy
www.nemo.cassina.it

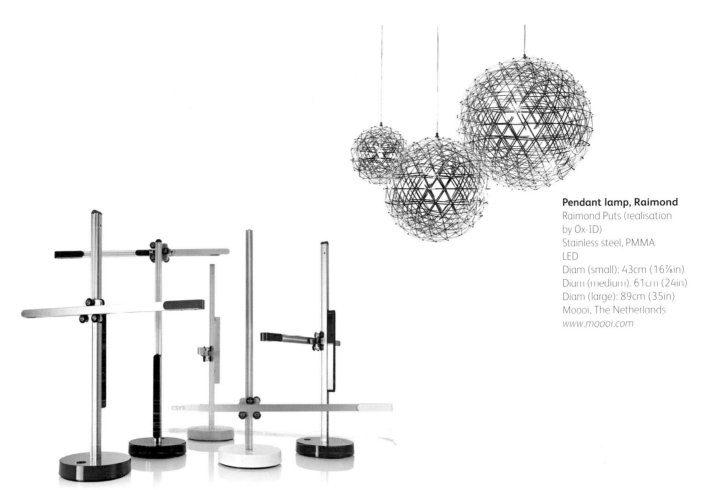

Pendant lamp, Raimond
Raimond Puts (realisation
by Ox-ID)
Stainless steel, PMMA
LED
Diam (small): 43cm (16⅞in)
Diam (medium): 61cm (24in)
Diam (large): 89cm (35in)
Moooi, The Netherlands
www.moooi.com

Jake Dyson grew up in a household where design ruled his father is Sir James Dyson, inventor of the bagless vacuum cleaner and the high-speed hand-dryer, as well as the Dyson Air Multiplier fan and the Dyson Hot fan heater (page 277). At the age of 17, Jake made his first foray into mechanics when he went to work for his father, helping him in the production of prototypes. Jake maintains that this introduction to the mill and lathe educated him on the limits of engineering. After studying industrial design at Central Saint Martins College of Art and Design in London, he founded his eponymous company in 2004 and went on to gain recognition in his own right with the now iconic Motorlight Floor and Wall lights. 'My taste is quite minimalist, which is why lighting is so important to me. If you don't have a lot of things, you need to use light to create the atmosphere in a room. I think lights themselves should be interesting to look at. I hate what I call "morphous" design, where a shape is imposed on something for no reason. The visual should be worked out around the mechanics of an object, rather than trying to cover them up.'

By investigating current developments in thermal-management systems and bringing the heat-pipe technology used in satellites and processor chips to LED lighting, Dyson has created a desk light that marries the latest know-how with sleek aesthetics, while also addressing environmental issues. A copper pipe conducts heat away from the light source, ensuring greater longevity (over 160,000 hours of continual use) and brightness from the high-intensity LEDs, which, at only 8 watts, are five times more energy efficient than a comparable halogen bulb. The CSYS requires no replacement bulbs; in addition, it contains no mercury, making it suitable for landfill disposal. Inspired by construction cranes, the lamp is adjustable on three axes and challenges the status quo of mechanical movement in existing lighting. Dyson concludes, 'We believe that the CSYS will change people's minds about LED lighting.'

LED task light, CSYS
Jake Dyson
Machined aluminium,
copper, polycarbonate
8.8W LED
H: 65.3cm (25in)
W: 52.7cm (20in)
D: 17.7cm (7⅛in)
Jake Dyson Products, UK
www.jakedyson.com

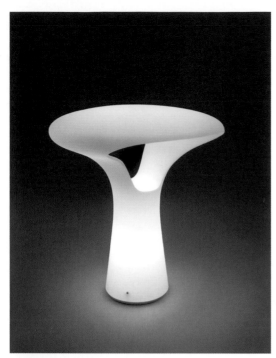

Table lamp, Ferea
Emmanuel Babled
Satin blown glass
100W incandescent
H: 49cm (19¼in)
W: 45cm (17¾in)
Vistosi, Italy
www.vistosi.it

**Suspension fixture
for spot lighting,
Mini Mini Led**
Habits Studio
Aluminium extrusion
5W LED spot
H: 66.4cm (26in)
Diam: 2.5cm (1in)
Luceplan SpA, Italy
www.luceplan.com

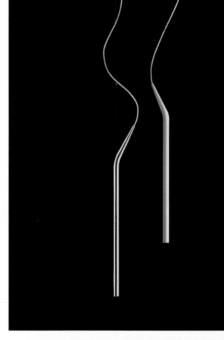

OLED panels, Lumiblade
Philips Lumiblade
Small molecule organic
materials, glass plates
OLED
L (square): 7cm (2¾in)
W (square): 7cm (2¾in)
Diam (circle): 7cm (2¾in)
L (triangle): 8.5cm (3⅜in)
W (triangle): 5cm (2in)
L (rectangle): 13cm (5⅛in)
W (rectangle): 5cm (2in)
Philips Lumiblade, Germany
www.lumiblade.com

**Modular lighting system,
Synapse**
Francisco Gomez Paz
Polycarbonate
3 x 0.4W RGB LED, changing
colour
Diam (module): 34cm (13⅜in)
Luceplan SpA, Italy
www.luceplan.com

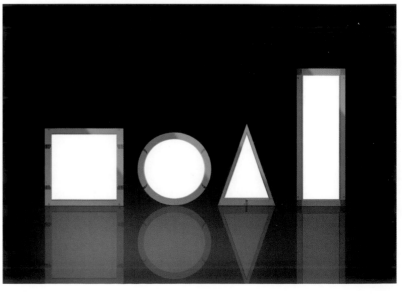

Wall-mounted/pendant lamp, Up & Away
Outofstock
Stainless steel with powder-coated finishing, active glass technology from Quantum Glass™
LEDinGlass
H: 2cm (¾in)
W: 60 or 91cm (23 or 35in)
L: 51 or 80cm (20 or 31in)
Saazs, France
www.saazs.com

Wall/ceiling lamp, Balance
Pio and Tito Toso
Blown glass
2 x 100W incandescent/energy saver
W: 40cm (15¾in)
L: 40cm (15¾in)
D: 17cm (6¾in)
Vistosi, Italy
www.vistosi.it

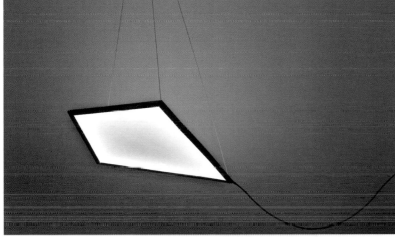

Desk lamp, Otto Watt
Alberto Meda and
Paolo Rizzatto
Aluminium
8W LED, tuneable white
W (base): 18.5cm (7¼in)
D (base): 18.5cm (7¼in)
L (arms): 48.5 + 45.5cm
(19¼ + 18⅛in)
Luceplan SpA, Italy
www.luceplan.com

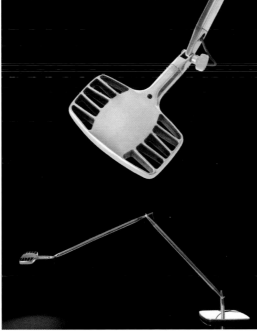

Table lamp, Bot
Gregorio Spini
Blown glass
3 x 100W incandescent/energy saver
H: 35cm or 17cm (13¾ or 6¾in)
Diam: 35cm or 16cm (13¾ or 6¼in)
Vistosi, Italy
www.vistosi.it

**Series of pendant
lamps, Ray**
Claesson Koivisto Rune
Steel with cord fabrics
LED
H (yellow): 8.9cm (3½in)
Diam (yellow): 16.7cm (6¾in)
NgispeN, The Netherlands
www.ngispen.com

**Pendant lamp,
Space Time**
Karim Rashid
Painted polythene
Max 20W E27
H: 42.5cm (16⅞in)
Diam: 55cm (21in)
Zero Lighting, Sweden
www.zero.se

**Pendant lamp,
0.5 KG Lamp**
Diederik Schneemann
Recycled flip-flops
Energy saver
H: 26.5cm (10⅝in)
Diam: 22cm (8⅝in)
Studioschneemann,
The Netherlands
www.studioschneemann.com

In one of the more inspiring examples of reuse in recent years, young Dutch designer Diederik Schneemann worked with the Kenya-based environmental initiative UniquEco to add his range of playful products to the FlipFlop Project. The story has its origins in 1997, when local women on the islands of the Lamu Archipelago, situated off the northeast coast of Kenya, started to collect the flip-flops that contaminated their beaches, turning them into jewellery and toys. In 2005, environmental scientists Julie Church and Tahreni Bwaanali saw the potential of developing a local industry whilst also protecting the area's ecosystem, and the FlipFlop Project emerged.

The Lamu Archipelago lies at the confluence of two major ocean currents and is an important conservation area where protected mangrove stands, sea-grass beds and coral reefs support a wide variety of marine life, including sea turtles. Because of these currents, thousands of flip-flops are deposited on Lamu's shores from the world's beaches, threatening both the turtles' nesting sites and, because of the eyesore they cause, the tourism on which the islands depend. The Project resolves the problem in a sustainable way: it offers

fair living wages to local women to collect the discarded sandals. Once gathered, the flip-flops are sent to Nairobi, where UniquEco's twenty full-time staff sand them back to their original bright colours, melt them down and transform them into a range of craft artefacts and gifts.

To build global awareness, Church and Bwaanali have sought media exposure and commissioned elaborate art pieces. The collaboration with Schneemann is their entrée into the international contemporary design world. His series consists of a range of colourful and idiosyncratic objects, including a tulip vase on wheels, a vase with a drawer in the front and a lamp with a power outlet in the base. At the time of the collection's debut at the 2011 Milan Salone Internazionale del Mobile, the press release read: 'They are discoloured, worn, torn, patched up and eventually tossed away or lost. After a long trip through Asia or Africa they end up in sewers and in the ocean. Then they are washed up on the shores of Eastern Africa. There they are found, collected, and eventually reclaimed. Turned into a collection of sustainable design objects in which the eventful travel tales of worn flip-flops is captured and translated.'

Pendant lamp, Roofer
Benjamin Hubert
Flexible silicon polymer tiles,
steel frame
Various dimensions
3 x CFL
Fabbian, Italy
www.fabbian.com

**Flexible ceiling
lamp, Greta**
Whats What
Textile pleats
Low energy
H: 55cm (21in)
Svenskt Tenn, Sweden
www.svenskttenn.se

Pendant lamp, Carmen
Héctor Serrano
Polished painted metal, steel,
satin methacrylate
3 x 70W halogen energy saver/
3 x 20W E27 fluorescent
H: 33cm (13in)
Diam: 51cm (20in)
FontanaArte SpA, Italy
www.fontanaarte.it

Desk light with integral dock for iPod, iPhone or iPad, D'E-Light
Philippe Starck
Chrome-plated aluminium, extruded aluminium, chrome-plated zamak
LED
H: 31.7cm (12⅝in)
W (top): 21.6cm (8⅝in)
W (bottom): 12cm (4¾in)
Flos, Italy
www.flos.it

Pendant lamp, Grand Trianon
Paula Arntzen
White Tyvek®, steel
Max 60W
H: 71cm (28in)
Diam: 59cm (23in)
Artecnica, USA
www.artecnica.com

Table lamp, Trash Me
Victor Vetterlein
Paper pulp
Max 40W E27/ 7W low energy
H: 52.4cm (20in)
W: 16.5cm (6½in)
L: 25.4cm (9⅞in)
& Tradition, Denmark
www.andtradition.com

Mobile rechargeable lamp, Lantern
Tong Ho
Ceramic, bamboo, plastic
LED
H: 45cm (17¾in)
Diam: 20cm (7⅞in)
Yii, Taiwan
HAN Gallery, Taiwan
www.yiidesign.com
www.han-gallery.com

Pendant lamp, Cristal de Luz (Light Crystal)
TT Leal
Plastic globe, brushed aluminium finish, crochet cotton cover
Diam: 50 or 38cm (19 or 15in)
COOPA-ROCA, Rocinha Craftwork Cooperative, Brazil
www.coopa-roca.org.br

The Coopa-Roca (Rocinha Seamstress and Craftwork Co-operative Ltd) brand presented its first collection, a small range of fashion items, accessories and light shades, at the Salone Internazionale del Mobile in 2011, heralding a new phase in the collective's development. The initiative had originated in the early 1980s to help the women of the Rio de Janeiro's Rocinha favela – possibly the largest in South America – to earn an income and hence contribute to their family budget whilst working from home. It was founded by Maria Teresa Leal, a sociologist and arts educator who turned her attention to the children of Rio's urban slums, setting up free Saturday craft classes. It wasn't long before she recognized the skill of the mothers who attended the sessions and worked alongside their offspring, encouraging them by demonstrating traditional Brazilian handwork techniques such as patchwork, crochet and fuxico (a form of embroidery that uses scrap fabric gathered at the centre to form flowers). A cooperative was formed to organize the women and train them to improve and standardize their work, which at first they sold in local markets. Today the group numbers over one hundred artisans, and over the years has established links and collaborated with international fashion houses, retailers, designers and installation artists, including Cacharel, Paul Smith, Agent Provocateur, Lacoste, C&A, Tord Boontje and Ernesto Neto.

Pendant lamp, Beads (Octo and Penta)
Winnie Lui
Spun stainless steel
20W E27 CFL/ max 100W clear incandescent
H (Octo): 41cm (16⅛in)
Diam (Octo): 77cm (30in)
H (Penta): 48cm (18⅞in)
Diam (Penta): 54cm (21in)
Innermost Ltd, UK
www.innermost.net

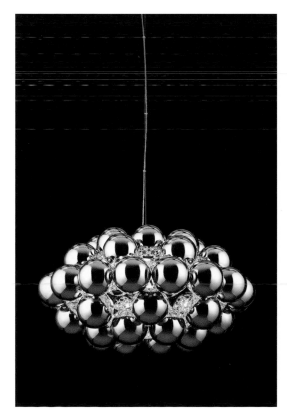

Pendant lamp, Cage
Diesel
Blown glass, lacquered metal
20W E27 CFL/50W E27
energy-saving halogen
H: 76cm (29in)
Diam: 46cm (18⅛in)
Foscarini, Italy
www.foscarini.com

Pendant lamp, Le Soleil
Vicente Garcia Jimenez
Polycarbonate
3 x 60W G9 halogen energy
saver/1 x 75W GU10 halogen
H: 43cm (16⅞in)
Diam: 62cm (24in)
Foscarini, Italy
www.foscarini.com

Pendant lamp, Wonderlamp
Studio Job and
Pieke Bergmans
Bronze fusion, glass bulbs
LED
H: 230cm (90in)
Diam: 50cm (19in)
Dilmos, Italy
www.dilmos.it

Occasional light, Work Lamp
Form Us With Love
Steel, chrome/gold
plating, rubber
Opal oversized halogen
H: 21cm (8¼in)
Diam: 15cm (5⅞in)
Design House Stockholm,
Sweden
www.designhousestockholm.com

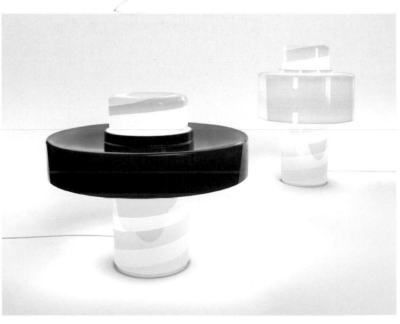

Table lamp, Elix
Emmanuel Babled
Handblown Murano glass
40W G9 halogen
H (large): 43cm (16⅞in)
Diam (large): 30cm (11¾in)
H (small): 30cm (11¾in)
Diam (small): 38cm (15in)
Venini, Italy
www.venini.it

**Desk lamp,
Chipperfield w102**
David Chipperfield
Brass
1–4W LED
H: 42.4cm (16½in)
W: 11cm (4⅜in)
L: 33.7cm (13⅜in)
Wästberg, Sweden
www.wastberg.com

**Pendant lamps, Valentine
and Baby Valentine**
Marcel Wanders
Crystal-clear blown glass
with lacquered shade
Max 105W E27 eco halogen,
type A (Valentine)

H (Valentine):
29.5cm (11¾in)
Diam (Valentine):
35.5cm (14⅛in)
Moooi, The Netherlands
www.moooi.com

Floor lamp, Foglie
Matali Crasset
Injection-moulded opaline
polycarbonate
30W 220V E27 CFL
H: 182cm (72in)
Diam: 68cm (26in)
Pullucco, Italy
www.pullucco.com

**Indoor/outdoor pendant
lamp, Wind**
Jordi Vilardell
Fibreglass, acrylic
40W 230V 2GX13 T5C
fluorescent tube
H: 48cm (18⅞in)
Diam: 60cm (23in)
Vibia, Spain
www.vibia.es

8.

ELECTRONICS

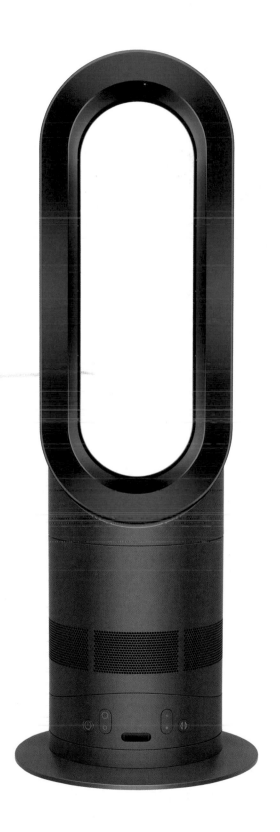

**Bladeless fan heater,
Dyson Hot™ (AM04)**
James Dyson
ABS
H: 57.9cm (22in)
W: 15.2cm (5⅞in)
D: 10cm (3⅞in)
Dyson, UK
www.dyson.co.uk/fans

The motto of Younicos, a Berlin-based renewable-energy company, is 'Let the fossils rest in peace'. The Yill Mobile Energy Storage Unit is the first in a range of environmentally sustainable products designed by Werner Aisslinger to demonstrate how green energy can be integrated into modern buildings. The cordless energy-storage unit takes the form of a wheel about the size of a bass drum, sleek and modern in appearance. It is primarily intended for use in office environments and, through its rechargeable lithium titanium battery, can provide all the energy necessary to power a workstation for two–three days. Yill can supply 300 watts of electricity and store 1 kilowatt hour of energy. The unit is recharged by plugging into a normal socket drawing power from the national grid, or into a charging station that derives energy from renewable sources.

Mobile energy-storage unit, Yill
Werner Aisslinger
Silicon PU, aluminium, ABS
H: 52.6cm (20in), plus handle
that can be extended up to
40cm (15¾in)
W: 28.3cm (11in)
L: 52.6cm (20in)
Younicos, Germany
www.younicos.com

Mobile hard drive, CLS
Sylvain Willenz
Injection-moulded plastics
H: 1.35cm (½in)
W: 7.95cm (3⅛in)
L: 10.98cm (4⅜in)
Freecom, Germany
www.freecom.com

Power station, Power Station Universal USB Solar
Philips Design
Plastic
H: 32.3cm (12⅝in)
W: 13.3cm (5⅛in)
L: 18.5cm (7¼in)
Philips, The Netherlands
www.philips.com

**Wall shelf with integrated
sound system and iPod
dock, Hohrizontal 51**
Bernd Brockhoff
MDF
H: 5.1cm (2in)
W: 100cm (39in)
D: 30cm (11¾in)
Finite Elemente GmbH,
Germany
www.finite-elemente.de

Speakers, Zikmu Parrot
Philippe Starck
ABS and PMMA resins
H: 74cm (29in)
W (bottom): 29cm (11⅜in)
L (bottom): 32cm (12½in)
Parrot, France
www.parrot.com

Universal remote, Peel
fuseproject
Nylon, IR translucent
polycarbonate
H: 9cm (3½in)
Circumference: 23cm (9in)
Peel, USA
www.peel.com

Peel combines a free app for searching TV listings with a fun
and friendly piece of hardware called the Peel Fruit that relays
the signal from your iPhone to your TV (an Android version
was in development at the time of writing). The product
itself has been designed to be displayed and celebrated, and
revolutionizes the aesthetics of TV equipment – available as a
stylized orange, apple or pear, the peripheral keeps its cutting-
edge technology hidden within its slightly angled base. Peel
aims to change the way we watch and discover content on TV.
Rather than surfing the hundreds of channels now available,
with this intuitive and handy product system, users can click
on a movie or programme, search by name, or consult their
viewing habits, which have been learned by the system, thus
'peeling back' the tedious layers of a channel guide.

**Bluetooth audio speaker,
Jambox**
fuseproject
Silicone rubber, steel grate
H: 5.7cm (2¼in)
L:15cm (6in)
D: 3.8cm (1½in)
Jawbone, USA
www.jawbone.com

**Computer speakers,
Sound2 Speakers**
Neil Poulton
ABS
W: 14cm (5½in)
L: 20cm (7⅞in)
LaCie, with technology by
Cabasse, France
www.lacie.fr
www.neilpoulton.com

**Wireless optical computer
mouse with USB receiver,
Oppopet**
Nendo
Plastic, silicone
H: 3.8cm (1½in)
W: 6cm (2⅜in)
D: 8.8cm (3½in)
Elecom, Japan
www.elecom.co.jp/global/

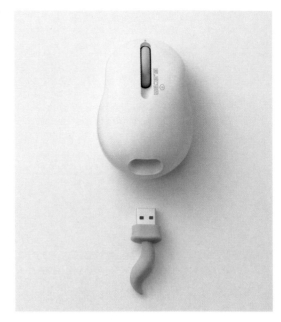

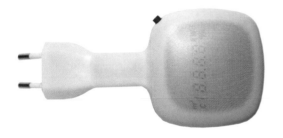

Marcel Wanders designed Wattcher to be the 'ticking heart of
the home'. He says, 'The design is very clean and has urgency
in pointing out your energy consumption. Wattcher is more
than just a product; it is a strategy that stimulates awareness.'
The device plugs into a standard socket and displays electrical
expenditure, encouraging users to reduce their usage. As well
as indicating the total number of units consumed, the display
glows brighter depending on the acceleration of energy use.
A year after its launch, there were over 12,000 Wattcher users,
and market research indicated a reduction in their energy
waste of up to 15 per cent.

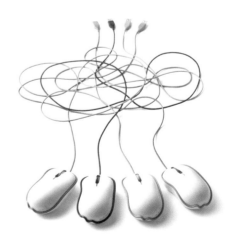

Energy monitor, Wattcher
Marcel Wanders
PE, TPE, electronics
H: 3cm (1⅛in)
W: 7cm (2¾in)
L: 15cm (5⅞in)
Wattcher bv, The Netherlands
www.wattcher.com

Computer mouse, Rinkak
Nendo
Plastic
H: 3.7cm (1½in)
W: 6cm (2⅜in)
D: 10cm (3⅞in)
Elecom, Japan
www.elecom.co.jp/global/

Such is the innovation of Sir James Dyson's designs that 'doing a Dyson' has become synonymous with the reinvention of everyday objects. His convention-defying appliances, such as the cyclonic bagless vacuum cleaner and the water-scraping high-speed Airblade hand dryer, owe their success not only to years of research and development (the Airblade, for example, went through over 5,000 failures and hundreds of prototypes before it was ratified), but also to careful consideration of the problems associated with domestic devices and how their designs can be improved. The Air Multiplier fan, launched in 2010, and the Hot fan heater, which followed a year later, are based on variations of the same patented technology that generates the fast flow of air to cool or warm a room without moving parts.

Neither looks anything like a typical fan or heater (essentially they are large loops sitting on top of sturdy cylinders without a blade or grille in sight), and both resulted from Dyson's disappointment with their predecessors. In the case of the Air Multiplier, he noted that fan design had not altered since the 1880s when they were first invented, explaining, 'Their spinning blades chop up the airflow, causing annoying buffeting. They're hard to clean. And children always want to poke their fingers through the bars. So we've developed a new type of fan that doesn't use blades.' The impetus behind his new heater was similar: 'The thing that I have always remembered about conventional heaters is that you switch them on and you get this terrible smell of burnt dust ... In terms of health and safety, they shouldn't be used at all. And fan heaters are such feeble blowers that they don't heat the air in the room, they only heat you fairly locally.'

The Air Multiplier works by sucking in air at the base and pushing it out at speed through a thin gap in the fan's ring. The expelled air moves over an airfoil-shaped ramp (similar in shape to the wing of an aeroplane), and surrounding air is drawn into this airflow. In all, 405 litres (107 gallons) of air are driven out every second. The Dyson Hot runs on the same principle of air propulsion but, unlike normal heaters, it does not pass over hot electrical coils but over twenty ceramic stones set to heat a room from anywhere from 1 to 37 degrees centigrade (33 to 99 degrees Fahrenheit). The advantages are numerous. There is no longer an acrid smell and, as none of the exposed parts get warm, it is impossible to burn yourself. In addition, the force at which the air is expelled means that heat flows to all corners of a room. It took twenty-two engineers, including experts in thermodynamics and fluid mechanics, more than three years to develop the technology.

Criticism has been levelled at the high price tag on both products. Justifying the initial outlay a consumer will have to make, Dyson responds, 'In hard times people want something that will last, rather than something cheap that they will have to throw away after a short time. We're appealing to somebody who wants to keep the product and have it provide pleasure over the years.'

**Bladeless fan heater,
Dyson Hot™ (AM04)**
James Dyson
ABS
H: 57.9cm (22in)
W: 15.2cm (5⅞in)
D: 10cm (3⅞in)
Dyson, UK
www.dyson.co.uk/fans

**Bladeless desk fan,
Dyson Air Multiplier™
(AM01)**
James Dyson
ABS
H: 49.6cm (19in)
W: 30.5cm (12in)
D: 15.2cm (5⅞in)
Dyson, UK
www.dyson.co.uk/fans

Steve Jobs, the visionary co-founder of Apple who revolutionized personal computing and changed forever the way we experience music, film and mobile communication, died on 5 October 2011, aged 56, after an eight-year battle with pancreatic cancer. If there is anything positive to be taken from his passing, it is the many discussions that have since taken place across the media underlining the role of design in our culture and its value to business. Famously quoted as saying that Apple sat 'at the intersection of the liberal arts and technology', Jobs's lasting legacy is to have made great design mainstream and affordable. In an interview with *Fortune* magazine in 2000, he was insistent on the importance of design: 'In most people's vocabularies, design means veneer. It's interior decorating. It's the fabric of the curtains and the sofa. But to me, nothing can be further from the meaning of design. Design is the fundamental soul of a man-made creation that ends up expressing itself in successive outer layers of the product.'

Apple Computers was founded in 1976 when the 21-year-old Jobs and his teenage friend Steve Wozniak recognized that computing was becoming personal. No longer relevant only in solving scientific and business problems, it could also be used for social and economic exchange. Apple I was launched from Jobs's parent's garage, followed quickly by the more successful and sophisticated Apple II, a lifestyle product with a sleek plastic chassis designed for use in the home environment. At a time when computers were identified by serial numbers, choosing a fruit as a name announced the unconventionality of the brand. The insides of the Apple II were the result of the self-taught engineering genius of Wozniak, but its styling and ease of use were the first signs of Jobs's instincts for the future. By 1980, when the company became public, the partners were millionaires. The following year, Wozniak was involved in a serious accident and it was Jobs who went on to shape Apple's destiny through the pioneering but ultimately unsuccessful Lisa computer and the Macintosh, the first commercially successful small computer with a graphical user interface and mouse.

Jobs was an inspiring but autocratic and high-maintenance co-worker, likened by his CEO John Sculley to Leon Trotsky and attracting complaints from his employees about his 'management by walking about frightening people' methods. Coupled with sluggish sales, this attitude resulted in Jobs being stripped of all power by his board in 1985, and his subsequent resignation. It was twelve years before he returned. During the interregnum he set up NeXT Computer and bought what became Pixar from George Lucas. Although NeXT failed as a business enterprise and Pixar seemed set to go in the same direction, Jobs still looked on this period of his career as one of his most creative. His ability to define the technological future saw him contracted by Disney to produce a number of computer-animated feature films including *Toy Story*, which went on to be the top-grossing movie of 1995 and was nominated for three Academy Awards.

This success helped him persuade Apple to buy NeXT and re-employ him, and in 1997 he rejoined a company that had been struggling without his expertise. With an advertisement campaign entitled 'Think Different' and his belief that survival meant innovation, Jobs oversaw the creation of one ground-breaking digital device after another, starting with the striking, colourful, all-in-one iMac designed by Jonathan Ive, followed by the iPod, iTunes digital-music software, the iPhone and the iPad. Each transformed not only product categories, such as music players and mobile phones, but also entire industries, from music to mobile communications. In 2011, Apple's market capitalization passed that of ExxonMobil, making it the world's most valuable company.

At the time of Jobs's untimely death, the English actor, director, author, TV presenter, self-confessed gadget freak and lover of all things Mac Stephen Fry wrote on his website:

> What was Steve Jobs? He wasn't a brilliant and innovative electronics engineer like his partner and fellow Apple founder Steve Wozniak. Nor was he an acute businessman and aggressively talented opportunist like Bill Gates. He wasn't a designer of original genius like Jonathan Ive, whose achievements were so integral to Apple's success from 1997 onwards. He wasn't a software engineer, a mathematician, a nerd, a financier, an artist or an inventor … The quality I especially revered in him was his refusal to show contempt for his customers by fobbing them off with something that was 'good enough'. Whether it was the packaging, the cabling, the use of screen space, the human interfaces, the colours, the flow, the feel, the graphical or textural features, everything had to be improved upon and improved upon until it was, to use the favourite phrase of the early Mac pioneers, 'insanely great'.[1]

Fry's tribute was only one of many that flooded in from legions of Apple users, media companies and leaders of the technology industry, including the founders of social-networking sites Twitter and Facebook. Even the President of the United States, Barack Obama, paid his respects: 'Steve was among the greatest of American inventors – brave enough to think differently, bold enough to believe he could change the world and talented enough to do it … The world has lost a visionary. And there may be no greater tribute to Steve's success than the fact that much of the world learned of his passing on a device he invented.'[2] However, it is a simple and poignant message from Twitter user Matt Galligan that best sums up the unique role Jobs played in redefining the digital age: 'R.I.P. Steve Jobs. You touched an ugly world of technology and made it beautiful.'[3]

1. Stephen Fry, 'Steve Jobs', http://www.stephenfry.com/2011/10/06/steve-jobs/.
2. The White House Blog, 'President Obama on the Passing of Steve Jobs: "He Changed the Way Each of Us Sees the World"', http://www.whitehouse.gov/blog/2011/10/05/president-obama-passing-steve-jobs-he-changed-way-each-us-sees-world.
3. Matt Galligan, Twitter feed (@mg), October 5, 2001, https://twitter.com/mg/status/121733036600598528.

Laptop computer, MacBook Air
Apple
Aluminium
W: (13in)
Apple, USA
www.apple.com

In 2011, major electronic companies tried to take on the Apple iPad, as evidenced by the number of competitive tablets on offer during that year's Consumer Electronics Show in Las Vegas. Apple started selling the original iPad in April 2010, and introduced the updated iPad 2 twelve months later. The device is already Apple's biggest source of revenue after the iPhone, with 9.25 million units sold in the quarter that ended 25 June 2011 alone. Samsung's Galaxy Tab 10.1 has fallen foul of Apple's lawyers for having allegedly infringed technology patents, resulting in temporary injunctions on its sale, while the other main challengers, the Motorola Xoom and the Blackberry Playbook, are either priced higher than the iPad or come with carrier contracts, or both. Furthermore, none of the competitors has the combination of content and cachet that Apple does, nor do they have the variety of music, video and apps of the iTunes Store. Android tablets are set to stay but need to develop before they can seriously challenge Apple's 80 per cent share of the market.

Tablet computer, iPad2
Apple
Aluminium, glass, plastics
W: 24.6cm (9⅝in)
D: 0.9cm (⅜in)
Apple, USA
www.apple.com

Interchangeable-lens digital camera, NEX-5
Noriaki Takagi
Die-cast magnesium, aluminium
H: 5.88cm (2⅜in)
W: 11.08cm (4⅜in)
D: 3.82cm (1½in)
Sony Corporation, Japan
www.sony.co.jp

Interchangeable-lens digital camera, K-01
Pentax and Marc Newson
Machined aluminium, natural rubber, aluminium alloy
H: 7.9cm (3⅛in)
W: 12.1cm (4¾in)
D: 5.9cm (2⅜in)
Pentax, Japan
www.pentax.com

Digital still camera, DSC-TX55
Kenzo Nakajima, Noriaki Takagi, Mitsuo Okumura, Masahiro Takahashi, Manabu Fujiki, Chiya Watanabe, Yui Yamaoka
Aluminium
H: 5.44cm (2⅛in)
W: 9.29cm (3⅝in)
D: 1.32cm (½in)
Sony Corporation, Japan
www.sony.co.jp

Light-field camera, Lytro Light Field Camera
Lytro
Anodized aluminium, silicone rubber
H: 4.1cm (1⅝in)
W: 4.1cm (1⅝in)
L: 11.2cm (4⅜in)
Lytro, USA
www.lytro.com

The Lytro completely redefines what we expect from a camera. 'Camera 1.0 was film. Camera 2.0 was digital; 3.0 is a light-field camera that opens all these new possibilities for your picture taking,' says Ren Ng, who worked on the technology of this innovative device at Stanford University before founding Lytro, originally called Refocus Imaging, in 2006. A two-tone elongated box with an LCD touchscreen display at one end and a lens at the other, the Lytro not only looks completely different to conventional cameras but it also handles focus differently as well. In light-field photography, instead of a lens focusing a subject so that it is sharp on the image sensor, the light from all directions falls on each part of the sensor and the camera records and maps the information three-dimensionally. Once the picture is stored, the image can be manipulated on the 3.7 centimetre (1½ inch) LCD display or on a computer, allowing users to choose what they want to bring into definition. Because the camera captures depth information, the photograph can be viewed in three dimensions on a 3DTV. Ng says, 'It's got an instant shutter. You press the button ... bang! It takes the picture right away. We have that unique feature: shoot first, focus later. The camera doesn't have to physically focus while you take the shot.'

The Sony Bloggie MHS-FS3 offers a feature that only a handful of other pocket camcorders share: it has two lenses on the back, so you can record 3D video and capture 3D stills simultaneously. Swapping between 3D and 2D is quick and easy, although it cannot be done while filming. The 3D footage can be viewed on the camera itself. The camcorder has a USB dongle on the side that allows it to be connected directly to a computer without a cable.

**3D mobile HD camera,
Bloggie MHS-FS3**
Kenzo Nakajima
Aluminium, plastic (ABS)
H: 10.8cm (4⅜in)
W: 5.5cm (2⅛in)
D: 1.73cm (¾in)
Sony Corporation, Japan
www.sony.co.jp

Digital camera, X-Pro1
Jun Sato (design manager)
Die-cast aluminium
H: 8.18cm (3¼in)
W: 13.95cm (5½in)
D: 4.25cm (1⅝in)
Fujifilm, Japan
www.fujifilm.com

The Samsung MultiView MV800 is a response to customer demands for maximum flexibility and ease of use in a camera. The compact, ultra-slender body boasts a 7.6-centimetre-wide (3-inch-wide) flip-out touchscreen, ensuring that even the most challenging shot can be achieved, whether the user is behind or in front of the lens.

**Digital camera, MV800
16.1 Megapixel MultiView
Compact Digital Camera**
Samsung Electronics
Black magnesium,
aluminium, glass
H: 5.1cm (2in)
W: 9.2cm (3⅝in)
D: 1.8cm (¾in)
Samsung Electronics, Korea
www.samsung.com

The LX 9500 LED TV was the first 3D HDTV released by LG Electronics and, at the time of going to print, boasted the highest specifications amongst all brands of LED TV. At 22.3 millimetres (⅞in) in depth, it is ultra-slim and looks elegant whether switched on or off. The 3D effect is powered by Active Shutter spectacles that alternate which eye is able to see the picture at any given moment. They last up to 40 hours between charges.

LED 3D TV, LX9500
LG Electronics
Metal
W: 140cm (55in)
D: 2.2cm (⅞in)
LG Electronics, Inc., Korea
www.lg.com

Full-HD LCD TV with E-LED backlight, Loewe Individual 40 Compose 3D
Loewe
Chrome
H: 118.8cm (47in)
W: 113.3cm (45in)
D: 6cm (2⅜in)
Loewe AG, Germany
www.loewe-int.de

LCD TV, Cinema 21:9 LCD TV
Philips Design
Metal
H: 58cm (22in)
W: 124.2cm (49in)
Philips, The Netherlands
www.philips.com

HD TV, Reference 52
Loewe
Aluminium
H: 120.1cm (47in)
W: 129.5cm (51in)
D: 6cm (2⅜in)
Loewe AG, Germany
www.loewe-int.de

3D 3-chip full-HD video projector for home theatre, LUMIS 3D-S
Giorgio Revoldini
Polycarbonate, stainless steel, die-cast aluminium
H: 21cm (8¼in)
W: 45.8cm (18⅛in)
D: 45.5cm (18⅛in)
SIM2 Multimedia SpA, Italy
www.sim2.com

LED TV, LED 8000 Series Smart TV
Samsung Electronics America
Ultra-clear panel, metal frame, LED
H (with TV stand): 79cm (31in)
W (with TV stand): 123cm (48½in)
D (with TV stand): 24cm (9½in)
Samsung Electronics, Korea
www.samsung.com

By completely rethinking every aspect of manufacture, assembly, use and recycling, Philips has created the most environmentally conscious high-performance TV to date. The winner of a prestigious iF Award in 2011, the Econova is a landmark in ecological design: extremely light, making maximum use of recycled aluminium and employing the absolute minimum of plastic. The remote control has an aluminium body with a solar-charging panel, which means that the batteries will never need to be replaced.

LED TV, Econova
Philips Design
Recycled aluminium
H: 65.3cm (25in)
W: 108.1cm (43in)
Philips, The Netherlands
www.philips.com

Smartphone, Lumia 800
Anton Fahlgren
Polycarbonate, hardened
glass, metal
H: 11.65cm (4¾in)
W: 6.12cm (2⅜in)
D: 1.21cm (½in)
Nokia, Finland
www.nokia.com

Over recent years, the consumer preference for Nokia –
one-time leader in the mobile-phone market – has declined
worldwide, with only one in five people in the UK now opting
for the brand. Nokia CEO Stephen Elop has himself likened
the stricken company to a burning oil rig, ignited by its lack
of innovation amidst the competitive smartphone industry.
All this is set to change with the Lumia 800. Launched in
November 2011, this sturdy yet elegant handset, made from
a single piece of polycarbonate, was immediately acclaimed.
The slightly convex screen dominates the design, and its
crisp and legible display works differently from those of its
competitors, with tiles that show live information about
e-mails received and a daily diary. Flicking the screen to the
left brings the user deeper into the menu with easy and
intuitive controls. Rather than use the Android operating
system, Nokia has opted to collaborate with Microsoft and has
provided a wealth of apps, which means that the Lumia 800
offers a real alternative to Apple's and Google's smartphones.

Mobile phone, X-Ray
Tokujin Yoshioka
Reinforced polycarbonate
H: 11cm (4⅜in)
W: 4.9cm (2in)
D: 1.57cm (⅝in)
KDDI Corporation/
Fujitsu Toshiba Mobile
Communications Limited,
Japan
www.iida.jp

Cordless phone, DP01
Jasper Morrison
ABS
H: 15.5cm (6⅛in)
W: 4.8cm (1⅞in)
D: 2cm (¾in)
Punkt, Switzerland
www.punktgroup.com

Smartphone, Galaxy S II
Samsung Telecommunications
America
Plastic, metal
W: 6.6cm (2⅝in)
L: 12.6cm (4⅞in)
D: 0.9cm (⅜in)
Samsung Telecommunications,
Korea
www.samsung.com

Smartphone, Nexus S
Samsung Telecommunications
America
Plastic, metal
W: 6.3cm (2½n)
L: 12 cm (5in)
D:1cm (⅜in)
Samsung Telecommunications,
Korea
www.samsung.com

**Mobile phone, Æ+Y
Mobile Phone**
Yves Béhar
Stainless steel
H: 11.4cm (4½in)
W: 4.98cm (2in)
Æsir, Denmark
www.aesir-copenhagen.com

**Smartphone,
Xperia™ arc S**
Sony Ericsson
Plastic
W: 6.3cm (2½in)
L: 12.5cm (4⅞in)
D: 0.87cm (⅜in)
Sony Ericsson, Japan
www.sonyericsson.com

**Smartphone,
HTC EVO 3D**
HTC
Plastic, glass
W: 6.54cm (2½in)
L: 12.61cm (4⅞in)
D: 1.13cm (⅜in)
HTC, Taiwan
www.htc.com

The Philips SoundBar Home Theater with Ambisound addresses the problem of how to achieve surround sound without the clutter of multiple speakers and cables. The device, which is designed to sit below the TV screen, is slim in both height and depth, elegant and gently curved to optimize the virtual surround sound from the angled Ambisound speakers. The front display provides a minimum of information so as not to distract from what is being viewed above.

Sound system, SoundBar Home Theater with Ambisound
Philips Design
Metal
H: 15.7cm (6¼in)
W: 95.5cm (37in)
D: 9cm (3½in)
Philips, The Netherlands
www.philips.com

Tablet computer, BlackBerry PlayBook
BlackBerry
Glass, rubbery plastic
H: 13cm (5⅛in)
W: 19.3cm (7⅝in)
D: 1cm (⅜in)
BlackBerry, Canada
www.blackberry.com

Laptop computer, VAIO C series
Soichi Tanaka
Acrylic
H: 2.79cm (1⅛in)
W: 34.1cm (13⅜in)
D: 23.52cm (9½in)
Sony Corporation, Japan
www.sony.co.jp

The Dell Inspiron Duo's display is held by two joints, one on each side of the bezel. When pressure is applied to the screen, it flips backwards and turns a full 180 degrees, snapping into position the other way round. When the lid is shut, the laptop is transformed into a tablet.

Convertible laptop computer, Inspiron Duo
Dell
Plastic
W (screen): 26cm (10in)
Dell, USA
www.dell.com

The VAIO F series does not just play back precreated 3D content but also transforms 2D video into 3D. The transmitters that connect to the active-shutter 3D glasses are embedded in the lid, making the laptop itself heavy. However, the primary feature of the device is the ability to watch any movie or video footage in the round; portability is not its chief selling point.

**Laptop computer,
VAIO F series**
Yuki Kubota
Plastic resin (PC + ABS)
H: 3.31cm (1¼in)
W: 39.85cm (15¾in)
D: 27.15cm (10⅝in)
Sony Corporation, Japan
www.sony.co.jp

Laptop computer, Series 9
Samsung
Duralumin
W: 33cm (13in)
D: 23cm (9in)
Samsung, Korea
www.samsung.com

**Laptop computer,
Mini 210-3002sa**
HP
Plastic, glass
H (closed): 3.2cm (1¼in)
W: 26.8cm (10⅝in)
D: 19.1cm (7½in)
Hewlett-Packard Company,
USA
www.hp.com

**In-ear headphones,
Miles Davis Tribute**
Monster, Inc.
Metal, plastic, rubber
Monster, Inc., USA
www.monstercable.com

'We have brought magic to the simple everyday gesture of switching a light on and off,' says Alberto Vuan, business entrepreneur and founder of Think Simple, whose brainchild Vitrum sets new standards in home-automation products. He continues, 'The traditional light switch has remained unchanged for the last one hundred years. With Vitrum, we have radically improved on this, using innovative materials to create an intelligent switch with eye-catching styling.' The product was designed in collaboration with Italian industrial designer and architect Marco Piva, whose focus on research and development in technologies, forms and materials has resulted in a range of internationally recognized buildings and objects that combine clean, elegant lines with formal elegance. A simple rotary movement on Vitrum's large, circular, touch-sensitive control area is enough to alter the level of lighting in a room or to control the temperature inside the home. In addition, integrated wireless technology enables Vitrum to interface with remote handsets, tablet computers, laptops and smartphones. The design combines an electronic section with a glass decor front panel that can easily be customized and is simple and intuitive to use. The product uses completely recyclable materials and is energy efficient. Vitrum switches lights on at 65 per cent power; only when a second touch is applied does it increase to 100 per cent.

Switch, Vitrum Home Control
Marco Piva
Glass, LED
H: 9.5cm (3¾in)
W: 9.5cm (3¾in)
D: 0.8cm (⅜in)
Think Simple SpA, Italy
www.vitrum.com

The GS-TD1 is the first camcorder on the consumer market that offers 3D video recording in full high definition. Using two camera lenses and two imaging sensors – one for each lens – it captures 3D images in the same way that human eyes work.

3D full-HD camcorder, GS-TD1
Akihiko Miyamori (senior manager), Shuji Tanifuji (senior designer)
Polycarbonate resin, magnesium and magnesium alloy die-castings
H: 6.4cm (2½in)
W: 10.2cm (3⅞in)
L: 18.6cm (7¼in)
JVC, Japan
www.jvc.net

The DEV-5K (pictured here) and DEV-3 digital binoculars double as high-definition 3D video cameras. Unlike traditional binoculars, each eyepiece features an independent electronic viewfinder offering clear stereoscopic images. In recording mode they can capture exactly what is seen through the viewfinders either in 2D format or as 3D footage for playback on compatible TVs.

Digital recording binoculars, DEV-5K
Naofumi Yoneda
Plastic resin (ABS), plastic elastomer, rubber
H: 8.8cm (3½in)
W: 15.5cm (6⅛in)
D: 21.9cm (8⅝in)
Sony Corporation, Japan
www.sony.co.jp

**Digital audio system,
BeoSound 5 Encore**
Anders Hermansen
Anodized aluminium,
pressure die-cast aluminium,
coated glass
H: 19cm (7½in)
W: 31cm (12¼in)
D: 7cm (2¾in)
Bang & Olufsen, Denmark
www.bang-olufsen.com

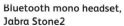

**Professional A3+ photo
printer, PIXMA Pro 1**
Canon
Metal chassis with
plastic panels
H: 23.9cm (9½in)
W: 69.5cm (27in)
D: 46.2cm (18⅛in)
Canon, Japan
www.canon.com

**Bluetooth mono headset,
Jabra Stone2**
Johan Birger
Polycarbonate/ABS,
polycarbonate, thermoplastic
elastomer
H: 5.8cm (2¼in)
W: 5cm (2in)
D: 2.5cm (1in)
Jabra, Denmark
www.jabra.com

**Bluetooth mono headset,
Nokia J**
Jose M. Perez
Stainless steel, moulded
plastic, silicon rubber
W: 1.3cm (½in)
L: 4.8cm (1⅞in)
D: 0.6cm (¼in)
Nokia, Finland
www.nokia.com

9.

MISCELLANEOUS

Watering can, Diva
Eero Aarnio
Thermoplastic resin
H: 31cm (12¼in)
W: 28cm (11in)
D: 10.8cm (4⅜in)
Alessi SpA, Italy
www.alessi.com

Sunshade, Ecran
Xavier Lust
Aluminium, marine fabric
H (base): 170–200cm
(66–78in)
W (shade): 122cm (48in)
L (shade): 152cm (60in)
Borella Design, Italy
www.borelladesign.com

Bicycle, Bamboo
Ross Lovegrove
Aluminium, bamboo
Diam (tyres): 66cm (26in)
Biomega Philosophy APS,
Denmark
www.biomega.dk

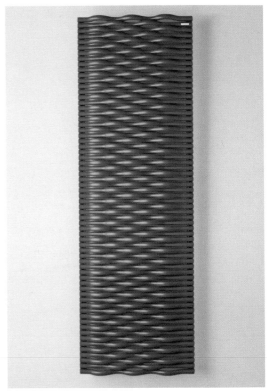

Radiator, Trame
Stefano Giovannoni
Steel
W: 51.5cm (20in)
Tubes radiatori, Italy
www.tubesradiatori.com

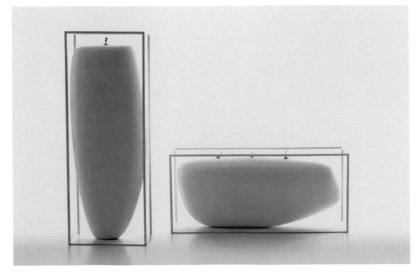

**Outdoor fire feature,
Overscale Flames**
Jean-Marie Massaud
Ceramic
H (tall version): 100cm (39in)
W (tall version): 36cm (14⅛in)
D (tall version): 19cm (7½in)
H (short version): 40cm (15¾in)
W (short version): 88cm (34in)
D (short version): 23cm (9in)
B&B Italia SpA, Italy
www.bebitalia.com

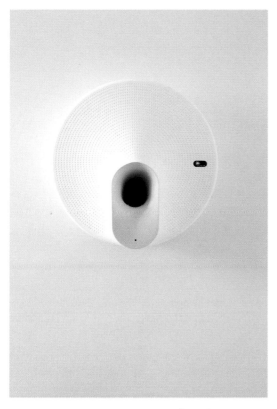

Air purifier, Plain AIR
Patrick Norguet
Plastic
D: 20cm (7⅞in)
Diam: 46cm (18⅛in)
TLV, France
www.tlv.fr

Screen, Paper Screen
Studio Job
Wood, paper, cardboard
H: 180cm (70in)
L (max): 175cm (68in)
Moooi, The Netherlands
www.moooi.com

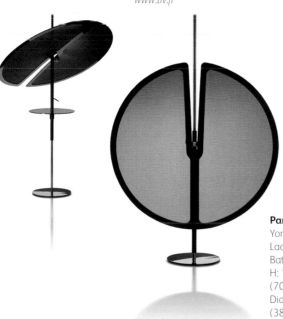

Parasol, Nenufar
Yonoh
Lacquered aluminium,
Batyline fabrics
H: 180 or 220cm
(70 or 86in)
Diam: 98, 148 or 178cm
(38, 58 or 70in)
Samoa, Spain
www.samoadesign.com

Mirror, Dawn/Dusk
Minale Maeda
Concrete, dichroic glass
H: 102cm (40in)
W: 77cm (30in)
D: 12cm (4¾in)
Droog, The Netherlands
www.droog.com

Javier Mariscal

You are the modern-day Renaissance man working on everything from identities, graphics and illustration to product, interior and exhibition design, and sculpture; and now with *Chico & Rita* (opposite page) you also have an Oscar-nominated animated feature-length film to your name. How do you account for your multidisciplinarianism?

It comes naturally. I can't remember having worked any other way. I was always interested in investigating new languages and new media. A few months ago I was given an iPad, and I haven't stopped drawing with my finger. It is now my notebook.

You studied philosophy and then graphic design at university and see yourself as an image-maker for different media and disciplines, rather than a designer or architect as such. Do you think this background and attitude allows your work to be spontaneous and emotional in a way that maybe it would not had you received a more formal training?

I identify a lot with emotion, freshness and spontaneity. I get very passionate when I work, and I hope to transmit this feeling to others. On the other hand, today, finally, almost all projects include different disciplines from their inception. It's not unusual. It's the norm.

Cobi, mascot of the 1992
Barcelona Olympic Games

The 2009 retrospective of your work at the London Design Museum was entitled 'Drawing Life'. How important is draughtsmanship to you?

Drawings, sketches and notes are the basic tools I use to construct my language. They are my alphabet and my syntax. It's a lot easier for me to express myself with drawings than it is with words. It's much more than a working method; it's my way of understanding the world and explaining it to others.

What was the intent of the exhibition and how much were you involved in the concept?

I believe that an exhibition has to provide the keys that best explain your work, as well as being a way for you to review it, to see it from another perspective and to question it. I get involved body and soul in all my exhibitions. I enjoy it and suffer from it at the same time. But I always need the support of the members of my team, who bring things that I alone would be unable to provide. They bring order, synthesis, the development of concepts and, above all, a different angle from my own that always surprises me.

There is a lot of humour in your work, some of which has an almost childlike quality. What attracts you to such playfulness?

I think that to survive in this world humour, joy and irony are indispensable. We're lost if we don't know how to laugh at ourselves and to learn to enjoy simple things.

Cobi (the 1992 Barcelona Olympics mascot; opposite page) was the most profitable mascot for the International Olympic Committee in the history of the games and is still popular today. What do you think accounts for his success?

We devised a symbol capable of capitalizing on all the energy and enthusiasm that the Olympics created for Barcelona. Cobi was also the host character that represented a new, happy Barcelona to the world, a democratic and creative city that within a few years became one of the references for modernity in Europe. The success consisted of associating these values with the character and then allowing it to have a life of its own.

Can you briefly describe what you consider to be the pivotal projects of your studio?

It would be very hard for me to be objective in my selection. However, when it comes to projects created by friends, it's very clear to see where they went wrong, or which piece is the best work they've done. The relationship I have with my projects is very personal and intimate. They mix with my life, which is why it's hard for me to answer this question. There are pieces, of course, that have meant a lot to me and to the studio, but there have also been people with whom I've collaborated who have been very important, encounters that changed my life, or times of crisis in which everything was turned upside down.

Chico & Rita, Fernando Trueba and Javier Mariscal (2010)

How would you describe the way you work within your studio?

I think that during the twenty years of the life of the studio I've been able to transmit a language and way of doing things to the team that we've together converted into a multidisciplinary methodology. We created a very particular dynamic that makes us evolve, and allows us to take on a variety of projects with a lot of freedom, but in a highly efficient way too.

Most designers and manufacturers today believe emotionally and intellectually in sustainability. What are your thoughts?

To be morally involved in the survival of our planet is so obvious that it should not be a demand on one product, one designer or one political party. In the twenty-first century, after all the atrocities that have taken place, the consensus should be universal.

In the 1960s Ettore Sottsass was quoted as saying, 'For me design is a way of discussing society, politics, eroticism, food and even design. At the end, it is a way of building up a possible figurative utopia or metaphor about life.' How much do you agree with this?

Like Ettore Sottsass, anyone dedicating him- or herself to creative work should be self-questioning. Not only designers.

Mirror, Aviator mirror
Nigel Coates
Mirror, wood, laser-cut
polished steel
H: 75cm (29in)
L: 105cm (41in)
D: 6cm (2⅜in)
Poltronova, Italy
Cristina Grajales Gallery,
New York, USA
www.poltronova.com
www.cristinagrajalesinc.com

Wall clock, Sundial
Front
Painted metal
Diam: 55cm (21in)
Porro, Italy
www.porro.com

**Crank-powered radio,
LA81H Safe Radio**
Pierre Garner and
Elise Berthier
Bamboo, PLA
H: 9.5cm (3¾in)
W: 4.6cm (1¾in)
L: 14cm (5½in)
Lexon, France
www.lexon-design.com

Divider, Zen Screen
Ludovica and Roberto Palomba
Canadian solid-wood red cedar
H: 180cm (70in)
W: 6cm (2⅜in)
L: 270cm (106in)
Exteta, Italy
www.exteta.it

**Swivelling luminous
double-sided mirror,
Perseus**
Xavier Lust
Stainless steel, Planilum
active glass technology
from Quantum Glass™
H: 189cm (74in)
W: 84cm (33in)
Saazs, France
www.saazs.com

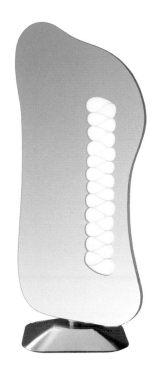

Perseus, On/Off and Lightstamp were three of the objects on
show in 'Material Matters', an exhibition staged during the
2011 Milan Salone Internazionale del Mobile to showcase the
innovative properties of interactive glass, which can be used
as a source of light and heat and produce alternately opaque
and transparent surfaces. Quantum Glass has patented six
technologies — Planilum, Electrochrome, Thermovit Elegance,
E-Glas, LEDinGlass and Priva-Lite — of which Planilum was
the first. A collaboration between Saazs (a French laboratory
for the design and dissemination of pioneering furniture
and concepts founded by Tomas Erel in 2007) and the
R&D department of the Saint-Gobain Group, Planilum is
the first ever light-emitting glass panel and was six years
in development. Though only 20 millimetres (¾in) thick, it
is a complex four-layered glass containing a rare gas and
serigraphed phosphors. It is environmentally certified and,
with a power consumption of only 100 watts, has exceptional
durability and a lifetime equating to twenty years' normal
usage. The light does not radiate from a distinct light source
but is distributed over the entire surface of the material on
both sides, creating a soft, emotional and nondazzling effect.
With a temperature close to that of the human body, it can be
safely touched and no filter or protection is required. Planilum
was so successful when it was first launched in Milan in 2008
that Erel was encouraged to carry out a broader study, which
three years later resulted in 'Material Matters'.

Tomas Erel and Xavier Lust have both incorporated Planilum
into their designs, Erel in his lacquered composite screen
Timestamp and Xavier Lust in his luminous, softly curved
Perseus mirror. Daniel Rybakken, long fascinated by the
atmospheric effects of colour and light, used Priva-Lite in
his On/Off, a hybrid object that, when approached, reveals a
tri-fold mirror floating at the heart of a coloured box. Priva-Lite,
a laminated glass with a liquid-crystal film, allows immediate
switching between transparency and translucency, creating
a magical effect. A further example of Quantum Glass's
inventions, LEDinGlass, can be seen in the series of playful
lights Up & Away by design collective Outofstock (page 265).

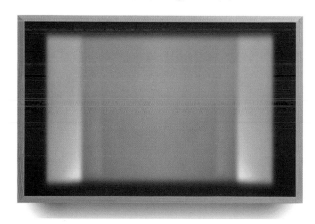

Mirror/light box, On/Off
Daniel Rybakken
Priva-Lite active glass
technology from
Quantum Glass™
H: 70cm (27in)
W: 104cm (41in)
D: 20cm (7⅞in)
Saazs, France
www.saazs.com

Screen, Lightstamp
Tomas Erel
Lacquered aluminium
composite, Planilum
active glass technology
from Quantum Glass™
H: 162cm (64in)
W: 174cm (68in)
D: 3cm (1⅛in)
Saazs, France
www.saazs.com

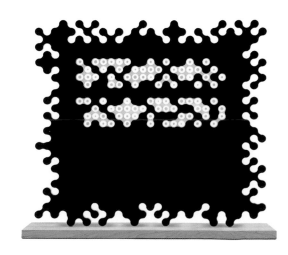

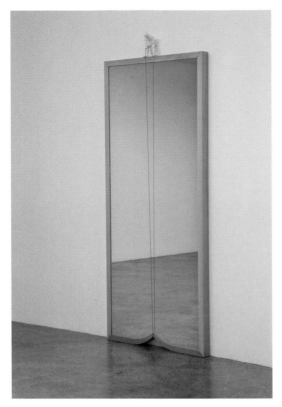

Mirrors, IX Mirrors
Ron Gilad
Wood, mirror
H: 200cm (78in)
W: 90cm (35in)
Dilmos, Italy
www.dilmos.it

Mirror, IX Mirrors
Ron Gilad
Wood, mirror
H: 140cm (55in)
W: 354cm (139in)
D: 24cm (9½in)
Dilmos, Italy
www.dilmos.it

My Moon My Mirror
Successful Living from Diesel
with Moroso
Print on mirrored surface
Diam: 100cm (39in)
Moroso, Italy
www.moroso.it

Bookends, Eco
Ross Lovegrove
White Carrara marble
H: 25cm (9⅞in)
W: 10cm (3⅞in)
L: 23cm (9in)
Marsotto Edizioni, Italy
www.marsotto-edizioni.com

Partition, Entre-Deux
Konstantin Grcic
Anodized aluminium
H: 90cm (35in)
W: 90 + 90cm (35 + 35in)
D (max): 90cm (35in)
Azucena, Italy
www.azucena.it

Radiator, Therme Radiator
Karim Rashid
Printed single steel plate
H: 182cm (72in)
W: 54cm (21in)
Caleido, Italy
www.caleido.bs.it

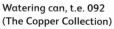

**Watering can, t.e. 092
(The Copper Collection)**
Aldo Bakker
Copper
H: 20cm (7⅞in)
W: 23cm (9in)
D: 1.6cm (⅝in)
Thomas Eyck,
The Netherlands
www.thomaseyck.com

Ice bucket, Gelo
Filipe Alarcão
Agglomerated cork,
recyclable plastic
H: 31.5cm (12⅝in)
Diam: 30cm (11¾in)
Amorim Cork Composites, S.A,
Portugal
www.corkcomposites.amorim.com

**Speaker, Change
the Record**
Paul Cocksedge
12-inch records
H: 19cm (7½in)
Diam: 30cm (11¾in)
Paul Cocksedge Studio, UK
www.paulcocksedgestudio.com

This is not the first time that Paul Cocksedge has found a use for all those unwanted vinyl records gathering dust in the attic. Back in 2006 he made them into fruit bowls by heating, moulding and fusing two together. Now he has revisited the concept, adding that element of genius for which he has become known. Looking for a way to magnify the sound from miniaturized, inadequate smartphone speakers, he applied heat to old records until they softened and then formed them into the perfect 'horn' shape. No electricity or power is needed for amplification – the phone is simply placed inside.

**Alarm clock, AC01
Alarm Clock**
Jasper Morrison
ABS
H: 10.7cm (4⅜in)
W: 9cm (3½in)
D: 3.4cm (1⅜in)
Punkt, Switzerland
*www.punktgroup.com
www.jaspermorrison.com/shop/*

**Screen, Xraydio 3
Natura Morta**
Diesel
Glass with printed
photographic image
H: 176cm (69in)
D: 61cm (24in)
Moroso SpA, Italy
*www.moroso.it
diesel.foscarini.com*

Vacuum cleaner, DC26
James Dyson
ABS
H: 26.6cm (10⅝in)
W: 21cm (8¼in)
L: 32.5cm (13in)
Dyson, UK
www.dyson.co.uk

Screen, Origin part I: Join
BCXSY
Hinoki (Japanese cypress)
H: 160cm (63in)
W: 170cm (66in)
D: 2cm (¾in)
BCXSY, The Netherlands
www.bcxsy.com

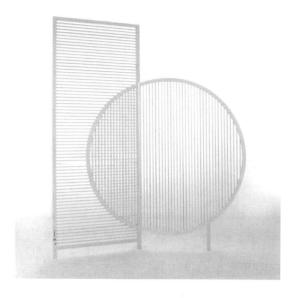

**Laundry furniture,
Laundry Room Collection**
Terry Dwan
Cedar wood
Made to order
Riva 1920, Italy
www.riva1920.it

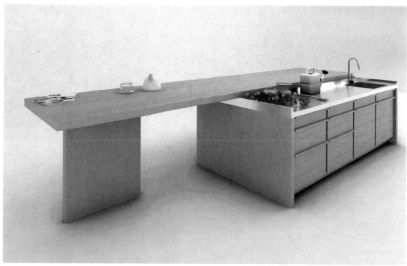

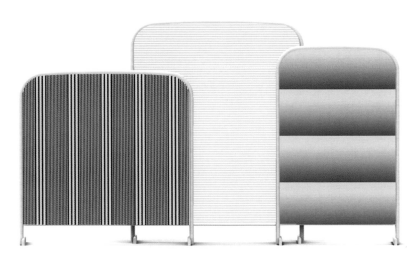

Screen walls, Boge
Anderssen & Voll
Biri Tapet straw textile
made from oats and cotton,
solid steam-bent ash wood,
brass capping
H: 168 and 140cm
(66 and 55in)
W: 100 and 140cm
(39 and 55in)
Biri Tapet AS, Norway
www.biritapet.no

Bicycle, Local
Yves Béhar, Josh Morenstein,
Nick Cronan, Noah Murphy-
Reinhertz and Jeremy Sycip
Steel
H (handlebars to ground):
107cm (42in)
L (back tyre to front of
basket): 183cm (72in)
Sycip, USA
www.sycip.com

Room divider/sound
absorbent, Button
Mia Cullin
PP/viscose felt laminated
with wool felt
H (single module):
36cm (14⅛in)
W (single module):
36cm (14⅛in)
Assemble modules to
create a unit of any size
Mia Cullin, Sweden
www.miacullin.com

The Tiltpod was designed to avoid the time-consuming effort of screwing a tripod into the base of a camera and potentially missing the shot of the century. By using simple but powerful magnets to attach the base to a pivot permanently screwed into the camera's tripod socket, vital seconds are gained. The base's underside is covered in a material created to grip just about any surface, from the rough rocks to smooth car bonnets.

Camera tripod, Tiltpod
Mike Strasser and Clint Slone
of Think2Build
Plastic, metal
H: 1cm (⅜in)
W: 3.8cm (1½in)
L: 5.1cm (2in)
Gomite, USA
www.gomite.com

Dumbbells/candlesticks, Light&Heavy
Tove Thambert
Cast iron
H (Light): 19.2cm (7½in)
H (Medium): 25cm (9⅞in)
H (Heavy): 28.2cm (11in)
Diam (bottom): 10.9cm (4⅜in)
Tove Thambert, Sweden
www.tovethambert.com

Compact photo/video light, 40 LED Photo/Video Slim Lighting Panel
Hama
Battery-operated LED lamp, plastic, aluminium
H: 5cm (2in)
W: 8cm (3⅛in)
D: 2cm (¾in)
Hama GmbH & Co KG, Germany
www.hama.de

The Hama LED light panel offers a valuable alternative to a heavy cinematographic lamp when something more than a flash is needed to take the perfect picture. The compact, battery-operated LED lamp is approximately the size of a cigarette packet, and its 20 millimetre (¾ inch) depth is sufficient to hold forty dimmable daylight LEDs. It is attached to a swan neck that can be bent in all directions and is connected to the camera via the flash shoe. Users can make the light softer with a diffuser or add warmer tones with an orange filter.

Stove, Toba
MCZ
Steel, cast iron, ceramic/
soapstone, Alutec
H: 111cm (44in)
W: 52.3cm (21in)
D: 51.2cm (20in)
MCZ, Italy
www.mcz.it

**Fireplace (gas or wood),
Scenario**
Emo Design
Painted steel, glass ceramic
H: 75cm (29in)
L: 205cm (80in)
D: 10cm (3⅞in)
MCZ, Italy
www.mcz.it

Mirror on stand, Iconic
Dan Yeffet and Lucie Koldova
White Carrara marble, mirror
H: 185cm (72in)
W: 38cm (15in)
L: 75cm (29in)
La Chance, France
www.lachance.fr

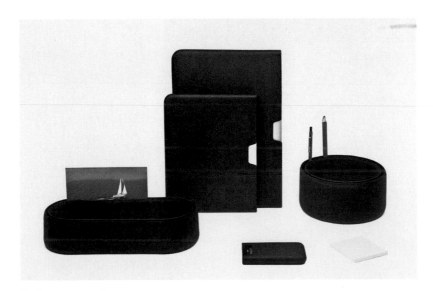

**Desktop accessories,
Matt Collection**
Sylvain Willenz
Plastic
H (Oval): 6.5cm (2⅝in)
W (Oval): 30cm (11¾in)
D (Oval): 12cm (4¾in)
Objekten, Belgium
www.objekten.com

**Pen, Pentagon
Fountain Pen**
Industrial Facility
Precious resin, 18K gold nib,
ionized plated clip
H: 15cm (5⅞in)
Diam: 1.8cm (¾in)
Elephant & Coral, Singapore
www.retailfacility.co.uk

**Rechargeable 2-in-1 stick/
handheld vacuum cleaner,
Daily Duo**
Philips Design
Recycled aluminium
H: 111cm (44in)
W: 21cm (8¼in)
L: 25cm (9⅞in)
Philips, The Netherlands
www.philips.com

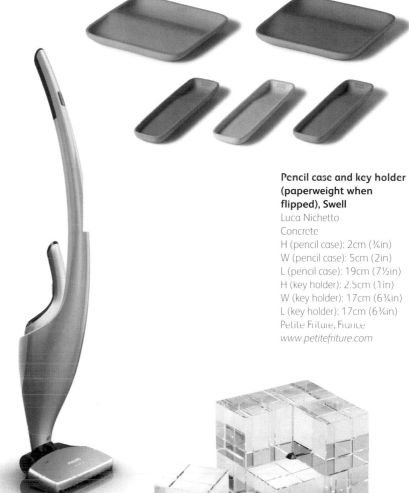

**Pencil case and key holder
(paperweight when
flipped), Swell**
Luca Nichetto
Concrete
H (pencil case): 2cm (¾in)
W (pencil case): 5cm (2in)
L (pencil case): 19cm (7½in)
H (key holder): 2.5cm (1in)
W (key holder): 17cm (6¾in)
L (key holder): 17cm (6¾in)
Petite Friture, France
www.petitefriture.com

**Paperweight collection,
Puzzle**
Nendo
Glass with Swarovski elements
H: 10cm (3⅞in)
W: 10cm (3⅞in)
D: 10cm (3⅞in)
Gaia & Gino, Turkey
www.gaiagino.com

Biofireplace, Bubble
Serge Atallach
Fibreglass polyester laminate,
white gloss, stainless steel
H (base): 36cm (14⅛in)
H (total): 61cm (24in)
Diam: 92.5cm (36in)
Planika, Poland
www.planikafires.com

Watch, Jak
Karim Rashid
Polyurethane
Diam: 4.7cm (1⅞in)
Alessi SpA, Italy
www.alessi.com

Watch, Issey Miyake Vue
Yves Béhar, Josh Morenstein,
Bret Recor and Gabe Lamb
Steel, aluminium, crystal
Diam: 4cm (1⅝in)
Issey Miyake, Japan
www.isseymiyake.com

**Vibration alarm watch,
An Alarm**
Industrial Facility
Stainless steel with
ionized plating
H: 3cm (1⅛in)
W: 3cm (1⅛in)
D: 1.1cm (⅜in)
Idea Japan, Japan
www.retailfacility.co.uk

Hybrid solar watch, Sol
Shin Azumi
Polyurethane, stainless steel,
watch circuits with solar cell
L: 24.4cm (9½in)
W: 3.9cm (1⅝in)
D: 1cm (⅜in)
Idea International Co., Ltd.,
Japan
www.idea-in.com

Watch, Hacker Watch
Michael Young
Stainless steel, mineral glass,
PU plastic
D (case): 0.9cm (⅜in)
Diam (case): 4.2cm (1⅝in)
o.d.m., Hong Kong
www.odm-design.com

Watch, Iconograph
Werner Aisslinger
Soft touch silicone, chrome
L (total length of watch):
24.5cm (9⅞in)
W (watch band): 2cm (¾in)
Diam (display): 4.5cm (1¾in)
Lorenz, Italy
www.lorenz.it

**Watch, r5.5 XXL
Chronograph**
Jasper Morrison
Platinum, matt high-tech
ceramic finish, brushed
platinum dial
H (case): 4.9cm (2in)
W (case): 4.1cm (1⅝in)
Rado Watch Co. Ltd.,
Switzerland
www.rado.com

Watch, O
Tokujin Yoshioka
Stainless steel, plastic
W: 3.3cm (1⅜in)
D: 1.21cm (½in)
Issey Miyake/Seiko
Instruments Inc., Japan
www.isseymiyake-watch.com

Paper knife, Uselen
Giulio Iacchetti
Stainless steel
L: 23cm (9in)
Alessi SpA, Italy
www.alessi.com

**Dual-power desktop
calculator, LC69H Safe
Calculator**
Pierre Garner and
Elise Berthier
Bamboo, PLA
W: 8.6cm (3⅜in)
L: 15cm (5⅞in)
D: 1.05cm (⅜in)
Lexon, France
www.lexon-design.com

**Solar pocket light, LL99H
Safe Pocket Light**
Pierre Garner and
Elise Berthier
Bamboo, PLA, LED
W: 3.4cm (1⅜in)
L: 10cm (3⅞in)
D: 0.8cm (⅜in)
Lexon, France
www.lexon-design.com

Bicycle, Cityspeed Bike
Michael Young
Aluminium
H: 95cm (37in)
W: 65cm (25in)
L: 170cm (66in)
Giant, Taiwan
www.giant-bicycles.com

**Camera case, Case for
Leica D-Lux 5**
Paul Smith
Leather
W: 8cm (3⅛in)
L: 13cm (5⅛in)
D: 6cm (2⅜in)
Paul Smith, UK
www.paulsmith.co.uk
www.leica-storemayfair.co.uk

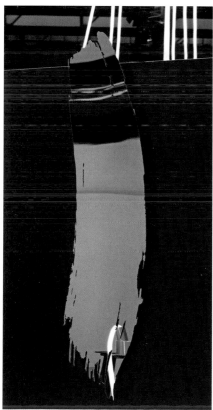

Mirror, Brush Mirror
Ron Gilad
Mirrored-polished steel
L: 195cm (76in)
Established & Sons, UK
www.establishedandsons.com

**Furnishing accessory,
Zen Apple**
Ludovica and Roberto Palomba
Solid wood red cedar
from Canada
H: 34cm (13⅜in)
Diam: 54cm (21in)
Exteta, Italy
www.exteta.it

Folding knife, Il Canif
Pierre Charpin
18/10 stainless steel,
AISI 420 steel
L: 19cm (7½in)
Alessi SpA, Italy
www.alessi.com

PICTURE CREDITS